W9-BYA-364

A Never Ending War

MICHAEL CAPPI

Note for Librarians: A cataloguing record for this book is available from Library and Archives Canada at www.collectionscanada.ca/amicus/index-e.html
ISBN 1-4251-3081-x

Offices in Canada, USA, Ireland and UK

Book sales for North America and international:
Trafford Publishing, 6E–2333 Government St.,
Victoria, BC V8T 4P4 CANADA
phone 250 383 6864 (toll-free 1 888 232 4444)
fax 250 383 6804; email to orders@trafford.com
Book sales in Europe:
Trafford Publishing (UK) Limited, 9 Park End Street, 2nd Floor
Oxford, UK OX1 1HH UNITED KINGDOM
phone +44 (0)1865 722 113 (local rate 0845 230 9601)
facsimile +44 (0)1865 722 868; info.uk@trafford.com
Order online at:
trafford.com/07-0019

10 9 8 7 6 5

To Susan, my thanks for her support.
She gave more then she will ever know.

and

To Those Muslims who are part of the solution
for their moral courage is great.

"The battle Sir, is not to the strong alone; it is to the vigilant, the active, the brave."

–Patrick Henry

*"The majority of politicians are interested
not in truth but in power
and in the maintenance of that power.
To maintain that power, it is essential
that people remain in ignorance;
that they live in ignorance of the truth
of their own lives."*

–Harold Pinter,
from his Nobel Prize for literature
acceptance speech "Art, Truth and Politics"

Contents

Preface

On the morning of September 11, 2001 I was in the vicinity of the World Trade center a mere few blocks away. The events that ensued were horrendous for anyone to see on TV but to be an eyewitness was especially affecting. I spent the day watching the enfolding tragedy including the early spectacle of seeing many people jumping from the towers to avoid the hellfire unleashed by an act of pure irrational hatred in the guise of a religion. Some unfortunates were too late to avoid the flames for they were on fire as they fell to their deaths.

To say the least the events of that day were deeply disturbing to any sane human but the aftermath of seeing on TV tens of thousands of people in the Islamic World cheering the event was surreal. Certainly shock would be an accurate description of my reaction but more than that in the succeeding days I felt that I had witnessed an irrevocable shift in the direction of the evolution of civilization. The shift was not one that could bode well for the U.S. and for the culture of Western civilization. The ensuing years did little to shake the feeling. I began to view much of the world in the same way one would view a landscape after an enormous earthquake changed the topology. Although it was sort of the same, it was actually quite different.

Dramatic changes in the course of civilization's forward march seem to happen because of some major event but this is never exactly true. The event itself is the result of an evolving set of beliefs and seemingly unimportant events. To find the actual cause of the society altering "incident" it is critical to identify and review the many trends and changes in society's philosophy, politics and economics that converged to cause a horrendous occurrence.

As the years passed and seemingly endless activities resembling a horrific nightmare continued unabated, I began to read and research the religion and history of Islam. I also read extensively about the relationships among the Middle East, Europe and The United States and the evolving nature of Islam and its expansion; and in fact its ascendancy (at least in the context of its current world position compared to a generation ago). There were two thoughts that became clear. The first was that the idea that a small number of fanatics were driving the current major shifts in history was nonsense, perhaps they are responsible for terrorism but they are not the driving force behind the bigger strategic picture and shift in civilization's evolution. The second realization was that I could not find a book that covered the breadth of the enfolding historical events from all aspects of the complex problem. It was this book that I set out to write.

Although in doing the research for the book I read many quotes from Islamic writers through the centuries and across a broad range of modern Islamic leaders and representatives the quote that best encapsulates the issue that the West faces was declared by the Ayatollah Khomeini:

> "I am decisively announcing to the whole world that if the world-devourers [i.e., the infidel powers] wish to stand against our religion, we will stand against their whole world and will not cease until the annihilation of all of them. Either we all become free, or we will go to the greater freedom which is martyrdom. Either we shake one another's hands in joy at the victory of Islam in the world, or all of us will turn to eternal life and martyrdom. In both cases, victory and success are ours."
>
> A passage from the Ayatollah Khomeini, quoted in an 11th-grade Iranian schoolbook.

The thought expressed by Khomeini is not the isolated ravings of a deranged mind. Quite the contrary although it is true that Khomeini was a fanatic he was a brilliant and clear thinking fanatic and the quote is at the heart of the issue the West faces with Islam because Islam embraces the essence of that quote with every fiber of its existence and every lesson from the *Qur'an*. It will be the task of this book to make that point clear and to propose appropriate solutions. The first of these solutions is to recognize that...

> "For evil to triumph it is only necessary for good men to do nothing."
> Edmund Burke

Author's Notes

The *Qur'anic* quotes used throughout this book are taken form: "The Koran" by N.J. Dawood, Penguin books. For reference and comparative purposes "The *Qur'an*" by Richard Bell, B.D., D.D. and "The *Qur'an*" by M.A.S. Abdel Haleem were also used but are not quoted.

The reason for utilizing several versions of the *Qur'an* was to understand the real intent of the Islamic holy book with as little translation ambiguity as possible. The three versions used all agree in intent if not in their literal translation.

The Arabic language does not lend itself to easy phonetic translation into English and therefore there are many English spellings of any Arabic name. I have chosen the following because they seem to be the most popular.

"*Qur'an*" as shown here is used in lieu of other forms except where it is part of a quote; the same is true of Muslim, al-Qaeda, Shari'a and Hezbollah.

Introduction

If all the harm and death done in the name of religion and its stepchildren "the –isms" of the world disappeared there would exist a heaven of sorts on earth.

I believe that the sameness of human nature across all races is not disputable from either a scientific or a philosophical context. All humans are born the same. We may have different capacities and potentials. However, these do not change the basic premise of equality per se or equality under the law. The real strength of the human species is that the brain at birth is blank. There are no ideas, no hate, no love and no thoughts. What will develop and form the human over time are the experiences of life and the information and knowledge a person integrates into his growing base of perceptions and understanding. This is the essence of what will make a person develop within a wide range of possible human behaviors, namely every degree and nuance of rational, good, productive, generous or at the other end of the spectrum, irrational, evil, criminal, abhorrent. Further it is this essential element of the human being that makes the formation of knowledge and the teaching of that person incredibly important to the future of the person and the society.

This book deals with the results of a set of teachings that I have come to believe are inimical to human beings individually and to society on the whole. The unfortunate thing about a formed human and his set of beliefs is the difficulty of altering what he believes. To re-educate is perhaps the hardest task in the sphere of human experience, it is truly difficult to give up what we have learned. However, with rational thought and an open mind, truth can be a powerful agent for change.

The evolution of western culture and philosophy has been oriented toward the development of the individual and a society that supports and protects individual rights. The Age of Enlightenment saw this evolution reach its zenith in philosophy (metaphysics, epistemology, ethics, etc.), the arts and humanities and in the recognition of the individual human being as existing for his own happiness, development and productivity. The forms of government that evolved from this concept recognized the sanctity and uniqueness of the individual, and their rights. The most advanced form of a government that is individual centric is the United States of America.

The concept of an individual's "inalienable rights" is paramount in the formation of the laws and norms of any free society. It is the purpose of the State to protect these inalienable rights and its citizens in the exercising of those rights. The choices of freedom of thought and expression, freedom of speech, of occupation, education, religion, marriage, life-style, sexual preferences, mobility, property ownership all in the context that the actions of an individual are free and unencumbered by the State as long as they do not infringe on the physical welfare and equal rights of another.

When religious "law" or norms are substituted for, or supercede the set of secular laws that exist to protect these inalienable rights, then the citizen, whether a believer in that religion or not, becomes the victim of a degree of arbitrariness that does not exist in rationality based secular law. Of course one can posit many secular codes that are in fact arbitrary however this is less likely when the laws are based on the supposition that they exist to protect the individual from the power of the state. On the contrary religious law's purpose is to execute an extreme degree of arbitrariness over the citizen so as to "protect him" from himself. In reality the purpose is aimed at controlling the citizen and assuring their adherence to the rules set forth in the religious code.

And so we see many cases throughout history where citizens exercising personal choice (where no victims exist as a result of that choice) are punished by the most extreme forms of punishment. In many cases both societies and religions have implemented these extreme forms of punishment, e.g., death, dismemberment, torture, imprisonment, etc. all in the name of a State, a religion or a God. From the dark ages into the middle ages it was The Inquisition, in today's world it is in the name of Islam. The result is the same, the subjugation of the individual to the state or the religion.

Philosophically this is no different than Nazism, Marxism, Communism or any ism of a totalitarian nature. The repressive nature of all totalitarian regimes is foreign to Western thought and experience. That is not to say that Westerners do not know of its existence but in a personal living context it is fortunately foreign to them. As such it is often difficult to intellectually and viscerally come to terms with the nature of this evil. There is the tendency to not want to believe what is in front of their eyes.

Islam is in that mode today. Westerners, particularly Americans, find it hard to except that a religion is intrinsically capable of instigating human actions that are evil. We will blame these actions on extremists or fanatics and their interpretation of the religious teachings but not on the religion itself. Certainly the Catholic Inquisition was an example of a perversion of religion on a grand scale but it was a moment, a long moment perhaps, but a passing period in history non the less. The same cannot be said of Islam. Since its inception it has been a religion of war and conquest. And as one studies the *Qur'an* it becomes quickly evident that Islam is a religion that is inimical to Western society and its way of life.

Whenever the State is supreme and the individual subservient, the individual will be destroyed, literally or spiritually, in the Western secular sense of sprit.

WW II and Nazism was an "easy" enemy as was Communism. You could see them and fight them and they could be defended against with the normal mechanisms of politics and warfare. What we face with Islamism is insidious and deadly. Like the inexorable spread of a cancer through the human body Islam is spreading and taking control of more and more of Western Society. This is a far more effective way of destroying an organism or a society than any other means. It is subtle, slow and not quickly identified until it is almost too late. Many readers will decry this as just another "conspiracy theory" but in fact it is not a conspiracy in any ordinary sense. There is no group of Islamic fundamentalists led by a mad dictator following a master plan for world domination. Nor is Islam being lead by a single madman or group of madmen (although there are many of these afoot). It is precisely that there is no specific conspiracy as we generally use that term that makes the quest by Islam so dangerous.

It is one of the goals of this book to demonstrate the decentralized and diffuse way in which Islam spreads and the way it gradually insinuates itself within a culture. To be successful at achieving this insinuation requires that Islam be presented as benign and peaceful, tolerant and benevolent. However there is a great difference between what Islam says and what it does. The methods Islam uses to achieve their goals and how we in the West help them will also be examined. Lastly there are actions that the West can take to curtail and ultimately defeat this insinuation and they will be discussed as well.

Religion is the most powerful of all the "isms". It can only be defeated by a greater idea skillfully used and consistently voiced.

A last point that is critical to understand while reading the early chapters of the book. Man's inhumanity to man is universal. There is nothing in the realm of brutality or subjugation or conquest that Islam will be accused of, that has not also been done by other religions and people throughout history. The point that will be dealt with that makes Islam so different is that with Islam the behavior is fundamental to the religion and often obligatory and not passing or aberrational as it sometimes was with other religions.

I

THE MYTHS OF ISLAM

1 Peaceful

When a person spends a great deal of time shouting his own praises to all who will listen you can be sure your are dealing with a person who is hiding something. In the case of organizations, political parties and religions you are in the presence of "the big lie." The big lie is an untruth that is said often and loud. And if the lie is said often enough for a long enough period of time and is unchallenged, people begin to believe it. This is what is happening with Islam today. The constant shout is that Islam at its heart is a "religion of peace, tolerance and benevolence" and any Islamic actions to the contrary are defensive and in reaction to hostile forces. The hostiles of today are almost always Israel or The United States (The Great Satan) but these hostile forces can be any nation or people in the path of Islam.

With respect to Islam's self-designation as the "Religion of Peace" the mass of evidence is just too overwhelming for the big lie to work for long. The best way to gage the truthfulness of Islam's claim to these virtues is to examine each claim in the context of "Islam's words vs. Islam's actions". Even with a cursory examination of Islam through history it becomes clear that Islam, contrary to its claims, is a religion of conquest, violence, subjugation, intolerance and malevolence. So it always was and so it will always be. As we shall see it is written in the *Qur'an*.

INVASIONS

The earliest manifestation of the "Islam vs. the Non-Islamic World" problem began immediately following The Prophet's death. The Islamic world began a series of invasions of Europe that lasted more than 1000 years. One can say that in effect the hostilities continue right into modern times and is on going today, albeit in different forms but non the less aimed at conquest.

> Mohammad's death 632 C.E.,
>
> 638 C.E. an invasion of Christian Syria and Palestine (Palestine was Christian not Moslem) and Jerusalem by the Islamic horde,
>
> 640 C.E. the invasion of Persia, Armenia, Mesopotamia (Iraq), Christian Egypt, Christian Tunisia, Algeria and Morocco
>
> In 668 C.E. Islam began a 16 year siege of Christian Constantinople
>
> In 711 C.E. Islam invaded the Iberian peninsula and conquered it.
>
> From 731 to 733 C.E. Islam conquered most of what is today the south of France.
>
> In 837 C.E. Islam invaded Sicily
>
> By 846 C.E. Islam sacked most of the Italian cities of size along the Adriatic and Mediterranean coasts.
>
> In 889 C.E. Islam invades Provence (France)
>
> In 9/11 C.E. Islam crossed the Alps and lay siege to Piedmont and Turin and continued into Switzerland.
>
> In 940 C.E. the Islamic horde entered Toulon.

All this conquest and war was prosecuted by the Islamic state ***before the first Crusade***. It is interesting how modern apologists for Islamic militancy blame the root of this militancy on The Crusades. Granted that many of the crusades were either ill conceived or just morally wrong, it also must be granted that a history of over 300 years of war and invasion predated the first crusade and thereby greatly helped to set the stage for the crusades. No one looking at the historical record can honestly say that the root of today's problem stems from the Crusades. So why is this justification so important to the Islamic world? Why are they so vociferous on the point that they are "fighting back," that the West through the Crusades started the confrontations with Islam? The answer can be found in the *Qur'an*.

There are few sayings in the *Qur'an* that admonish against violence one of the major quotes is:

> "Fight for the sake of God (Allah) those that fight against you, but do not attack first. God does not love the aggressor." *Qur'an* 2:190

In the context of the Crusades this is easily translated into "since Islam has been attacked by the "crusaders" we are not held to this admonishment since we are defending Islam. This certainly does disregard the several centuries of Islamic attacks on Europe before the first Crusade, but then we shall see that ignoring reality and inconvenient historical events is very much a central part of Islam. Furthermore long after the last crusade the Islamic expansionism began anew without the existence of a crusade as a reason.

In 1356 C.E. Gallipoli was conquered and used as a base to invade Thrace, Macedonia and Albania. From the Greek peninsula the Islamic armies invaded Serbia.

Following these events there was a five-year siege of Constantinople (which was still at that time Christian).

> In 1420 C.E. Islam occupied Venetian Salonica.
>
> In 1444 C.E. Walachia, Moldavia, Transylvania, Bulgaria and Romania fell.
>
> In 1453 C.E. the Muslim horde finally took Constantinople.
>
> In 1456 C.E. Islam conquered Athens.
>
> By 1476 C.E. the forward march of Islam once again turned to

> Venice. In this campaign they took Friuli and the Isonzo Valley followed by Puglia.

Over the next century the Ottoman Empire was formed and expanded into Hungary and Austria. The Ottoman Empire to a large extent lasted until the First World War. In 1529 C.E. an attempted Islamic invasion of Austria was repelled. With this success the West succeeded in halting, the spread of Islam into Europe.

Finally in 1571 C.E. an alliance of Spain and Italy (the independent states of Genoa, Florence, Turin, Parma, Mantua, Lucca, Ferrara, Urbino, Malta and the Papacy) defeated the Islamic armies at the Battle of Lepanto. (It is interesting to note that France refused to join the alliance.) Even with this victory the Ottoman Empire continued its relentless push into Europe by invading Poland in both 1672 C.E. and 1683 C.E. Also in 1683 C.E. the Islamic armies turned once again to Austria. However an alliance of English, Spanish, Ukrainians, Poles and Italians (once again France declined to participate) defeated the Ottoman Empire decisively and Islam was temporarily stopped as they fled greater Europe.

Throughout history there has never been a more aggressive and constant desire on the part of one people to conquer another as Islam's desire to conquer and dominate Europe and convert it to Islam. The conquest and conversion is central to their religious beliefs. If the actions of the past 1400 years are not sufficient to demonstrate this point, some quotes from Islamic "scriptures" should help clarify why violence seems to be constant and central to Islam.

Note: These quotes are taken from the Hadith (the literature recounting the sayings and actions of the Prophet):

The Hadith:

> "dictates that only three choices are acceptable for non-Muslims according to Islam, "conversion, paying the non-Muslim tax (*dhimminitude*), or death".
>
> "*Jihad* is your duty under any ruler, be he godly or wicked.
>
> "A day and a night fighting on the frontier is better than a month of fasting and prayer.

"Nobody who dies and finds good from Allah would wish to come back to this world even if he were given the whole world and whatever is in it, except the martyr, who upon seeing the superiority of martyrdom, would like to come to the world and get killed again, in Allah's cause.

"He who dies without taking part in a campaign dies in a kind of unbelief.

"A single endeavor in Allah's cause in the forenoon or in the afternoon is better than the world and whatever is in it.

"Paradise is in the shadow of the sword."

And from The *Qur'an*:

As for those who are slain in the cause of God (Allah), He will not allow their works to perish." *Qur'an* not 47:4 ?

"God (Allah) has purchased from the faithful their lives and worldly goods, and in return has promised them the Garden. They will fight for the cause of God, they will slay, and be slain...." *Qur'an* 9:111

"Muhammad is God's (Allah's) Apostle. Those that follow him are ruthless to the unbelievers but merciful to one another." *Qur'an* 48:29

"Do not take for friends or helpers unbelievers rather than believers. If any do that, in nothing will there be help from Allah; except by way of precaution, that ye may guard yourselves from them." *Qur'an* 3:28

"Fight against such of those to whom the Scriptures were given (Jews and Christians) as believe in neither God (Allah) nor the Last Day, who do not forbid what God and His apostle have forbidden, and do not embrace the true Faith, until they pay the tribute (the non Muslim tax) out of hand and are utterly subdued." *Qur'an* 9:29

"I shall cast terror into the heart of the infidels. Strike off their heads, strike off the very tip of their fingers." *Qur'an* 8:12

"When you meet the unbelievers in the battlefield strike off their

> heads and, when you have laid them low, bind your captives firmly. Then grant them their freedom or take a ransom from them, until War shall lay down her burdens." *Qur'an* 47:4

There are few admonitions to be peaceful in The *Qur'an*, with the exception of the one quote given earlier in referring to not attacking first.

And dictates from the "Pulpit":

> "The Prophet, Allah bless him and grant him salvation, has said: 'The Day of Judgment will not come about until Moslems fight the Jews (killing the Jews), when the Jew will hide behind stones and trees. The stones and trees will say O Moslems, O Abdulla, there is a Jew behind me, come and kill him. Only the Gharkad tree, (a certain kind of tree) would not do that because it is one of the trees of the Jews.'" Abdel Aziz Dweik a Moslem cleric.

The following quote from the *Qur'an* assures that peace between Islam and the Jews can never be.

> "There is for you an excellent example to follow in Abraham and those with him, when they said to their people: "We are clear of you and of whatever ye worship besides Allah; we have rejected you and there has arisen between us and you enmity and hatred for ever, unless ye believe in Allah and Him alone." *Qur'an* 60:4

From the Prophet's farewell address to his followers:

> "I was ordered to fight all men until they say, 'There is no god but Allah.' "

Muhammad spent the last years of his life fighting to unify Arabia under his reign; within a decade of his death, Islamic conquest had already built an Arab-Muslim empire that is viewed by many historians as "one of the most remarkable examples of empire-building in world history."

The legacy of Mohammad lives on. Extensive readings and research could not yield a single instance of a secular, or for that matter, any civilization that could exist peacefully with Islam for any length of time. The West has endured in relative peace for the past two centuries because of its overwhelming technological advantages in science and weaponry. The unfortunate thing is that the advantages of technology ceased being the sole domain of the West when Islam became increasingly wealthy from vast amounts of money derived from oil and thus was able to purchase the tools for a modern *jihad* and with these once again begin its expansion.

2 Tolerant

A dictionary definition of tolerance; "a fair and permissive attitude toward those whose race, religion, nationality, opinions, practices, etc. differs from one's own, free from bigotry."

In practice a tolerant society and people when confronted by ideas, beliefs, sentiments and opinions that are not central to their culture nevertheless support another's right to hold these beliefs and even practice them to the extent that they are not inimical to the existing culture and society. Furthermore the tolerated beliefs must be viewed in a context of not inflicting physical harm or curtailment of the rights of others in the mainstream society or of violating fundamental practices of that society. Within this context of tolerance the rights and beliefs of all people need to be protected by a set of laws designed to support human liberty and freedom of thought.

There is nothing within the religion of Islam that expresses a concept even remotely similar to this nor did it ever exist in practice anywhere in the world of Islam, yet Islam claims to be tolerant. In all of the Islamic invasions through the centuries the conquered people were told to convert to Islam or be put to the sword. Alternatively the sale of conquered people into slavery was a lucrative business and still exists today in many Islamic countries in Africa. This approach to the conquered people actually never changed, and was prevalent, well into the 20th Century.

TOLERANCE FOR OTHER RELIGIONS

Dr. Ahmed Abu Halabiya (a member of The Palestinian Authority) from one of his *Fatwa*s:

> "Allah the almighty has called upon us not to ally with the Jews and Christians, not to like them, not to become their partners, not to support them and not to sign agreements with them. Allah said:
>
> 'O ye who believe! Take not the Jews and the Christians as allies for they are allies of one another. Who from among you takes them as allies will indeed be one of them. Have no mercy on the Jews, no matter where they are, in any country. Fight them, wherever you are. Where ever you meet them kill them.'" *Qur'an* 5:51 (As

> quoted herein the intent of *Qur'an* 5:51 is the same as that of the *Qur'anic* source used in this book however the literal quote was taken as part of the quote from Ahmed Abu Halabiya's fatwa.)

> "slay the idolaters wherever ye find them. Arrest them, besiege them, and lie in ambush everywhere for them." *Qur'an* 9:5

To Islam an idolater is anyone who is not a Muslim.

> And slay them wherever ye find them, and drive them out of the places they drove you." *Qur'an* 2:191

A now infamous case of "Islamic religious tolerance" is the Afghan Mr. Abdul Rahman. Mr. Rahman converted to Christianity from Islam and by doing so created a political furor and Muslim enmity. Under the interpretation of Islamic (*Shari'a*) law on which Afghanistan's constitution is based, Mr. Rahman's conversion to Christianity was illegal and warranted extreme punishment. A *fatwa* was issued for his death and he was arrested. Rahman faced the death penalty unless he reconverted back to Islam.

Imagine being sentenced to death for choosing to believe in God in a different way. Such has always been the way of Islam and still is. All of the schools of Islamic jurisprudence agree on this issue.

> "The Prophet Muhammad has said several times that those who convert from Islam should be killed if they refuse to come back," says Ansarullah Mawlafizada, the trial judge.

> "Islam is a religion of peace, tolerance, kindness and integrity. That is why we have told him if he regrets what he did, then we will forgive him," the judge told the BBC News. (Of course if he doesn't regret it he will be executed.)

Both these statements demonstrate quite explicitly the way in which Islam acts even though Islam strongly states its position as the exact opposite of what it does.

The attitude implicit in the *fatwa* against Mr. Rahman is not isolated to a tiny minority of extremists it is what an overwhelming number of average Afghans believe, i.e., Mr. Rahman has erred and deserves to be executed.

This position was applauded throughout the entire Muslim world.

> "At Friday prayers in mosques across the Afghan capital, the case of Abdul Rahman and the consequent international outcry (Western) was the hot topic of discussion and the major theme of sermons. 'We will not let anyone interfere with our religious practices,' declared cleric Inayatullah at Kabul's Pulakasthy mosque, one of the city's largest. 'What Rahman has done is wrong and he must be punished.' 'What is wrong with Islam that he should want to convert? asks an agitated Abdul Zahid Payman." (1)

> "The courts should punish him and he should be put to death."

Few were willing to listen to the growing condemnation in the West.

> "According to Islamic law he should be sentenced to death because God has clearly stated that Christianity is forbidden in our land," says Mohammed Qadir, another devout worshipper.

And from the *Qur'an*:

> "Whoever changed his Islamic religion, then kill him."

The situation was pragmatically solved by declaration that Mr. Rahman was insane and therefore not responsible for his actions. He was then snuck out of the country to an unknown destination. This solution was utilized as an expedient only because the case received such intense focus from the West and because of the presence of U.S. and UN troops throughout Afghanistan. Normally Mr. Rahman would have been executed if he did not convert back to Islam.

More Expressions of *Tolerance* Within Islam:

In Saudi Arabia neither Christian Churches nor priests are allowed in the country.

In March 2006, Algeria passed a law that forbids members of religions other than Islam to seek converts or to worship in public without a license. Violators would face imprisonment of up to five years and a fine of up to 10,000 Euros.

From the Shafi'i manual 'Umdat al-Salik, (University in Cairo), it is quite clear that apostates must be killed:

> "Someone raised among Muslims who denies the obligatoriness of the prayer, zakat, fasting Ramadan, the pilgrimage, or the unlawfulness of wine or adultery, or denies something else upon which there is a scholarly consensus...and which is necessarily known as being of the religion...thereby becomes an unbeliever (kafir) and is executed for his unbelief"...(f1.3)

And:

> "When a person who has reached puberty and is sane voluntarily apostatizes from Islam, he deserves to be killed. (o8.1) 'Umdat al-Salik continues: In such a case, it is obligatory for the caliph...to ask him to repent and return to Islam. If he does, it is accepted from him, but if he refuses, he is immediately killed."

TOLERANCE FOR OTHER PEOPLE

To Islam a non-Muslim is an *infidel*. Actually the Islamic view of many people is that they are far lower than *infidels*. Christians and Jews are considered "people of the book" and can be viewed as *infidels*. People not of the book such as Hindus, Buddhists, et al are filth, lower than dogs.

> "There are ten types of filth and impurities: urine, feces, semen, carrion, blood of carrion, dogs, pigs, disbelievers." Muhaqqiq al-Hilli (2)

In addition the al-Hilli writings include a chapter on *jihad*, setting down the conditions under which Muslims are supposed to fight Jews and Christians. The fact that statements of this type were made in the thirteenth century is of no matter to Islam. They are as valid and accepted today as they were then.

The Muslim historian Ibn Khaldin (15th century) is recognized as the greatest historical mind of his time. In his writings he describes the Arab treatment of conquered lands as follows:

> "Places that succumb to the Arabs are quickly ruined. The reason for this is that the Arabs are a savage nation, fully accustomed to savagery and the things that cause it. Savagery has become their cause and nature. They enjoy it because it means freedom from authority and no subservience to leadership. Such a natural

disposition is the negation and antithesis of civilization." (3)

The Islamic treatment of subjugated people was never good from before Khaldin's time and right up to the present; but the single worst example of intolerance occurred in the early 20th century.

The Holocaust may be a word that was penned to describe the horrendous attempted extermination of the European Jews during the 1930s and World War II, however unfortunately for mankind there were many other holocausts. In the late 19th and early 20th century Turkey prosecuted a holocaust against Christian Armenians. The number of deaths associated with this nightmare is 1.2 million out of a population of 1.35 million. 150,000 survivors remained from an entire people. At the time of this tragedy the Western world decried it but as in the case of the Jews little was done. To this day the Turks deny that this extermination ever occurred. As recently as 1994 any Turk that spoke out about these events received death threats. (This seems to be a "standard operating procedure" in the Muslim world; when confronted with that which you do not like or agree with one threatens death to the *infidels*.)

It is a belief system, extreme, fanatical and strongly held that leads societies to perpetrate atrocities of the magnitude of a "holocaust." What is critical to the understanding of Islam and its view and treatment of non-Muslim people and societies is the belief system that is at its foundation. The thoughts expressed by the *Qur'an* and preached and enforced by Islamic scholars and imams past and present is as real and pertinent to Muslims today as it was 1400 years ago. The religion of Islam does not change; it has been unaltered through the centuries and is not to be altered today, nor is it to be re-interpreted. This is in fact the source of the West's major problems with Islam.

TOLERANCE FOR EXPRESSION

One of the greatest and most important freedoms of western society is "free speech." No society has ever remained free for long without free speech. Curtail free speech and in no time the ruling powers will be curtailing all freedoms.

In John Milton's eloquent essay on free speech, *The Aeropagitaca*, (4) he concludes: *"truth comes from books promiscuously read."* The more one reads and observes the better the chance of seeing and knowing the truth. Every totalitarian state that has ever existed has worked tirelessly to stamp out free speech and the free flow of information. Islam is no different. From the earliest dictators through the middle ages of the Inquisition, from Fra Savonarola to today's dictators and Islamic Mullahs the one thing that all of them cannot allow is an environment with free speech. With free speech there will always come free thought and learning and eventually truth.

The following incidents are included for the purpose of demonstrating and providing a flavor of how Islam, despite its claims to the contrary, is absolutely the least tolerant major religion in history. The incidents span events within Islamic countries, within Europe and even actions taken by Westerners on behalf of Islam.

ACTIONS WITHIN ISLAMIC COUNTRIES

"*23 Years: A Study of The Prophetic Career of Mohammad*", by Ali Dashti (5). In this work Mr. Dashti writes extensively about The Prophet's violence and how the prophet himself stooped to political assassinations, murder, and the elimination of all opponents. To his followers murders were presented as "services to Islam." Dashti also stated that the *Qur'an* lacks common morality. The *Qur'an* he said:

> "contains nothing new in ideas not already expressed by others. All the moral precepts of the Koran are self evident and generally acknowledged. The stories in it are taken in identical or slightly modified forms from the lore of the Jews and Christians, whose rabbis and monks Muhammad had met and consulted on his journeys to Syria, and from memories conserved by the descendants of the peoples of 'Ad and Thamund'.... In the field of moral teachings, however, the Koran cannot be considered miraculous. Muhammad reiterated principles which mankind had already conceived in earlier centuries and many places. Confucius, Buddha, Zoroaster, Socrates, Moses, and Jesus had said similar things. Many of the duties and rites of Islam are continuous of practices which the pagan Arabs had adopted from the Jews."

For his efforts he was tortured during his three-year incarceration in Iran's prisons (under Khomeini) and executed at the age of 82 in 1984. The numbers of these events abound throughout the Islamic world.

ACTIONS BY MUSLIMS IN WESTERN COUNTRIES

More then twelve years ago Salman Rushdie wrote a book, "The Satanic Verses." The book was in part mildly critical of Islam and contained depictions of the Prophet. (This is forbidden in the *Qur'an.*) In response to the book's publication the Ayatollah Khomeini of Iran issued a *fatwa.* A religious ruling, that declared that it was permitted for any Muslim to kill Mr. Rushdie. In fact it was every Muslim's duty to attempt to kill him and to help them along to this goal the Ayatollah offered a reward of several million dollars for Rushdie's murder. To this day Mr. Rushdie, a British citizen, lives under a death threat and is forced to live in hiding. He has constant bodyguards.

Theo van Gogh a Dutch filmmaker wrote a number of articles entitled *"Allah Knows Best"* that were irreverent to European Islamic pieties. Subsequently he made a documentary film that was critical of Islam's treatment of women. Although the film was accurate in its depiction of the plight of women under Islam it is the kind of scrutiny that Islam cannot tolerate. A Muslim executing a Fatwa against Mr. Van Gogh murdered him in Amsterdam.

In March 2006 a Danish newspaper published 12 cartoons depicting The Prophet in various contexts. For the most part they ranged from humorous to, arguably, bad taste, but none of them were of the "hate filled" type that appear in the daily Islamic press and TV to depict "the Great Satan" or the Jews in the most outrageous and slanderous contexts. In addition the cartoons were not disgusting as were both art works and cartoons that depict icons of the Catholic Church. However the resulting Islamic outcry was out of all proportion to the "offense". *Fatwas* were issued against the authors and bomb threats were made against the publishers, demonstrations were prevalent for some time in the streets and in front of Danish embassies throughout the Muslim world. Car bombings followed and stone throwing became daily events.

> From Reuters: "At least 50 people have been killed in protests in Asia, Africa and the Middle East after Danish paper *Jyllands-Posten* published 12 cartoons about the Prophet last year."

The twelve Muhammad cartoonists now live underground and with police protection. The Muslim actions caused the Western press to capitulate and remove the cartoons from circulation. Only a few stalwart publications and Web sites rebelled against these threats and displayed the cartoons.

The imam Ahmed Akkari, not content with stirring up international cartoon rage, then issued death threats against Naser Khader, a Muslim politician in Denmark who is not sufficiently Islamic by imam Akkari's standards. Mr. Khader is not a fundamentalist; he is the founder of Denmark's Democratic Muslims. Mr. Khader's organization spoke out against the cartoon rage and for his courage he was targeted by Iman Akkari. A French TV documentary crew secretly filmed the imam threatening to have Naser Khader bombed.

In a French border town with Switzerland, Saint-Genis-Pouilly, a cultural group organized a reading of one of Voltaire's plays (March 2006). *"Fanaticism, or Mahomet the Prophet."* In the play Voltaire used Mohammad to lampoon all forms of religious intolerance and extremism. News of the production predictably created a furor in the Muslim community. "This play constitutes an insult to the entire Muslim community," said a letter to the mayor, signed by Said Akhrouf, French-born of Moroccan decent, and three other Islamic activists representing Muslim associations. They demanded the performance be cancelled. The Mayor, Hubert Bertrand, refused to capitulate and permitted the play to go forward. On the night of the performance the mayor had the police protect the theater. In response many Muslim youths from the community rioted, set fire to cars (a French Muslim protest staple) and attempted to halt the play. The rioters were controlled and the play was performed. The Mayor commented: "For a long time we have not confirmed our convictions, so lots of people think they can contest them." Unfortunately the mayor seems to stand as an exception in Europe.

In a sermon at Filadelfia church in Stockholm in March 2005 the Norwegian celebrity evangelist preacher Runar Søgaard, questioned the Prophet's morality since his wives included a girl aged nine years old. Søgaard was placed under police protection after receiving death threats. The sermon triggered fears of a religious war in Sweden. Muslim radicals posted a very explicit threat to launch a wave of terrorist attacks against Sweden for the "insult."

In February 2005 a Swedish museum removed an erotic painting plastered with verses from the *Qur'an* from an exhibition about AIDS. Some vocal members of the Muslim community launched a letter-writing campaign that resulted in hundreds of e-mails, among them messages along the lines of "remember what happened in Holland" (eluding to the murder of Theo Van Gogh). It would appear that Sweden has already lost freedom of speech.

What corner stone of a free society will they voluntarily relinquish next?

In the cities of Rotterdam and Amsterdam there are districts where Muslim women are subjected to genital mutilation and where the Dutch police are afraid to enter or interfere. Ironically these very cities were where refugees from Catholic France and the Spanish Inquisition sought refuge centuries ago. It is also where Spinoza was anathematized for his opposition to Jewish fundamentalism. (What is it about religion that it creates so many "refugees"?)

A trendy European jeans company emblazons its products with anti-religious symbols and slogans. While there is a jean-line insulting Christianity and a line insulting Hinduism, there are no plans for an anti-Muslim line. The motive, again, is simple fear.

"Two terrorist groups beheaded two teachers in front of their students in the Amna and Shaheed Hamdi primary schools in Shaab district in Baghdad," a ministry statement said, he believed the attacks were aimed at "intimidating pupils and disrupting learning." The studies contained subject matter not approved by Islamic clerics. (6) The real telling point of this incident is that it occurred during the American occupation and after untold "propaganda' about democracy in Iraq.

ACTIONS BY WESTERNERS AGAINST WESTERNERS ON BEHALF OF ISLAM

The pressures created within Western societies by implied threats of Muslim violence over slights, insults and behavior ***not viewed by Islam as appropriate*** has created a climate of fear and intolerance in every European country as well as elsewhere in the West. The environment of fear has led to the absurd situation of Western countries censoring many aspects of the free expression of their citizens because of Muslim intolerance to any type of criticism.

Italian journalist Oriana Fallaci criticized Islam in her book *The Force of Reason*. Muslims in Italy filed charges essentially for expressing her ideas in a supposedly free country.

In Australia, two Christian pastors were convicted of violating the anti-vilification law when they read some of the scarier parts of the *Qur'an* in public and taught that Islam is a false religion.

The Borders bookstores have carried *Free Inquiry*, an intellectual and liberal publication for many years. *Free Inquiry* planned to publish the Danish cartoons (one of the few that actually did). The Borders response was to inform *Free Inquiry* that they would not stock the April/May 2006 issue, (the issue that carried the cartoons). Borders cited security. "For us, the safety and security of our customers and employees is a top priority, and we believe that carrying this issue could challenge that priority." Borders went on to say "We absolutely respect our customers' right to choose what they wish, to read and buy and we support the First Amendment, and we absolutely support the rights of *Free Inquiry* to publish the cartoons. We've just chosen not to carry this particular issue in our stores." All the right words followed their fear driven actions.

A student group at New York University (NYU) planned to display the Danish cartoons for the purpose of having a panel discussion (March 2006). The University prohibited the display of the cartoons and the discussion thereof if it were open to the public (which these events normally are). "In a seemingly mundane (to them) decision, New York University has sacrificed the principle underlying the survival of civilization—free speech," said Dr. Yaron Brook of the Ayn Rand Institute. Under the pretense of maintaining campus security, the administration contradicted its own stated policy on free speech by requiring that, if the cartoons are displayed, the event be limited only to "members of the NYU community." The student group had to turn away more than 150 members of the public who had planned to attend the panel.

The government of Sweden has been busy closing down websites that republish the Danish cartoons.

"South Park," a wickedly funny, satirical and politically incorrect animation show for adults that deals with the politics and issues of the day, recently (April 2006) had an episode that dealt with the Danish cartoons. In addition the episode depicted the Prophet. However the show did not only deal with Islam it also contained a blasphemous scene involving Jesus, the American flag and President Bush. Comedy Central, the cable station that broadcasts "South Park" ***blacked out the depiction of Muhammad but kept the other objects of South Park's humor***. So America and Christianity are fair game to be satirized but not Islam. I would say that this action constituted an

Islamic privilege over all others. There is no question that the managers of the station acted out of fear.

Perhaps what may be one of the most extreme examples in the Northern Hemisphere of subjugating the host county's laws and norms to an emigrating group is in Canada. Canada has accepted *Shari'a* law for Muslims in cases dealing with disputes over property and family issues, including marriage and divorce. Imagine the surprise of a woman expecting to lead her life in a free country with a legal system that protects individual rights must instead submit to an Islamic council. Canadian courts will enforce the council's rulings. How can a country endure when it has two sets of laws for its citizens based on their religion?

Throughout the academic world religion is constantly being examined and criticized. Christianity is routinely criticized. The *Jesus Seminar* casts doubt on the Bible, but there is no *Muhammad Seminar* to cast doubt on the *Qur'an*. They don't dare. In all of academia Islam is treated with kid gloves.

The *generation of fear* is an appropriate motivator according to "Islam the Tolerant."

TOLERANCE OF NATIONAL SOVEREIGNTY

The world of Islam shows no respect for the sovereignty of other countries. This is demonstrated in many ways and incidents.

With respect to the Danish cartoons incident mentioned above, Kofi Annan, the Head of the U.N. said:

> "The offensive caricatures of the Prophet Muhammad were first published in a European country which has recently acquired a significant Muslim population, and is not yet sure how to adjust to it."

Adjust to it!! Since when does the host country have to adjust to immigrants? Throughout history it is the immigrant that adjusts to the host country–there has never been an exception until the Muslims immigrated to Europe and the U.S. Now the world of Islam expects all people to adjust to their norms, beliefs and eventually their rule. The latter point is never stated explicitly of course but will become clear shortly.

Pressuring a country to change its culture is only one form of disrespect for the sovereignty of a country and intolerance for its norms. A more pernicious form of disrespect is used constantly by Islamic mullahs in the form of *fatwa*s against citizens of foreign countries. The mullahs do this with total impunity from the West and from their own governments. The local Muslim governments by not stopping this practice show their tacit approval of the "custom."

The Salman Ruhdie affair was one of the first cases that demonstrated Islam's total disrespect for the sovereignty of a country. The Ayatollah Khomeini issued a *fatwa* against Rushdie who is a British subject living in Britain. In doing so Iran was claiming jurisdiction over the nationals of a foreign state. Imagine the gall; he was passing a death sentence on a British citizen and inciting other British citizens (Muslims) or Muslims of other countries to carry out this murder on British soil. Iran's supreme leader instructed Muslims around the world to serve as executioners on behalf of the Islamic Republic. The result was tragic on two levels.

First: since Rushdie was placed under British security he himself was relatively safe but within an outrageous context. However not so safe were those associated with his book. Rushdie's Japanese translator was murdered, his Italian translator was also killed, and the Italian publisher was stabbed. Three-dozen innocent people, that had no connection to the book, were killed when a Muslim mob burned down a hotel where Rushdie's Turkish translator was staying. To say that these acts are outrageous is to minimize the real significance, which brings us to the critical issue.

Secondly: the West's reaction, as always, was at best or worst depending on your view, a tongue lashing and shock. "War" was essentially declared and launched against a number of Western countries (certainly England at minimum) and nothing was done about it. Iran proved that it could do what it liked with complete impunity. And is doing so today in every possible way.

One of the cornerstones of international diplomacy is the sanctity of the foreign embassy. Diplomatic missions are recognized as the sovereign territory of the state that occupies those grounds and no one is allowed to infringe on that territory under any circumstances. Any violation of this is considered an act of war. Even in the event of an actual war, normally the diplomatic staff of both countries would be allowed to safely depart. The seizure of the U.S. embassy (November 4, 1979) in Tehran by "students" acting with Khomeini's blessing demolished that bastion of sovereignty with this one incident. Khomeini thought that the West in general, and the U.S. in particular, would do nothing if he violated this protocol. Khomeini was accurate in his assessment. The U.S did nothing for over three years. We will return to this particular incident and its further ramifications later in the book.

There should be no illusion that Islam has any tolerance for national sovereignty. It is a concept that is essentially the antithesis of the foundations of Islam. ***Islam, through the Qur'an, recognizes only two worlds–dar al-Islam (the realm of Islam) and dar al-harb (the realm of war).*** (Dar can be translated as house, law or world as well as realm.) If all those who oppose you are *infidels* (at best) then they clearly exist in the "realm of war" by *Qur'anic* definition. In all of history this is the only manifestation of this concept. Islam does not believe in any borders per se. The world is composed of only the realm of Islam (Muslims) and the realm of war (non-Muslims). This was the first realization of a "virtual world" in History. Given this concept and belief, which is strongly and widely held in the Islamic world, then the inconvenience of national borders is easily ignored.

On the surface this concept may appear to be at odds with the current existence of many Islamic nations. In Arab countries especially there is a pervading consciousness of being one nation even though there are over twenty plus "independent nations" that have evolved. In reality this "mind set" transcends the fact that there may be any number of fratricidal wars, denunciations or sworn enemies. An ancient proverb that is still used throughout the Arab-speaking world is: "I against my brother; I and my brother against my cousins; I and my cousins against the world." And they mean it.

The question that logically follows this "world view" is what of the non-Islamic people that exist within *dar al-Islam*. The answer is: they are considered *dhimmis,* people inferior to Muslims, second-class people in a state of permanent inferiority, ***dhimminitude***. When they are conquered, through whatever means, they are treated as *dhimmi*.

3 Dhimminitude

The lack of tolerance is a significant problem throughout the world. However the injustices caused by intolerance are rarely as pervasive and systematized as they are within Islamic culture wherein non-Muslims are either slaves or *dhimmis*. The slave has no rights in actuality while the *dhimmi* has virtually no rights.

Slavery, despite the prevailing opinion in the West, is prevalent throughout the world. The British Anti-Slavery Society estimates that there are 2.7 million humans enslaved in Asia and Africa and even Europe and the U.S. as well. (Other organizations put the number at many times the British estimate.) (1) In the West, most often the form of "slavery" is sexual in nature and in numbers is comparatively miniscule (non the less a tragic but aberrational element of our culture). In other parts of the world the forms of slavery run the gamut from sexual enslavement for purposes of prostitution, concubines, etc. to hard labor. In the Islamic world slavery is most prevalent in the United Arab Emirates (UAE), Mauritania, Indonesia and the Sudan where in total there are approximately one million human slaves. The practice of enslaving conquered people has existed throughout the entire history of Islamic conquests, however not all the people of the subjugated land are made slaves.

Through the belief in, and the practice of, *dhimmitude* non-Muslims become second-class citizens and are held with a degree of contempt while being forced to live with limited rights and freedoms in a semi-subjugated state. The oppression is administered through the concept of "*dhimmi*.

> "The term "'*dhimmi*' refers to the subjugated non-Muslim individuals or people that accept the restrictive and humiliating subordination to an ascendant Islamic power to avoid enslavement or death." (3)

The monotheistic populations, what Muslims call "people of the Book" i.e., Christians and Jews, living under Islam (*dar al-Islam*) can retain their religion as long as they accept the status of *dhimmi*. This entails paying a special tax, which is in reality tribute money to Islam. They thereby accept second-class citizenship, and must follow special laws limiting the practice of their religion and keeping Islam as supreme. In addition they are subject to *Shari'a* (Islamic religious law). In many Islamic countries *dhimmis* cannot walk on the sidewalk if a Muslim is walking toward him. A *dhimmi* cannot testify at a trial if it involves a Muslim. In short there exists a set of rules that completely and exactly describe what a *dhimmi* can do and how he can do it within the Islamic society.

It would be a mistake to think that the practice of *dhimminitude* is an ancient construct of law not relevant in today's western societies. In actuality the West has already accepted a degree of *dhimmi* status without realizing what they have done or its significance. Every time the West allows "special considerations" for Muslims that are not in keeping with the norms of a western society we are allowing Islam to become a privileged religion over all others and as such we are implicitly accepting a role as *dhimmi*. It would be easy to think that this position is an exaggeration of the implications of granting an "exception" for Muslims. However the case will be made that the "exceptions" are in fact the first subtle steps on a long road to the state of *dhimminitude*.

In the context of "special considerations" as used here it does not include the basic respect and deference western societies allow all religions nor are these an issue. The exceptions that fall into the "special" category are the ones that counter commonly accepted behavior and norms. These are realized in the form of accommodations for Muslims that have never been permitted to another group. Some examples:

Freedom of speech in the press or TV is almost gone in the context of ever saying anything negative about Islam itself or portraying any image that might be construed by Muslims as inappropriate. Many stations (TV and radio) prefer to use terms such as "freedom fighters" or "insurgents" instead of terrorists when it is possible. And when terrorist is used it is often not "Islamic terrorist", just terrorist. It is interesting how during the entire coverage of the Russian theater hostage crisis in Chechnya where 147 students were tortured and murdered, CNN never once mentioned that the terrorists were Muslims. The reason may clearly lie in the context of trying not to be perceived as against a particular religion. But Islam views this type of "easy treatment" as its due.

The following items are indicative of the kinds of things that are allowed in deference to Islam.

Refusal to "profile" Muslims when in fact, given many contexts, profiling is exactly what is needed as a successful screening agent to investigate possible terrorism. (Certainly not all Muslims are terrorists but all terrorists are Muslim.)

Special rules for Saudi students in the US wherein they do not need licenses to study in the US while other foreign students do.

Special consideration in schools by allowing the disruption of college classes so Muslims can pray five times a day.

The acceptance of polygamy by means of turning a blind eye in Canada, parts of Italy as well as many other countries throughout Europe.

The passing of anti-vilification laws in many countries including the U.S. is reasonably common.

Even exceptions from strikes exist in some cases. During a strike of cemetery workers, Christians waited for their relatives to be interred but Muslims were exempted from the ban on religious grounds. (Blackburn, Lancashire UK)

In Italy the Muslins actually tried to pass a law allowing female circumcision. However this was too much even for the placating Europeans and the Italians defeated the proposal for now.

As mentioned previously Canada has implemented *Shari'a* law for Muslim citizens of Canada.

There are sections of Italy, Sweden, Holland, etc. where *Shari'a* is actually the law (although not yet sanctioned legally) and Muslim enclaves are essentially autonomous from the host country.

Many companies in America and Europe have made special prayer arrangements for Muslim workers who must pray five times a day. The problem is that one particularly critical prayer is the sunset prayer but of course the sun sets at a different time everyday. So companies (Dell, Spherion, Whirlpool, etc.) have tried to accommodate the Muslims requirement but have experienced assembly line disruptions.

The Muslim Students' Association (MSA)'s National Religious Accommodations Task Force (RATF) directs local MSA chapters to insist that universities provide separate housing and meals for Muslims only. MSA is a Saudi funded organization that stridently espouses advocacy of the Saudi-style Wahhabi interpretation of Islamic fundamentalism. It is a nationwide organization.

In Europe Muslims demanded that a pro Islamic version of history be taught in schools and universities. The Europeans revised the History texts to accommodate this request even to the point of changing depictions of actual events.

Stories unfavorable to Islam are rarely carried by mainstream media and when carried they are relegated to the back of the paper or are softened in their tone. (This item does not refer to incidents of terrorist violence or war related activity but to Islamic specific issues.)

This is not an exhaustive list by any means (keep *dhimmitude* in mine as you read the many cases of exceptions and accommodations that appear in different contexts throughout the book) but it is indicative of the way the West accommodates Islam. In every case above, the "exception for Muslims" would not even be considered for any other culture or religion living within the West even though many of them have special needs. In the non-Islamic cases the group (Jewish, Christian, etc.) ***privately*** acquires any special requirements while working within the norms of the society. By making the exception for Islam the West is in a very real way voluntarily accepting a position of *dhimmitude* or at minimum moving on the path to becoming *dhimmis* in their own countries. Anytime a society creates a "privileged class" regardless of the reason, it is creating, at least to a degree, an inferior class. The fact that it is subtle in the early stages changes as the accommodations grow. It becomes more difficult to say "no" once the premise has been established and impossible to reverse a thing that is once granted. Taking away is always an extreme act while granting always seems easy, for a while anyway.

4 Limits to Tolerance

The fact that Islam is intolerant does not mean that the West should be intolerant to Muslims, quite the contrary. The values that are fundamental to Western society would be seriously compromised if we practiced intolerance to any group. This is not a situation of an "eye for an eye." The often-stated (by Muslims) moral superiority of Islam is a poor and distant second to even the West's imperfect realization of tolerance. Even during periods in history when horrific abuses to tolerance occurred at the hands of the West, it was in spite of the prevailing philosophy and not because of it. And most importantly the return to the basic beliefs always followed any behavioral aberration. Tolerance is one of modern Western societies' central traits, at least on a comparative basis. But can a society be too tolerant?

Is there a limit to tolerance? If the act of tolerance undermines the foundations of freedom that the premise of tolerance is constructed upon, then tolerance, in fact, is devoid of meaning. A good example is the Danish cartoon "fiasco" in early 2006. Sensitivity may state that certain publicized images or statements might offend some group; therefore one should be conscious of this and perhaps avoid or tone down the offending material. However, often sensitivity will undercut "freedom of expression". The publication of the 12 cartoons depicting The Prophet was clearly in the realm of exercising free speech. The cartoons were by most standards mild compared to some of the cartoons and condemnations hurdled at Jews and Christians by various hate groups and even artists in recent times. The Western reactions to these hate expressions of art and word are often quite strong but well within the range of acceptable public behavior and objection. The Islamic reactions to the Danish cartoons were not only irrational but also completely immoral by any objective standard of "morally acceptable behavior". The outburst of death threats to publishers and authors of the cartoons, actual murders and peripheral deaths, bomb threats, rioting, destruction of property–both in Europe and in the Muslim world was barbaric even for the "Religion of Peace." Should the West tolerate such attitudes and actions?

The result of this extreme behavior, as we have seen, was that much of the "free press" in European countries, as well as many American counterparts, refused to publish the cartoons. Many excuses were stated but the truth is there was only one real reason–fear. The truth of this statement is easy to see given that the same press consistently defends their right to publish the most extreme forms of anti-Christian and anti-Jewish art, literature and cartoons all in the name of freedom of expression. And although one may find the published material disagreeable or even disgusting, the press does have the right to publish it in a free society.

So the Islamic world succeeded in limiting one of the West's basic rights, i.e., free expression. This is particularly interesting in light of the endless hate literature and actions perpetrated by Islam on Israelis and Americans over the years. Is there an aura of hypocrisy in this or is it a part of *dhimmitude*?

Free speech cannot exist without tolerance, tolerance of expression in words, ideas and art. Perhaps satire is one of the most important forms of expression. It is satire in both words and images that often dramatically demonstrate human foibles and offer a pause for honest thought and wise humor. However, the Danish Cartoons may have hit too close to real truth to be tolerated by the adherents of Islam. Let's look at the words of a leading Islamic spokesperson in Denmark, Imam Abu Laban. Laban was one of the prime movers in making the cartoons a major international issue:

> "We want to internationalize this issue so that the Danish government will realize that the cartoons were insulting, not only to Muslims in Denmark, but also to Muslims worldwide".

"Insulting"–so because a single incident of "freedom of expression" in a particular country is viewed as insulting, the entire world must pay a dear price in the form of mass destruction, rioting and death.

Although the cartoons might have been perceived as insulting to many Muslims the real issue was much bigger than the cartoons themselves. The incident was used to instill fear and thereby gain control. The objective was, and continues to be, to control the exercise of rights in a (host) free society by the implied intimidation of the people that would exercise those rights. Regardless of the country, the Islamic sense of tolerance does not extend to the acceptance of the norms, laws and sovereign rights of the country they live in. This is a very real example of the mind-set of *dar al-Islam*. There is no rights or sovereignty outside of the embrace of Islam.

While the Islamic Arabs demand that Europeans respect the religious, political and human rights and sensibilities of Muslims in the West, no significant show of resentment came from the Europeans concerning the impingement on their freedoms of expression in their own country as a result of the outbursts of Muslim violence. Also there is never a protest against the Islamic countries' continued abuses of freedoms. Most of the editorials written about the cartoons and its aftermath said the right words in defense of free speech but virtually none of the periodicals that published the editorials published the cartoons.

When tolerance is practiced in a "one-way direction" it is really another name for cowardice.

> "Tolerance becomes a crime when applied to evil." Thomas Mann

The use of tolerance as a mechanism to undo a basic freedom such as freedom of expression is evil. And in the Islamic world tolerance in one direction translates to *dhimminitude.*

5 Benevolent

Benevolence and charity are variations of a common theme. Benevolence is the attitude of being kind, helpful and generous to others, while charity is the virtue of giving alms and material as well as a generosity of spirit. Belief in, and the practice of these virtues in the West are meant to be universal. In Western philosophy artificial obstacles should not create boundaries on these virtues; they should be applied universally within the context of willingness. Benevolence and charity should never be forced or be confused with altruism. In today's Islamic world it is difficult to find either the concepts as stated here or the application of their principles except between individual Muslims. And the *Qur'an* bears this out.

From the *Qur'an*:

> "Muhammad is Allah's Apostle, Those who follow him are ruthless to the unbelievers but merciful to one another." *Qur'an* 48:29

> "Let not believers make friends with infidels in preference to the faithful–he that does this has nothing to hope for from God (Allah)." *Qur'an* 3:28

> "Fight against such of those to whom the Scriptures were given as believe in neither God (Allah) nor the Last Day, who do not forbid what God and His apostle have forbidden, and do not embrace the true Faith, until they pay the tribute out of hand and are utterly subdued." *Qur'an* 9:29

It should be noted that the last quote is the admonition from Allah to place non-Muslims into a state of *dhimmi.*

From Historical Writings:

> "Ever since the religion of Islam appeared in this world, the espousers of it have been as wolves and tigers to all other nations, rending and tearing all that fell into their merciless paws and grinding them with their iron teeth; that the numberless cities are raised from foundation, and only their name remaining; that countries, which were once as the garden of God are now a desolate wilderness; and that so many once numerous and powerful nations are

vanished from this earth! Such was, and is at this day and age the fury, the revenge, of these destroyers of human kind." (1)

EXAMPLES OF ISLAMIC TOLERANCE AND BENEVOLENCE

Since its creation Islam has been the least tolerant of any religion. It is now and always has been, with only brief respites, conquest driven. In achieving its objectives it has been ruthless and resourceful in using every tactic at its disposal.

The objective of Islam, from the days of Mohammad to the current day, is to destroy any opposition to the installation of Islam as the reigning religion in the world. Chapter 3 - *Peaceful* presented a number of quotes from the *Qur'an* that clearly commanded the faithful to embark on world conquest. Although the dictums of the *Qur'an,* as handed down by Mohammad, are 1400 years old they are completely embodied in today's realization of *Shari'a* law. They are to Muslims as compelling today as they were when Mohammad wrote them. For the Muslim who accepts the *Qur'an* as the literal word of Allah there is no equivocation about the meaning of these words. It is a serious mistake that Westerners make in thinking that the literal interpretation of the *Qur'an* is not widespread among Muslims. The contrary is very much true, after all heresy within Islam is punishable by death and not to accept the *Qur'an* literally is heresy.

The conquered lands always had, by definition, an indigenous culture and people that were not Islamic since the *Qur'an* spoke of going forward and conquering the lands of the *infidels.* The conquerors, demonstrating their degree of tolerance enslaved the conquered. This process is recorded as early as 712 C.E. with the invasion of what is today Pakistan (then Kshatriya) where all males over the age of seventeen were executed and all others were enslaved. In subsequent conquests in the Indian sub-continent more than 60,000 people were enslaved and thousands more put to the sword. In 1001-1002 C.E. another 500,000 persons were enslaved. By 1019 C.E. the total number had reached 750,000 people. A contemporary historian by the name of Abu Nasr-Muhammad Utbi recorded these numbers. (2) A similar pattern and numbers can be found as a result of the wars with Turkey. Keep in mind none of these "target" countries were Muslim at that point in history. In fact the original conquest by Islam of the Arabian Peninsula followed a similar pattern only the numbers were smaller.

In all cases the total lack of any degree of tolerance or benevolence on the part of the conquering Muslims quickly caused the indigenous religions to be abandoned. The following table shows this process of religious persecution continuing into more recent times. Now the focus of Islam was the Jew.

Pogroms and organized massacres of Jews by country and year (all dates are C.E.):

Morocco 1728,1790, 1875, 1884, 1890,1903,1912,1948, 1952, 1955
Algeria 1805, 1934
Tunisia 1864, 1869, 1932, 1967
Persia (Iran) 1839, 1867, 1910
Iraq 1828, 1936, 1937, 1941, 1946, 1948, 1967, 1969
Libya 1785, 1860, 1897, 1945 1948, 1967
Egypt 1882, 1919, 1921, 1924, 1938, 1939, 1945, 1948, 1956, 1967
Palestine 1929, 1936 (a larger area of land then current "Paleatine."
Syria 1840, 1945,1947, 1948, 1949,1967
Yeman 1947 (3)

As the reader can see most of the pogroms occurred before the 1947 C.E. formation of Israel. An event that allegedly started the Islamic rage against Jews. However this outline of pogroms clearly demonstrates that the Jews only needed to exist in an Islamic country to be persecuted.

There is no question that the Jews are the people most despised by the Muslims, slightly ahead of Americans. However the Christians, Hindus, Buddhists and Zoroastrians have not faired well under Islam either. In the following slaughter the Jews were not singled out. The sword of Islam through the use of *jihad* wielded by the converted Ottoman (Turkey) ravaged villages and towns throughout Western Asia Minor (39 towns), Eastern Asia Minor (13 towns) and Northern Asia Minor (14 towns). In addition, the areas surrounding the towns were laid waste to. (4)

From 1463 to 1694 C.E. *jihad* slave raids throughout Poland, Russia, Ukraine, Kiev and the surrounding area captured more than 2.8 million slaves to serve Islamic masters. This is truly a mind-numbing amount of human suffering. (This number is said to be extremely conservative.) (5)

In much of Europe the tide of war surged or ebbed over the centuries eventually working against the Islamic Empire. Europe survived the Muslim threat and Christianity became the dominant religious force until modern times. Outside of Europe and specifically in the areas of the Arabian Peninsula, Islam kept its hold on the countries and people. And in the following set of statistics lies a very telling picture of intolerance.

The population numbers are from the year 2002 and are taken from the Internet web site of *Worldwide Population Statistics.* (6)

Afghanistan	(22.7 mm)	98% Muslim
Bangladesh	(129mm)	86% Muslim
Egypt	(69mm)	87% Muslim
Indonesia	(213mm)	81% Muslim
Iran	(68mm)	99% Muslim
Pakistan	(57mm)	97% Muslim
Saudi Arabia	(22mm)	93% Muslim
Sudan	(30mm)	65% Muslim
Turkey	(70mm)	99.7% Muslim
Uzbekistan	(25mm)	84% Muslim

Note the extremely low non-Muslim populations in these countries. The pogroms listed above along with the on going expulsion or subjugation of non-Muslims through *dhimmitude* created an environment that is dangerous to any non-Muslim.

> "The basis of Islamic attitude towards unbelievers is the law of war; they must be either converted or subjugated or killed". (7) (Note: The source of the above uses the word "law" in the above quote. This is translated from dar *al-harb* where the *dar* is often also translated by house, *world, realm* or *law*. In this book I use realm.

> "As a matter of doctrine, the Muslim's conception of tolerance is one in which non-Muslims have been politically and economically subdued, converted to Islam, or put to the sword." (8)

However true this may be it is only part of the story.

From *Shari'a* :

> "The Iman (ruler) may condemn the population of the conquered

> countries, in case they do not accept Islam and the Imam does not demand that they work and pay tribute, to be enslaved and be divided among the *Jihadists* as ghanimah (spoils of war). The owner of a slave had the liberty to treat him anyway he liked. If the slave is a woman, he was allowed to have sexual connection with her without marriage. (9)

Islamic law (*Shari'a*) brought to the horror of slavery legitimacy by stating that the enslavement of non-Muslims captured in the course of *jihad* was acceptable. What major religion has ever done anything but speak out against slavery?

In an eloquent demonstration of the Islamic sense of peacefulness, tolerance and benevolence a religious *fatwa* was issued in Iran that stated that it was permissible to use nuclear weapons in the cause of *jihad*. Further pursuant to this *fatwa* the two "extremes" of Iranian politics expressed their political positions on Israel. Rafsanjani, one of the more moderate of Iranian politicians stated that Israel is "the most hideous occurrence in history." The Moslem world "will vomit (Israel) out from its midst." Rafsanjani proposes that: "a single atomic bomb has the power to completely destroy Israel, while an Israeli counter-strike can only cause partial damage to the Islamic world." Countering this "moderate view" is the comment from the Iranian president Ahmadinejad. He has called for Israel to be "wiped off the map." This statement is certainly less "eloquent" but quite clear in its intent.

What is most telling about their position is the fact that although nuclear fallout knows no boundaries they don't seem to mind collateral damage of horrendous proportions resulting from the dropping of a nuclear bomb on Israel. For those not familiar with the geography of the Middle East let me point out that a nuclear bomb dropped on Israel could kill, depending on its radioactivity level and the prevailing winds, millions of Muslims in Egypt, Iraq, Syria, Jordan, etc. as well as most of the Israeli population. Furthermore, it is well known that Israel has its own nuclear arsenal. Do the Iranians think that they in turn will not be annihilated as retaliation? They fully understand this scenario and claim they are "a bigger country with many more people and we can absorb the damage". Insane does not begin to describe the mental capacity of the leader of Iran! No doubt to the Islamic fundamentalist a small price to pay to rid the Middle East of the Jew.

II

THE ISLAMIC–JEWISH RELATIONSHIP

6 The Roots of Hatred

THE ROOTS

What is it about the Jews that cause Muslims to harbor such a deep and abiding hatred? As we saw earlier the hatred existed long before the country of Israel existed so it clearly can't be the prime reason. Actually the Muslim's hatred of the Jews has spanned the 1400 years of Islamic history and is rooted in Islamic writings. Muslim eschatology (the body of religious doctrines concerning the human soul in its relation to death, judgment, heaven and hell) claims that the Jews were and always will be hostile to Islam because the Dajjal is Jewish. (The Dajjal is the Muslim equivalent of the Anti-Christ). Although the Muslim tradition believes that the Dajjal is Jewish this is not stated in the *Qur'an*. It is found in other writings extemporaneous with Mohammad.

The mythology states that the Dajjal along with 70,000 men from Isfraham (Jews) with shinning swords, will invade Islam for the purpose of conquest. However the Dajjal will be defeated. George Vajda (a historian) wrote an essay in 1937 analyzing the origins Muslim animosity to the Jews.

> "Not only are the Jews vanquished in the eschatological war, but they will serve as ransom for the Muslims in the fires of hell. The sins of certain Muslims will weigh on them like mountains, but on the day of resurrection, these sins will be lifted and laid upon the Jews." (1)

The shift of guilt from Muslim to Jew implied in the referenced mythology defies any concept of logic or justice from the perspective of the Western mind. However it appears to be quite an incentive (one of two actually) in the Muslim mind to fight the Jews.

Examples of Jew hatred and vilification can be found in the *Sira* (an Arabic term for Mohammad's biography) and the early Sunni historical accounts. In addition many verses in the *Qur'an* speak poorly of the Jews and in (5:82) the Jews are said to be: "malevolent enemies of Islam." These same writings also accuse the Jews of knowing that Mohammad was the true prophet but refusing to convert to Islam out of envy and private interests. To support their position the Jews are accused (there was never any evidence presented) of falsifying their Hebraic scriptures to prove they were correct in their denial of Mohammad as a true prophet. The Jews hurled oaths at Mohammad and plotted to assassinate him and even used sorcery against him. They are even accused of having poisoned Mohammad, from which he died three years after the poisoning, very slow poison indeed.

> "The analysis presented in Vajda's essay indicates that all these archetypes are used to justify Muslim animus towards the Jews, and the admonition to, at best, 'subject [the Jews] to Muslim domination', as *dhimmi*, treated 'with contempt', under "humiliating arrangements". (2)

The research found in Vadja's essay becomes very timely and real when one examines its premises in the context of terrorist organizations.

> "Hezbollah and Hamas have constructed core ideologies based upon this Islamic theology of Jew hatred, which one can glean readily from their foundational documents, and subsequent

> pronouncements, made ad nauseum. Hamas further demonstrates openly its adherence to a central motif of Jew-hatred in Muslim eschatology. Article 7 of the Hamas Charter concludes with a verbatim reiteration of the apocalyptic hadith:
>
> 'The Last Hour would not come unless the Muslims will fight against the Jews and the Muslims would kill them until the Jews would hide themselves behind a stone or a tree and a stone or a tree would say: `Muslim, or the servant of Allah, there is a Jew behind me; come and kill him'; but the tree Gharkad would not say, for it is the tree of the Jews.'" (Sahih Muslim, Book 40, Number 6985). (3)

The most senior clerical authority for Hezbollah, Husayn Fadlalah has stated:

> "We find in the Koran that the Jews are the most aggressive towards the Muslims...because of their **aggressive resistance** (emphasis added) to the unity of the faith."

It is clear from this that the Jew must convert or die. A reasonable person might conclude that if the Arab countries disarmed there would be peace in the Middle East whereas if Israel disarmed it would be destroyed as almost all of Islam has sworn to do. Husayn Fadlalah further clarified:

> "Either we destroy Israel or Israel destroys us." (4)

THE HATRED IN ACTION

It is historically interesting to note that modern genocidal anti-Semitism is deeply rooted in Arab nationalism, which is a 20th century phenomenon. It began with the Arab collaboration with the Nazis.

Many papers and books written in recent times reveal that there was extensive collaboration between the Arabs and Nazis with respect to exterminating the Jews in Arabia.

> "'One of the Nazis' main collaborators as well as an unconditional anti-Semite was the Mufti of Jerusalem, Haj Amin El-Husseini', the historians point out, and add that he reflected exemplarily the decisive role played by Jew-hatred in German-Arab friendship', the historians say. According to the study's findings, Haj

> Amin el-Husseini prepared in minute detail the extermination of Jews during several meetings with Adolf Eichmann, the SS officer responsible for carrying out the Holocaust." (5)

At the Nuremberg Trials, Eichmann's deputy Dieter Wisliceny (subsequently executed as a war criminal) testified:

> "The Mufti was one of the initiators of the systematic extermination of European Jewry and had been a collaborator and adviser of Eichmann and Himmler in the execution of this plan....He was one of Eichmann's best friends and had constantly incited him to accelerate the extermination measures. I heard him say, accompanied by Eichmann, he had visited incognito the gas chamber of Auschwitz." (6)

As a young man, al-Husseini worked with a native Jew, Abbady, who documented this comment:

> "Remember, Abbady, this was and will remain an Arab land. We do not mind you natives of the country, but those alien invaders, the Zionists, will be massacred to the last man. We want no progress, no prosperity. Nothing but the sword will decide the fate of this country." (7)

And long before the thought of a separate Palestinian state existed:

> "Haj Amin El-Husseini, a relative of Yasser Arafat, was the leader and father of Palestinian Arab nationalism, as well as a close ally of the Muslim Brotherhood. He was Mufti of Jerusalem from 1921 to 1937 and spent the war in exile in Germany where he frequently met with the highest echelons of the Nazi party, including Adolph Hitler. During the war, he helped form Muslim SS units in the Balkans. Though he was wanted for war crimes, France deported him after the war to Egypt. His memory is very much alive among Palestinians today and pictures of him are featured on the Palestinian Islamic *Jihad* website. (8)

His place as leader of the radical, nationalist Palestinian Arabs was taken by his nephew Mohammed Abdel-Raouf Arafat As Qudwa al-Hussaeini, better known as Yasser Arafat. In August 2002, Arafat gave an interview in which he referred to "our hero al-Husseini" as a symbol of Palestinian Arab resistance.

It is difficult to grasp how in the 21st Century a set of beliefs so lost in time and so completely mythological in nature could be the cause and justification of such pain and human suffering to the point of bringing the Middle East to a nuclear war.

From the brief history of Islamic conquest outlined above and given the behavior of today's terrorists/fundamentalists and the fact that Islam has maintained the longest hatred in history (against the Jews), one might conclude that peacefulness, tolerance and benevolence, when used in describing Islam, is at the very least a gross exaggeration. What then is the true nature of Islam?

III

WHAT KIND OF RELIGION IS ISLAM?

7 The Nature of Islam

THOUGHTS ON THE ESSENCE OF ISLAM

Although the major religions, Islam, Christianity and Judaism are monotheistic, Islam has quite a different view of God. In Islam Allah is not a God of atonement and redemption (both characteristics are present in the Christian and Jewish views of God) instead he is a God of vengeance and capable of arbitrariness. In addition in both Christianity and Judaism God has a "contract" or covenant with the religion's adherents. No such covenant or even concept of a covenant between God and humanity exists in Islam. Instead, Allah decrees his law:

> "by means of a unilateral pact, in an act of sublime condescension (that) precludes any notion of imitating God as is urged in the Bible." (1)

Compounding the theological split between the Judeo-Christian and Muslim concepts of divinity is an added critical difference:

> "Although Muslims like to enumerate the 99 names of God, missing from the list, but central to the Jewish and even more so to the Christian conception of God, is 'Father' - i.e., a personal God capable of a reciprocal and loving relation with men,"

> "The one God of the Koran, the God Who demands submission is a distant God; to call him 'Father' would be an anthropomorphic sacrilege." (1)

What begins to flow from this premise is a view of God more as an absolute ruler, a disciplinarian rather than a redeemer.

From the *Qur'an*:

> "The Jews say: 'God's hand is chained', May their own hands be chained! May they be cursed for what they say! By no means. His hands are both outstretched: He bestows as He wills." *Qur'an* 5:64

Here the *Qur'an* unequivocally lays down another reason to hate the Jew while at the same time also declaring Allah's absolute ability to do what it is He wishes completely arbitrarily with respect to any rules or humanly defined morality.

> "The idea that Allah's hand is 'not chained' is a reflection of his absolute freedom and sovereignty. If God is good, as Jesus says, His goodness may be discernable in the consistency of creation; but in Islam, even to call Allah good would be to bind him." (2)

The concept of a God "not chained" by anything releases into the realm of reality a ***destroyer of causality, logic and morality.*** Given this context all logic and science is built on sand, no rational framework can exist that could not arbitrarily be destroyed by a capricious God. ***With a belief system predicated on a view of God that is all-powerful, unforgiving, vengeful and arbitrary there can be no deviation from the "written word" for His followers.*** It is no wonder that the modern world is anathema to the fundamentalist and devout Muslim. Every aspect of modernity is, in one form or another, a sacrilege or an effrontery to the Muslim belief system.

Contrast this position with St. Thomas Aquinas' view of God:

> "Since the principles of certain sciences—of logic, geometry, and arithmetic, for instance—are derived exclusively from the formal principles of things, upon which their essence depends, it follows that God cannot make the contraries of these principles; He can not make the genus not to be predicable of the species, nor lines drawn from a circle's center to its circumference not to be equal, nor the three angles of a rectilinear triangle not to equal two right angles." (3)

Another philosopher put it succinctly when she stated the three laws of logic in this form: [A is A, either or, non contradiction]. Ayn Rand summarized Aristotle's logic and Aquinas's proposition when she wrote that a thing is what it is, it is one thing or it can be another but it cannot be both at the same time with respect to the same framework. By the nature of existence contradictions cannot exist. (4) Only in the world of Islam does it seem that the laws of logic and causality can be suspended.

The contrast here is so startling as to be almost shocking. It is clear why Islam is as backward today as it was 1000 years ago. Reality as it can be perceived is not accepted in the world of Islam. It is a world where "A can equal non-A", where contradictions can exist. In a single statement Mohammad laid the bedrock for a society that, if it accepted the *Qur'an* in a literal interpretation, could not advance, could not question. It is a religion that creates an absolutists' acceptance of its word. Why not kill an innocent, why not enslave women or enemies, why not destroy civilizations? If it is what Allah wants, if it is sanctioned in the *Qur'an* then it is what all Muslims can and often must do.

If the good is that which is life sustaining and affirming then evil is that which is inimical to the life of the individual. A review of Islam's epistemological framework yields a system of beliefs and a mode of thinking that cannot sustain life in the context of growth. In reality the Islamic world exists by virtue of the West's science, commerce and trade. In its own vacuum Islam would deteriorate into a pre Middle Ages culture much like the recent fundamentalists implementation of Islam achieved by the Taliban in Afghanistan, or as currently exists in the Sudan. The truth is that there does not exist an Islamic theology/philosophy that has integrated modernity in any form whatsoever. It is this glaring inability that underlies the absolute need to dominate the non-Muslim world. It is the mind-set of a barbarian; you destroy what you are unable to compete with. It is always *dar al-harb* (the realm of war), a must for Muslims.

VIEW'S OF ISLAM BY HISTORICAL FIGURES

No religion has garnered so many negative views. They can be found at every age throughout history. This is truly unique.

> Winston Churchill on Islam: "How dreadful are the curses which Mohammedanism lays upon its votaries! Besides their fanatical frenzy, which is as dangerous in a man as hydrophobia in a dog, there is this fearful fatalistic apathy. Improvident habits, slovenly systems of agriculture, sluggish methods of commerce, and insecurity of property exist whenever the followers of the Prophet rule or live. A degraded sensualism deprives this life of its grace and refinement, the next of its dignity and sanctity. The fact that in Mohammedan law every woman must belong to some man as his absolute property—either as a child, a wife, or a concubine–must delay the final extinction of slavery until the faith of Islam has ceased to be a great power among men.
>
> "Individual Moslems may show splendid qualities. Thousands become the brave and loyal soldiers of the Queen; all know how to die. But the influence of religion paralyses the social development of those who follow it. No stronger retrograde force exists in the world. Far from being moribund, Mohammedanism is a militant and proselytizing faith. It has already spread throughout Central Africa, raising fearless warriors at every step; and were it not that Christianity is sheltered in the strong arm of science–the science against which it had vainly struggled–the civilization of modern Europe might fall, as the civilization of ancient Rome." (5)

Like so many of Churchill's words these too were so very prophetic.

From Hillaire Belloc:

> "In the major thing of all, Religion, we have fallen back and Islam has in the main preserved its soul…We are divided in the face of a Mohammadan world, divided in every way–divided by separate independent national rivalries and dispossessed–and that division

> can not be remedied because the cement that once held our civilization together, the Christian cement, has crumbled. Perhaps before (these lines) appear in print the rapidly developing situation in the Near Nest will have marked some notable change. Perhaps that change will be deferred, but change there will be, continuous and great. Nor does it seem probable at the end of such a change, especially if the process be prolonged, Islam will be the loser." (6)

Like Churchill's words Mr. Belloc's quote is proving to be quite prescient.

Bertrand Russell on Islam:

> "Christianity and Buddhism are primarily personal religions, with mystical doctrines and a love of contemplation. Mohammedanism and Bolshevism are practical, social, unspiritual, concerned to win the empire of this world."

And the quote that perhaps best summarizes Islam comes from John Quincy Adams:

> "The essence of his (Mohammad's) doctrine was violence and lust: To exalt the brutal over the spiritual part of human nature." (7)

Alexis de Tocqueville on Islam more than two centuries ago:

> "I studied the Koran a great deal. I came away from that study with the conviction that by and large there have been few religions in the world as deadly to men as that of Muhammad. So far as I can see, it is the principal cause of the decadence so visible today in the Muslim world and, though less absurd than polytheism of old, its social and political tendencies are in my opinion more to be feared, and I therefore regard it as a form of decadence rather than a form of progress in relation to paganism itself." (8)

18th century philosopher Diderot.

> "Islam is the enemy of Reason."

And more recently Malek Chebel states:

> "Fundamentalist Muslims are true fanatics. They consider progress the enemy of Islam. They are narrow-minded ideologues who use the Koran to achieve sinister political aims." Chebel further defines

> Islam as "a backward political ideology." (9)

Ibn Warraq on Islam:

> "The theory and practice of *jihad* was not concocted in the Pentagon. It was taken from the Koran, the Hadith and Islamic tradition. Western liberals, especially humanists, find it hard to believe this...It is extraordinary the amount of people who have written about the 11th of Sept without once mentioning Islam. We must take seriously what the Islamists say to understand their motivation, (that) it is the divinely ordained duty of all Muslims to fight in the literal sense until man-made law has been replaced by God's law, the *Shari'a*, and Islamic law has conquered the world. For every text the liberal Muslim produce, the mullahs will use dozens of counter-examples (that are) exegetically, philosophically, historically far more legitimate." (10)

THE LITERAL NATURE OF THE QUR'AN

It is true that all religious scriptures have passages that range from silly to gruesome when viewed through the lens of modern reality and science. The very antiquity of these writings almost assure that a certain simplistic view of the universe would be present as well as modes of behavior that were natural or acceptable millennia ago. The Bible and the New Testament are of course in this category. In many passages both sets of scriptures call for their followers to perform acts that in today's world are viewed as immoral and horrendous. The *Qur'an* indeed has many passages as well that exhort the followers of the religion to perform acts that are, in the eyes of the West, barbaric and uncivilized. This would indicate a rather level field when comparing the religious scriptures. In reality the field is anything but equal.

The difference lies in the fact that Islam does not know the word allegorical. Every word of the *Qur'an* is taken literally today just as it was 1400 years ago. The entire concept of "progressive revelation" as it exists with respect to Judaism and Christianity does not exist in Islam. Progressive revelation allows for the interpretations of many of the stories, parables, even dictates of the scriptures. They are viewed as allegorical constructs for the purpose of guiding a believer from a state of sin and ignorance to a state of enlightenment. The *Qur'an* on the other hand is accepted as the literal commands from Allah to the faithful. There can be no interpretation. This single fact leaves the Muslim with a religion that at its central core is war like for the *Qur'an* admonishes its followers to conquer the infidel and convert the world to Islam.

If interpretation were permitted one might position these *Qur'anic* dictates as meaning: "the adherents of Islam are to ***proselytize*** throughout the world." (As opposed to conquer the world.) But in fact many of the quotes we have seen as well as others leave that option in the realm of wishful thinking.

THE RESULTS OF LITERALISM

As stated before, the world, from the point of view of Islam, has only two parts: "The Realm of Islam" and "The Realm of War". These designations taken from the *Qur'an* leave little doubt as to how non-believers will be dealt with and how the "collective" (the people of Islam) can be brought together for a declared goal. However, there is another aspect to the nature of Islam, and in many ways it is even more disturbing then Islam's militaristic compulsions, and that is its absolute requirement to control the individual. The core philosophy of Islam that is responsible for both its militaristic nature and its need to control the individual is *collectivism.* A collectivist philosophy can only endure within a dictatorial state. This leads us to ask the question is Islam at all compatible with a republic-based form of democracy? The answer is an emphatic no. (I say republic based because in its primitive form democracy can be little more than mob rule and this exists all over the third world.)

Collectivism and democracy are incompatible. Surely the examples of the 20th Century in Eastern Europe make that point all too clearly. Nothing short of the complete secularization of the religion/state entity that is Islam will allow democracy in any form to exist within Islam. (Turkey is an exception that we will review shortly.) In fact nothing less than this split will allow the individual even a modicum of personal freedom. To the degree that the religion dominates, the individual will be subjugated. Here are the words of a Muslim intellectual, A. K. Brohi who was the Minister of Law and Religious Affairs in Pakistan and has written extensively on human rights from the Islamic perspective.

> "Human duties and rights have been rigorously defined and their enforcement is the duty of the whole of organized communities and the task is specifically entrusted to the law enforcement organs

> of the state. *The individual if necessary has to be sacrificed in order that the life of the organism be saved.* (Emphasis added) Collectivity has a special sanctity attached to it in Islam. In Islam there are no "human rights" or "freedoms' admissible to man in the sense in which modern man's thought, belief and practice understand them; in essence, the believer owes obligations or duties to God (Allah) if only because he is called upon to obey the Divine Law and such Human rights as he is made to acknowledge seem to stem from his primary duty to God (Allah)."

A review of how societies that accept a literal interpretation of the *Qur'an* operate in a way completely compatible with Mr. Brohi's philosophy is useful in making the abstract point concrete.

Mullahs are appointed by the state to supervise the morality and actions of the population including dress and private behavior. Apart from peering into the bedroom, many more of them scrutinize the cinema, the press, and books. They monitor the public expressions of thought to assure complete adherence and conformity with *Shari'a* and the *Qur'an* and its official interpretation. A professor cannot say what he likes at school since the mullahs run a network of spies throughout all walks of everyday life. If an intellectual publishes his own views, he is risking his life or at least his freedom. Many people who think and express thoughts not in keeping with the orthodoxy are given free room and board in the local prison for extended periods. This was the way of life under the Taliban and it is the way of life in many other Muslim countries with Iran being the most extreme example.

The so-called moderate Islamic states are little better. The extreme in these states is somewhat less brutal but freedom does not really exist and democracy is a sham. Saudi Arabia is a repressive monarchy; Egypt and Syria are dictatorships, etc. Turkey is the only Islamic country that ever succeeded in achieving a secular state and as a result also achieved the highest standard of living and freedom in all of Islam. However the tragedy is that the new generation of Turks are slipping back into fundamentalism and it is questionable as to who will win.

> "Individualism is not a recognizable feature of Islam; instead, the collective will of the Muslim people is constantly emphasized. There is certainly no notion of individual rights, which only developed in

> the West, especially in the 18th century. The constant injunction to obey the Caliph, who is God's (Allah's) shadow on earth, is hardly inductive to creating a rights-based individualistic philosophy." (11)

Contrast the Islamic view of "human rights" with Thomas Jefferson's:

> "A bill of rights is what the people are entitled to against every government on earth, general or particular, and what no just government should refuse, or rest on inference."

Apologists for Islam dismiss many of the personal control characteristics of the religion as merely anachronistic cultural influences that will change with time as Islam enters the modern age. Nonsense! Nothing will change until the fundamentalist view of the religion changes. If Islam was capable of change then why in 1400 years of history has it not changed? Especially why hasn't it changed over the past 100 years of its exposure to modern ideas and technology? It hasn't changed because as it is practiced it cannot change. It will never change so long as the religion and the state are one.

A closing thought: the word "freedom" did not exist in the Arabic language for centuries because within the Islamic civilization the concept did not exist in any form. The word freedom was introduced into Arabic in 1774 C.E. (the word "hurriyya," meaning literally "entitlement") since it became a necessity when signing treaties with the West.

8 The Collective and The "Group Think" Phenomenon

One of the things most frightening about the religion of Islam is its "group think" characteristic. No "ism" or religion has been able to create within almost the entire population the type of universal way of thinking and reacting to events, as has Islam. In part this emanates from the concept of *dar al-Islam*, which transcends national boundaries. What affects one part of Islam affects all of Islam. In theory and practice there is only one gigantic brotherhood under Allah.

The second aspect that drives "group think" is that Islam is more than a religion, it is an entire belief system governing all behavior throughout life; included in this governance is all aspects of the individual's life and the society's practices. Islam controls all dimensions of human existence: politics, economics, law, worship, dress, sex, eating, attitudes, definitions of crimes, punishments, etc. There is no secular state or truly independent personal choice. There is only *Shari'a*.

From the earliest infancy the indoctrination begins and continues through all aspects of education into maturation with the end result being the creation of the "citizen automaton." This degree of indoctrination coupled with the myth of "when dying in battle for Allah, the martyr goes to Paradise, etc." makes a normal person in one context a very dangerous and fanatical person in another. The individual morphs into a "tool" for achieving Islam's goals.

> "Individualism is not a recognizable feature of Islam; instead, the collective will of the Muslim people is constantly emphasized." (1)

Take the case of Abdul Rahmam mentioned previously. The Taliban was gone, Mr. Rahman's religious conversion to Christianity occurred in a "free Afghanistan." In most of the world a religious conversion is a very personal event and not anyone's business but not so in Islam. Mr. Rahman was arrested and put on trial for the crime of "religious conversion from Islam." The sentence would be death if he were to be found guilty. This is so foreign to Western thought that it seems part of some piece of fiction from an ancient world. But what makes it into a modern nightmare is the overwhelming support by the entire Muslim world of this potential death sentence. There were virtually no objections. All Muslims were calling for his death. Very few Muslims even mildly disagreed with the actions of the Afghan authorities. If they accept the *Qur'an*, and since the entire religion is based on the literal acceptance of the *Qur'an*, then there is very little room for dissent in cases that violate the teachings of the *Qur'an*. All Muslims accept this premise; it is what makes the group, the collective so compliant to the demands of the mullahs.

It is the same phenomenon that we see when anything bad happens to Israel or the U.S. There is this uniform celebration because the Jew or the Great Satan have gotten what they deserve.

"The Daily Telegraph in London reported: 'Iran's hard-line spiritual leaders have issued an unprecedented new *fatwa*, or holy order, sanctioning the use of atomic weapons against its enemies.' Hmm. I'm not a professional *mullah*, so I won't speak about the theological soundness of the argument, but it seems a religious school in the Holy City of Qom has ruled that: 'the use of nuclear weapons may not constitute a problem, according to *Shari'a*.' Well, there's a surprise. How do you solve a problem like *Shari'a*? It's the one-stop source for justifying all your geopolitical objectives and the use of any method to achieve them." (2) And here again there was no outrage from the moderate Muslim. Islam in general is essentially fine with the thought of nuking Israel.

Confessed al Qaeda conspirator Zacarias Moussaoui at his death penalty trial stated "Americans think that if you fly a plane into a building you are crazy. We are not. It's in our religion." And there is a long line waiting right behind Mr. Moussaoui to take his place.

Muslims all over the world cheered after 9/11 because the Great Satin was humbled, the invasion of the American Embassy in Tehran was met with cheering as well. The Iranian supported terrorist organization Hezbollah successfully completes a terrorist attack against the American marine barracks blowing up American Marines and again there is cheering. There is no event that harms the West, regardless of how horrendous, that isn't met with an instantaneous group wide common reaction of joy. This then is the nature of Islam, an essentially collectivist's set of extreme beliefs in the form of a religion that demands unquestioned literal acceptance of all of its tenets by all of its adherents.

9 Islam and Martyrdom

A Westerner looks at the event of a suicide bombing and is incredulous. From one perspective a person might conclude that a belief can be so strong and a cause so great that a devotee might sacrifice themselves for the belief. Throughout Western history there are many stories of heroism and the sacrifice of one's life for a perceived greater good. Emotions and actions such as these are usually admired in that a significant element of the sacrifice is generally to prevent others' deaths and not to specifically cause the death to an enemy. In all cases the act is an exception to Western culture's overriding sense of life and the belief in the sanctity of human life. It is always viewed as a terrible loss but a sacrifice that is rendered to save lives not as an act of destruction to take lives.

For Muslims the act of suicide is completely different in that the concept of killing one's self is "institutionalized as a weapon" and the objective of the act is martyrdom in the process of murdering *infidels*, the more the better. On a metaphysical level the differences between the two culture's perspectives on suicide is so profound that scholars and philosophers are required to elucidate the many elements. Suffice it to say that the fundamental difference lies in a person's sense of life and the value placed on a human life.

The reason suicide became so ingrained in Islam does NOT specifically lie in the *Qur'an* which clearly states:

> "..do not with your own hands cast yourselves into destruction..." (*Qur'an* 2:195); "
>
> "Do not kill yourselves..." (*Qur'an* 4:29)

The justification therefore lays in the events of history and in "the way one views" the admonition in the *Qur'an*. (That does sound like an interpretation.)

Mohammad's succession was contested some time after his death. One of the candidates, Ahl al-Bayt, was ambushed and decapitated by his enemies. The followers of the murdered Imam became the Shiite Muslims (Shi'a). They represent only 10% of Islam. The followers of the victorious group became the Sunni Muslims. The Shiites have, since their beginnings, been taught to honor and revere martyrdom, given that their founder was martyred. During the festival of Ashura, a Shiite religious holiday, the young male Shiite adherents gash themselves in the head as a sign of emulation and homage to the decapitated slain leader. This then is the cultural root of Shiite martyrdom as a noble act. (Today the Muslims that are Shiites (Shi'a) are the Iranians, the Palestinians (Hamas) and the Iraqi insurgent-terrorists.")

The way the modern suicide bomber rationalizes the *Qur'anic* admonition against suicide is by referring to the many other quotes in the *Qur'an* that enjoin Muslims to fight the *infidel.* It is further argued that the admonition against suicide is directed at the act itself when it is a non-*jihadist* act, an act that is a personal desire for a personal reason. The suicide terrorist is performing and an act of murder in the service of Allah and Islam, this is acceptable. (Once again the individual is subordinated to the collective.) There can be no plea to conscience that innocent people are being killed since the suicide bomber is on a *jihadist* mission for Islam and is therefore beloved of Allah. In this way there is also no guilt.

What "sanctifies" the act in the Muslim's mind is that he is doing Allah's will and command. And in addition there is a personal payoff for the suicide terrorist, he or she receives the promise of paradise. The motivation is overpowering to the ignorant mind. He is doing Allah's command and will exchange the "veil of tears" that is this life for Allah's paradise.

10 The Hypocrisy of the Leaders of Islam

Islam authors endless diatribes against Jews, Christians and the U.S. However the slightest negative aimed at Islam is met with an extreme response and at times the response is violent. This is actually in perfect harmony with the literal teachings and practices of the religion. Yet any mention of this fact (or of Islam in any unfavorable light) and it is met with accusations of bigotry and *Islamophobia*, but as we see from the previously presented population ratio statistics, the Muslim countries allow no other religion (in a practical sense) unless its adherents exist as *dhimmis*. And of course this encourages non-Muslims to leave an Islamic country if at all possible.

A typical example of living in the state of *dhimminitude*:

> "On behalf of The Canadian Lebanese Human Rights Federation (CLHRF), I strongly condemn the barbaric, savage and fundamentalist attacks that targeted yesterday (April 14, 2006) on three Egyptian Coptic churches in the northern Mediterranean city of Alexandria. The assailants, three fanatic Muslim extremists who were equipped with swords and knives, attacked the Christian civil and peaceful parishioners during their celebration of the Good Friday Masses. One parishioner was killed and twenty others were seriously injured. Two of them are in the hospital on the verge of death.

The CLHRF went on to say that these attacks were commonplace.

> "Today's crime in fact uncovers Egypt's harsh, blunt and ongoing anti-Christian policies, laws and practices that openly infringe on Christian basic human rights, properties, and freedom of beliefs and expression.
>
> "This phenomenon of anti-human rights practices is widely encouraged, nurtured and cultivated through education of hatred, fundamentalism, rejection of the other and ignorance. What is unfortunate, pitiful and sad is that the governments of the above mentioned countries adopt such practices while the free world keeps a blind eye or in the best scenario limits its condemnation to mere rhetoric levels.

(Taken form a letter written by Elias Bejjani, a Human Rights activist, journalist & political commentator, as well as spokesman for the Canadian Lebanese Human Rights Federation (CLHRF) (1)

Contrast the actions of these Muslims in Egypt (as well as the endless other atrocities of this nature throughout Islam) against the demands of the Muslim leaders for respect, accommodations and deference to the Muslims living in the West. Nothing but the word hypocrisy can be used to describe it. Saying that these are two different sets of people is not really relevant in the context of evaluating the hypocritical nature of the Muslim behavior. The salient point and the reason why this is valid is that on no occasion do actions taken by terrorists groups like those that attacked the Coptic Christians ever illicit a single protest or comment of regret or condolence from the Western Muslim leaders that are at the same time demanding special treatment for Muslims. It is as though they were not part of the same Muslim religion. However when the West is viewed as guilty of an activity not deemed acceptable to Islam the entire Islamic world descends on the West both figuratively and literally.

Applied Hypocriscy:
Mohammed Hasan al-Tohami describes the *jihad* conquest of Jerusalem in the seventh century (638 C.E.) as follows: "Jerusalem was liberated by the Muslim armies and purged from the remnants of Romans and Zionists." (Romans are Christians and Zionists are Jews.) This quote demonstrates two things: first it clearly shows, from Islam's mouth, that the indigenous people occupying Jerusalem in the seventh century (actually much earlier and long before Mohammad was born) were the Christians and Jews; and that they were vanquished from ***their*** homeland by the Muslims, who before that time did not occupy Jerusalem. Yet al-Tohami refers to this act of war as "liberated". (Similar to the way Hitler liberated Poland.)

Secondly and most telling is how Islam is most comfortable arguing both sides of an issue as it suits them. Although they "liberated" Jerusalem from the Jews they say it is still theirs even though Israel re-won it in the 1967 war, which Islam started. So if Islam conquers a territory it's always theirs and never anyone else's including the indigenous people Islam took it from. But if another state takes recently held Islamic territory in a war, Islam wants it back.

The UN allowed Iran to send a delegate to the UN's new "Human Rights

Commission." As if Iran having representation on a Human Rights Commission wasn't hypocrisy enough the man they sent, Said Mortazavi, is a prosecutor notorious for jailing and torturing Iranian dissidents. In addition Mortazavi is accused of being present in July 2003 when photojournalist Ms Zahra Kazemi (an Iranian with Canadian citizenship) was killed while in Iranian custody. Mortazavi is also accused of managing the cover up of her death. It is not clear which is the worse hypocrisy Iran sending a butcher or the UN allowing him to be on such a commission. Actually the act of Iran being permitted representation on anything associated with humanity is a travesty.

The activities of many senior Muslim leaders throughout the West continually demonstrate the differences between the image they project to the West and what they preach to other Muslims. As a sample: the former Florida professor Sami al-Arian is now accused of running a front for funding terrorist activities and groups. Yet Professor al-Arien was perceived as a respected community leader who on many occasions appeared at the White House as a guest. He has posed for photos with both Clinton and Bush. However it has come to light that privately he refers to America as the Great Satan. He has also espoused, "dismantling the culture of the West." These allegations can be found in current federal court documents relating to his illegal activities. In addition to al-Arien's activities there are a considerable number of Muslim charitable organizations (designated religious charities) whose sole purpose is furthering the Muslim cause and clandestinely supporting terrorist networks. While these organizations are espousing a benign view of Islam, their leaders are busy supporting the networks of terrorists that are attempting to destroy the West. Many of these activities and organizations will be revisited in later chapters.

11 Islam and Women

In discussing the nature of Islam it is impossible not to cover the most repressed people on earth, Muslim women. When evaluating a culture's efficacy in the context of sustaining life and generating the conditions conducive to material wellbeing and happiness, it is critical to understand the way that all people within the culture are viewed and treated. The West has not always had a position that is perfect in this context, far from it, but the salient point is that the West's progress in building progressive societies that are inclusive of all of its' people has been a consistent theme with real progress to show for it. Even a cursory review of the Islamic human rights record will show a very different picture.

Since its birth Islam's view of woman is that she is inferior. Some quotes from the *Qur'an* on the subject of Woman:

> "Men have authority over women because God (Allah) has made the one superior to the other and because they spend their wealth to maintain them. Good women are obedient. They guard their unseen parts because God (Allah) has guarded them. As for those from whom you fear disobedience, admonish them and forsake them in beds apart, and beat them." (*Qur'an* 4:34)
>
> "Women are your fields: go, then into your fields whence you please. (2:223)
>
> Allah thus directs you as regards your children's inheritance: to the male, a portion equal to that of two females." (*Qur'an* 4:11)
>
> "if any of your women are guilty of lewdness take the evidence of four reliable witnesses from amongst you against them; and if they testify, confine them to houses until death do claim them. Or God (Allah) ordain for them some other way" (*Qur'an* 4:15)

Although this does not specifically authorize an execution of an offending woman, nor does *Shari'a* law require such, it is a common practice to execute the offending woman.

> The *Qur'an* on what awaits the martyr in Paradise (this is the complete objectification of woman):

"voluptuous women of equal age" 78:312

"They shall sit with bashful, dark-eyed virgins, as chaste as the sheltered eggs of ostriches." 37:48

"We shall wed them to dark-eyed houris." 44:54

"Therein are bashful virgins whom neither man nor jinnee will have touched before."" 55:56

"We created the houris and made them virgins" 56:36

Note: "houris" are the pure people of Paradise awaiting the Muslim.

From these quotations one could not be faulted for thinking that the Islamic view of woman even in Paradise is in fact as property to be used, toys to be played with, children to be punished when required, etc.

From The Hadith:

"'I was shown the Hell-fire and that the majority of its dwellers were women who were ungrateful.' I was asked, 'Do they disbelieve in Allah?' or, 'Are they ungrateful to Allah?' He replied, 'They are ungrateful to their husbands and are ungrateful for the favors and the good deeds done to them.'" Haddith 1.2.2

"The Prohet said: 'I looked at Paradise and found poor people forming the majority of its inhabitants; and I looked at Hell and saw that the majority of its inhabitants were women.'" Hadith 4.54.464

"....I stood at the gate of Fire and saw that the majority of those who entered it were women." Hadith 7.62.124

"Wives are playthings, so take your pick." Hadith 22.858

Once Mohammad was asked: "What rights does a woman have with a man?" He replied, "He should feed her if he eats, cloth her when he dresses, avoid disfiguring her or beating her excessively or abandoning her except at home."

From Other Sources:

"From the protected and seclude environment of the extended family, Muslim daughters are sent into marriage. In many cases, the bride and groom do not meet until the day of the wedding contract is signed. In Islam, marriage is as much a joining of two families as it is a joining of two individuals. For this reason the family has a large amount of participation in the choice of marriage partners." (From *Voices Behind the Vail* by Ergun Mehmet Caner)

"A Muslim woman's essential identity is determined by her relationships with men–her father, her husband, and her family. She is not defined autonomously, but in relationship to the males for whom she functions as a symbol of both honor and Islam." (1)

In addition the *Qur'an* sanctions polygamy. Mohammed had 13 wives (one of them was nine years old) although by Islamic law four wives is the limit.

"Marrying a girl before she begins menstruation is a divine blessing." A. Khomeini

"Do your best to assure that your daughters do not see their first blood in your house." A. Khomeini

Abu Hamza al-Masri called upon the faithful to murder female tourists in his native Egypt, saying: "If a woman, even a Muslim woman, is naked and you have no way of covering her up, it is legitimate to kill her."

In many places a woman can only receive a medical examination by a woman doctor, but of course women are for the most part denied education beyond the *Qur'an* so how are enough women doctors developed? What happens to women who are ill and can't see a woman doctor? In the Muslim countries the general health of women is worse than that of men (which is in itself not great). As one views the state of women across Islam, it is clear that the degree of suffering is directly proportionate to the degree of literal enforcement of *Shari'a*.

Perhaps the practice that most dramatically and negatively defines a woman's station in Islamic society is female circumcision.

FEMALE GENITAL MUTILATION (FGM)

With respect to this issue the voices of Muslims are more informative than anything a writer could possibly add.

"It's our religion. We pray, we do fasting, we do circumcision. For

14 centuries of Islam, our mothers and grandmothers have performed this operation. Those who are not circumcised get AIDS easily. [Sheik Yusef Badry, in news report "Egyptian Court Allows Female Circumcision," Toronto Globe & Mail, June 25, 1997]

"Circumcision is cleanliness if used moderately and is useful to women as well as men." [Mohammed Tantawi, leading Islamic religious scholar, quoted in the Arabic newspaper Asharq Al-Aswat, reported by Miriam Sami, Associated Press Writer in "Cleric Eases Stand on Female Circumcision, Alarming Activists," April 9, 1996]

"Our mothers, aunts and sisters have been doing this for years and no one was complaining." Dr. Munir Fawzi, Gynecologist at Cairo's Ain Shams University, Dallas Morning News, 12/25/96

Many here dispute claims that there is any health risk associated with the age-old operation..."Circumcision has no negative effects as (the government) claims and today, with the progress of medicine, the operation can be done without any danger." [Khaled al-Sharif, Abnob tribe member, quoted in news report, "Egyptian Fundamentalists Ignoring Female Circumcision Ban," 6 January 1998, Agence France-Presse]

"I do see a few cases (of emotional disturbance from circumcision), but when you compare their number to that of the number of women that are circumcised, they are very trivial indeed." [Dr. Yahia Oun Alla, Sudanese psychiatrist, interview, p. 137, Prisoners of Ritual: Odyssey into Female Genital Circumcision in Africa, Hanny Lightfoot-Klein, 1989]

"According to a government study earlier this year, 97 percent of 14,779 Egyptian women polled had been circumcised...Eighty percent of those circumcised said they were pleased with the results." [Excerpt from news report "Egyptian Court Allows Female Circumcision," Toronto Globe & Mail, June 25, 1997]

"To defend themselves from feelings of inferiority, many women deny that FGM damages their bodies or their sexuality." [Excerpt from booklet "FGM: A Call for Global Action," p. 37, published by RAINBO, 1995]

Other quotes can be found in Appendix A.

One might ask: why does this practice persist? The essence of the reason lies in the fact that women are viewed as property and by altering them you eliminate their ability to enjoy sex and therefore increase the likelihood that they will stay loyal to the property owner.

The practice of FGM is now being performed in many places in Europe. Although still illegal there have been Muslim pressures to allow the practice in several Western countries.

HONOR KILLING

Another Islamic tradition is "honor killing," whereby family honor is restored through the murder of a female relative who is seen as having sullied the family reputation by being raped or found to be adulterous.

> "The problem of 'honor killings' is not a problem of morality or of ensuring that women maintain their own personal virtue; rather, it is a problem of domination, power and hatred of women who, in these instances, are viewed as nothing more than servants to the family, both physically and symbolically.
>
> "Unfortunately, the legal safeguards to protect women and men from indiscriminate and unlawful enforcement of presumed Islamic injunctions have been forgotten. Indeed, the legal system and law enforcement agencies including police officers and prison guards, have been implicated in the perpetuation of the problem by their willful lenience towards men who have carried out an assault in the name of 'honor' and by their abuse and denigration of women who stand accused." (2)
>
> "In the last few weeks, Swedish society has been touched by the brutal and calculated murder of Fadima Sahindal; a young courageous woman who chose to live according to her will and paid the price by her life. In the last two months, two other young women in Denmark and Britain were killed by their fathers because of the honor of the family. Honor of men and the family took their lives. Honor killing is a tribal and Islamic practice prevalent in Islam- ridden countries and Muslim inhabited

> communities in the West. Being killed deliberately and brutally is, in fact, a price that victims pay to practice their minimal human rights such as how to dress, talk to men other than their male family members, live, work and study independently, and marry at will, or have voluntary sexual relations.
>
> "Hundreds of women get shot, burned, strangled, stoned, poisoned, beheaded or stabbed every year in Islam ridden countries because their male relatives believe their actions have soiled the family name. They die, so family honor may survive. According to this tribal and religious practice, woman is a man's possession and a reflection of his honor. It is the man's honor that gets tarnished if a woman is 'loose'. The murderers and their defenders refer to this verse of the Koran that allows husbands to beat their wives: 'As to those women on whose part ye fear disloyalty and ill - conduct, admonish them, refuse to share their beds, beat them', the Koran, chapter 4, verse 34. Honor killing is a tribal practice that has been incorporated in the religion of Islam, because of its anti - women nature and misogynist philosophy. And the law is usually on the man's side, not only in the Middle Eastern and the Central Asian countries, but shamefully, in the Western countries too. They often let murderers go unpunished or with a light sentence." (3)

Gordon Ash a British intellectual and Islamic apologist states in *Free World: America, Europe and the Surprising Future of the West* "to see your daughter raped in front of your eyes by a militia gang is as soul-rending for a Muslim mother as for a Jewish mother." Of course Mr. Ash is correct but he has left out an important part. The Jewish parent does not then murder her daughter for having dishonored the family. Such honor killings have actually become routine in Europe.

CHILD BRIDES

Under *Shari'a* nine is the legal marrying age for a "woman". This is not just a statute it is a reality. Legalized pedophilia is a better word for describing this practice. In Iran, which strictly follows *Shari'a,* it has been found that pedophiles do in fact take advantage of this legal age by marrying children from the provinces. They use them and then abandon them. Since the girls are no longer virgins their lives are also ruined. A study in Jordan indicates that 26% of domestic violence is committed against wives under eighteen. In Nepal 40% of all marriages are consummated when the bride is younger than 14 years of age. In parts of Muslim India 56% of women were married before the age of 15 and 17% were younger than 10. In an Afghan refugee camp two out of three second graders were married or betrothed. (4)

RAPE

In 2004 a leading Danish mufti said that Danish women not wearing the veil "were asking for rape," a comment seemingly less offensive to the Muslim community than a few cartoons (first published in Denmark).

The number of rape charges in Sweden has quadrupled in just over twenty years. The growth exactly parallels Muslim immigration. The experience in other European countries is not different.

THE VEIL

What is the symbolism of the veil? It is a symbol of being subservient.

Shortly after the French controversy over the wearing of head coverings in public schools (this is where the French government stated that women could not wear the traditional Muslim head coverings in public schools) an Iranian-born novelist (Chahadortt Djavann), living in Paris wrote: "I wore the veil for ten years. It was the veil or death." In another book *"What Does Allah Think of Europe"* she compared the veil to the yellow star forced on the Jews in Nazi Europe.

LACTATION

The inferior treatment afforded females in Islamic societies begins in the first year of life. Male children are breast fed roughly twice as long as a female child. A boy is breast fed for two to three years and a girl for one to two.

"Since the period of lactation is one in which, under the practice of demand feeding a child is almost automatically pampered, and since the folk mores call for pampering a boy but not a girl, the mother, by cutting short the breast feeding of a girl child, in effect terminates the period in which the baby girl is pampered. A second reason (for the practice) is the widespread belief that while the mother nurses a child she will not become pregnant again. Having experienced the disappointment of bearing a daughter, the mother wishes to conceive again as soon as possible in hope of presenting a son to her husband and his kin, and thereby compensating everybody (including herself) for the loss of prestige suffered through the birth of a daughter." (5)

The abused wives who fled to women's shelters, the toddlers subjected to the torture of clitoridectomy, the children sent abroad to prison-like *Qur'an* schools or forced marriages, the teenage girls compelled to wed illiterate bullies who think wife-beating is a God-given right, the woman killed because she is raped or in some way has "sullied" the family reputation these are among the most acute abuses of women in the world today. There are women today fighting this treatment and fighting for women's rights, they just happen not to be part of the *Women's Movement* in America

12 Human Rights

THE WORSE ABUSE OF HUMAN RIGHTS

Terrorism is the destruction of human rights on a near unprecedented scale.

The world is currently the victim of a human rights abuse second only to the Holocaust; it is called terrorism. The most extreme form of an abuse of a human's right is the taking of life. War is horrific by any measure of the word. However murder is just as evil, it is only the multiplier that is different. The Islamic fundamentalists have succeeded in "institutionalizing" murder and through a twisted religious zeal, made it a virtue. I once read that "selling" suicide (convincing someone to take their own life) was morally worse than murder (the issue had to do with the cowardice of the "seller"), perhaps; and if so, an entire society has dedicated itself to murder and the selling of suicide but has also positioned it as a moral value rather than the evil it is. Suicide bombers are being trained from earliest childhood to "glory in their own destruction" as long as they can take *infidels* with them.

The other aspect of terrorism is that it destroys the human expectation of living free of fear. The very act of terrorism is meant to rob the society, within which the act occurs, of its sense of safety and peace of mind. Living free of fear may not be thought of as a classic human right but when it is gone little else seems to matter. Of course this is the objective of the terrorists.

What a glorious "moral code" for a society to have and what a legacy it will create.

Since the 1972 Munich massacre the terrorists have been perfecting their craft to the point that it has become the scourge of civilization. Even before Munich the terrorists gave the West terror in Cologne, Hamburg, Geneva, Vienna Airport, then came Munich followed by Frankfurt, Lod Airport, Trieste, London, Paris, Brussels, Geneva, Vienna, Montreal, Ottawa, Buenos Aires, Kinshasa, Thailand, Karachi, Khobar Towers, Nairobi, Tanzania, the USS Cole, the 1993 World Trade Center attack, the 2001 World Trade Center, Madrid, London and thousands of suicide bombings in Israel as well as else where. All these cities were the victim of the human rights abuse known as terrorism.

For a sense of just how widespread and lethal terrorism has become see Appendix B for a summary of terrorist attacks across just a four-month period of 2006.

In the realm of "classical human rights" the section on *dhimminitude* lays out the reality that i*nfidels* do not have rights–not in Islam. The following quote is typical of the attitude found among Islamic leaders towards human rights.

> "The very concept of human rights was a 'Judeo-Christian invention' and inadmissible in Islam. According to the Ayatollah Khomeini, one of the Shah's most despicable sins' was the fact that Iran was one of the original group of nations that drafted and approved the Universal Declaration of Human Rights." (1)

SLAVERY

References to, and approval of, slavery abound in the *Qur'an* as we have seen from many quotes included herein. One can claim that the same is true of the Bible, however as stressed before the literal nature of the Bible is suspect in modern religious traditions. Concepts that appeared to be acceptable in ancient times are not so today. Furthermore the practice of humanism mitigated the extremes of both Judaism and Catholicism over the years. Humanism does not exist in Islam and the extremes are very much present with us today. The *Qur'an's* literal nature is absolute and eternal. And so we find that slavery is prevalent in many areas within Islam today just as it has been for 1400 years.

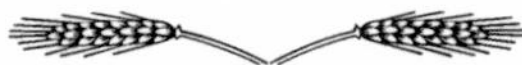

Through this brief examination of the "Nature of Islam" it is clear that the West and Islam have absolutely nothing in common, neither culturally, morally, nor attitudinally and most importantly not philosophically. What we are about to see is that we are in a battle with Islamic culture for our survival.

IV

THE CLASH "ABOUT" CIVILIZATION

13 The Nature of the Battle

The British Prime Minister, Tony Blair, speaking of the War On Terrorism told a press luncheon in London in early 2006 that: "This is not a clash ***between*** civilizations. It is a clash ***about*** civilization." President Bush in a speech to the nation on September 11, 2006 said: "This is a clash ***for*** civilization". Both of these men understand, at least implicitly, that the real nature of the clash with Islam is for the survival of civilization, as we know it. Intrinsic to Islam there exists a set of concepts that are inimical to the West while at the same time there exists a set of concepts within Western society that are inimical to Islam. Only one can win: only one will shape the future of civilization.

Two elemental and diametrically opposed philosophies are at the heart of the war with Islam. Simply put Islam is *collectivist* in every aspect of its belief system while the nature of the West is *individualist* based. From these vastly different philosophical foundations derive equally different concepts of man's relationship to the state. Within Islam the religion and the state are one and inseparable. Man exists to serve the Islamic state in the name of Allah. In the West the state exists to protect the individual and his inalienable rights.

Given these opposite views of the relationship of man to the state it is clear that the incompatibility of these philosophies is so extreme that only one can survive. From the West's perspective, an Islamic victory could very well end the forward march of civilization and its return to a repressive, religious dominated society more common to an age long past. Take a look at the current modern Islamic states, or at the Taliban and one can see the future civilization under Islam. From Islam's perspective the "Westernization" of Islam would mean the complete loss of the control of man through the force of religion. If this happens then the ability of man to think and act and strive for "his" own goals and desires and mode of living will dominate. Islam as it is structured today would change as dramatically as did the Catholic Church many centuries ago. This would be a catastrophe from the perspective of today's Islamic leaders.

To prevent this catastrophe, this threat to the traditional ways of life as defined by the *Qur'an* and the *Hadiths,* all forms of Western culture must be eliminated from the realm of Islam. Given the modern world's economic integration and its omnipresent communications capability it is absolutely impossible to achieve the complete isolation that the Islamists so fanatically strive for. And they know this. The question then becomes: if Islam can't be isolated from the West then Islam must convert the West through Islamization and at the same time fulfill a central directive of the *Qur'an* and that is the domination of the world by Islam. However the process of Islamization cannot be achieved without destroying Western culture since in fact the two cultures are diametrically opposite.

> "Within the Muslim world, Islamization means de-Westernizing everything: from political and cultural institutions to economic ones, even to the point of rethinking banking operations. On the outside, it means spreading Islam through vigorous missionary activity, in both Europe and the United States; this activity is supported above all by Saudi Arabia. But according to the most radical interpretations, Islamizing the West means violently

> attacking its political and economic power, without sparing the civilian population." (1)

This quoted view posited by Mr. Bertacchini and Mr. Vanzani is certainly in keeping with the Islamic scriptures and religious writings and especially within the speeches of Osama Bin Laden. To Islam everything about the West is a curse and unclean and must be destroyed. Many scoff at utterances such as these. However all the words of all of the "would be world conquerors" throughout history were often laughed at before their campaigns, but the tragedy of their actions were never avoided because the world avoided accepting the literal meaning and intent of their words. The world never thought "they" meant it *literally*. Unfortunately they always did and still do today! Believe the words of the Islamists for we are now in a World War with them and there is no prize for second place.

The veracity of stating that we are engaged in a world "conflagration" is really not difficult to prove, one merely needs to look at the scope of the conflict, as it exists today. In doing so keep in mind that the issue of weapons and conventional troops and battles do not need to be the same as prior world wars. The two central points of a world war are the desire for world conquest on the part of one of the antagonists and a near global scope of the fighting. The fighting can take many forms.

In the world war that we are currently engaged in only one philosophy will survive in the end. Either man and his inalienable rights will remain supreme or the religion-based state will dominate. Certainly this is in a very real sense a replay of many past battles throughout history. Battles fought for the same reasons but whose combatants had different names, Nazism, Communism, etc. At this time in history the war and its weapons have taken a somewhat different form. It is essential to understand the different nature of the war if the West is to fight the correct battles with the correct counter-weapons.

What follows is a review of the weapons used by Islam to achieve world dominance and how the West unsuspectingly aids Islam in its quest.

V

ISLAMIC METHODS

14 The *Ten Steps*

Islam's goal of world domination and the creation of a new Caliphate is well on its way to becoming a reality. The process by which this goal is being achieved is not like any prior attempt at world conquest in history. There is not the proverbial mad dictator forming a great army with the intent of instigating war and massive invasions. On the contrary, the method being used by Islam is more subtle and in the long run effective. There are two major components to Islam's process of conquest: "a slow corrosive process from within a targeted country" and " acts of terrorism from without." The slow corrosive process enfolds in many almost unnoticeable phases while the terrorism is blatantly used as a destabilizing force both to the targeted country and to the West in general. The two methods operate in parallel across all targets and phases simultaneously; and as such it is impossible to fight in any conventional way. The totality of the process appears to be nothing more than a type of awful chaos, but unfortunately it is more of a "planned chaos."

We are greatly indebted to two authors for the discovery and explanation of the methodology by which the conquest is achieved: *The Legacy of Jihad* by Andrew G. Bostom, M.D. and *Islamic Imperialism: A History* by Efram Karsh.

The following is a summary of the *Ten Steps* that the above authors identified.

By means of immigration, infiltration and gradual assimilation into organs of power such as political parties and organizations, business entities, educational institutions, even the military Islam gains an initial foot-hold, then moves to strength and finally to dominance. The "process" consists of ten phases, and it was in the past and is today replicated in country after country. It has been the Muslim way for hundreds of years.

Infiltration: The gradual migration of Muslim populations to a host country. Settlement is always in groups in suburbs, small towns or the countryside. Assimilation is avoided.

"Advertise": Explain how peaceful and tolerant Islam is and how good Muslims are. Any bad press or accusations are the result of "the hate mongers suffering from *Islamophobia*."

Acceptance: Through continuing works of charity for the poor and generosity to the locals become good members of the community. Encourage more immigration.

Converts to Islam: Convert locals focusing on the poor or in some way disenfranchised. In the U.S and Europe these groups include criminals in prisons, minorities, etc. Infiltrate human rights groups, etc. expand the number of mosques.

Agitation: Agitate for rights of Muslims. Demand protection of the Muslim's ways and traditions and agitate for laws against "*Islamophobia*".

Political Organization: Organize political parties sympathetic to the goals of Muslims, for example Muslim only enclaves. Force the host society to accommodate Muslim requirements, i.e., religious, marital, dress, food, etc. (Advanced in Europe and now unfolding in the US.)

Divide and Conquer: make pacts with anti-establishment and minority groups within the host country (Green Peace, National Lawyers Guild, lobbying, etc.) This furthers the formation of a power base.

Population Expansion and Violence: From the beginning increase the Muslim population through continued immigration but more importantly high birth rates. When the Muslim population percentage reaches 10-15% a destabilization process begins. This takes the form of strikes, violence, demonstrations, intimidation, street-violence, bribery, etc. (Most of Europe but particularly France is in this phase currently.)

Full Blown Terrorism: If the host country does not react strongly the next phase is implemented, i.e., full blown terrorism, Muslim leaders seek public office, move up the power structure and begin to restore peace. In this way they seem to be performing a great service for the host country when in reality they are amassing power for the next major push of Islam. (Process almost complete in Bangladesh)

Establish Shari'a: It is now possible to have *Shari'a* law (*Qur'an* based Islamic law) more widely enacted and eventually made the law of the land. At this point the mission is complete, the host country is effectively a Muslim state and the non-Muslim population becomes *dhimmis*.

The process in various forms evolves when the emigrating minority's culture, values and norms of behavior are the antithesis of the host country. A group that fanatically and absolutely literally follows a religion that is war like and vengeful and whose central dictum is world domination must be the victor when met with weakness and piece meal acceptance. At present a counter strategy does not exist in the West. What's worse is the fact that there is little to no awareness of the enfolding Islamic process as such.

One of the reasons that the process is not recognized in its entirety is that the process is not being "dictated" by a single identifiable dictator following an obvious master plan a' la a Hitler or as in previous century's endless numbers of egomaniacal would be conquerors. The process is decentralized and continuing on many fronts and at many stages simultaneous in different countries. The horror of the *Ten Steps* is, however, that it is inexorable and insidious. It is not impossible but it is incredibly difficult to fight and will be a long-lived battle. But if we don't identify the nature of the evolving battle in all of its enfolding contexts and fight this battle our culture and way of life are doomed.

15 As The Ten Steps Enfold

From Islam's mouth:
Algerian President Houari Boumedienne stood in the General Assembly of the United Nations in 1974 and declared,

> "One day, millions of men will leave the southern Hemisphere to burst into the northern one. But not as friends. They will burst in to conquer. They will conquer it by populating it with their children. Victory will come to us from the wombs of our women."

And again:
In 1997, a London-based Imam said, "We cannot conquer these people with tanks and troops. We have got to overcome them by the force of our numbers."

An ever-increasing population of Muslims, empowered by the freedoms offered by Western democracy is implementing the principles of *dhimmitude* in their new homelands at an ever-escalating rate without the West being aware of the process. Of course the skeptic can easily object to this since *dhimminitude* is not a process that is born extant and is therefore not easy to see. It is slow and evolutionary and as it progresses it eats away at our basic liberties. As an example of this process it is important to recall the way the Muslims in the Danish cartoon controversy demanded that non-Muslims obey the Islamic law against religious images (one of the *Shari'a* laws). The West capitulated. The cartoons were not published by most of western media. This is not the only incident of *Shari'a's* subtle insinuation into the West.

Below and throughout the book there will be many examples of this insertion of Islamic societal norms governed by *Shari'a* into Western countries. These are all exceptions to the indigenous culture's norms and are part of the slow process of a society's acceptance of *dhimmi* status. Many may seem, if not trivial, then at least not important. This may be true on the surface but when the totality of the accommodations and exceptions are considered the picture becomes more alarming. Many more examples will be presented to express different aspects of encroaching Islam.

> The recommendations for legalized polygamy for Muslims by an official commission in Canada. Canadian law is subordinated to Shari'a,

> The silent acceptance of polygamy in parts of Europe. European law and custom are subordinated to Shari'a and Islamic custom,
>
> The banning of the English flag in English prisons because it's an insensitive "crusader" emblem. This sets the precedent of subordinating patriotism to Islam,
>
> The introduction of gender-segregated swimming sessions in municipal pools in Puget Sound. The acceptance of the use the public treasury or property in support of Islamic customs,
>
> The elimination of any work of art works depicting Muhammad, et al from galleries, museums and print in many parts of the world. This is the subordination of freedom of expression to Islamic customs and Shari'a.
>
> Young women can be and are transported from the West to their country of origin for a forced marriage. In Norway the courts upheld that the parents right to force their daughter to leave the country to be married against her will was legal. Of course this is actually illegal. Once again this represents the subordination of common law to Shari'a's requirements and Islamic norms.

These are random events a "tip of the iceberg" occurring across the Western world. However in any one of these countries, from which the examples have been taken, there can be found many other "accommodations" for Muslims. Again no group or religion has ever received this degree of deference. ***In effect the existence of accommodations of this type is the first step toward accepting the jurisdiction of Shari'a over secular law.*** When one removes the nice words of the *multiculturalists* from the facts of the accommodation one can clearly see that in effect we really are accepting into our culture and society Allah's dictums for how to live. But it is our culture and our countries not Islam's. The accommodation of these types of extremes have never been allowed for any emigrating group to the West in the past–not Catholics, Hindus, Buddhists, Jews, ethnic groups, etc. All people were allowed to follow their religion and customs but not at the expense or loss of secular dominance and the rights and/or standards of the people of the hosting country.

Many will say that the level of accommodation is not significant. But they are wrong because it is a "creeping" set of accommodations that continues. It is one thing then another then another. It achieves the gradual surrender of the values and norms of the host country. *Dhimmitude* will eventually be achieved. As an example, no right is dearer to an American and to the West in general, then freedom of speech. There have been endless tests storming that fortress but all have failed until now. The Danish cartoons achieved censorship in the U.S. like nothing before it. The Comedy Central "censorship" of South Park because it depicted "The Prophet", and their subsequent letter of explanation (see below) is typical of the mealy mouth excuses for surrendering but the truth is fear drove the decision. And that is a tragedy and it is surrender. We must always keep in mind that in Islam there is no secular law there is only *Shari'a*! Religion and law are one!

The producers of "South Park" (see *Tolerance of Expression* in Chapter 2) decided to remove a segment of one of their episodes dealing with the Danish cartoon issue. After the announcement they wrote an open letter in response to many letters from viewers expressing concerns over Comedy Central's censorship of the "cartoons episode" of South Park. The following excerpt is most telling:

> "Comedy Central's belief in the First Amendment has not wavered, despite our decision not to air an image of Muhammad. Our decision was made not to mute the voices of Trey and Matt (South Park creators) or because we value one religion over any other. This decision was based solely on concern for public safety in light of recent world events.

They go on to say:

> "As a viewer of "South Park," you know that over the course of ten seasons and almost 150 episodes the series has addressed all types of sensitive, hot-button issues, religious and political, and has done so with Comedy Central's full support in every instance, including this one. "Cartoon Wars" contained a very important message, one that Trey and Matt felt strongly about, as did we at the network, which is why we gave them carte blanche in every facet but one: we would not broadcast a portrayal of Muhammad.
>
> "In that regard, did we censor the show? Yes, we did."

So they are willing to take on every subject and present any person whether from history or living today just so long as it does not offend Islam. Their complete letter was 580 words all of which tried unsuccessfully to mask the fact that they were afraid. The fact that they said in another paragraph that: "this decision was based solely on concern for public safety in light of recent world events," is a cop out. Whose safety were they concerned about? Where was the violence they were considering, Pakistan? Indonesia? It was fear plain and simple and of course they will most likely be afraid in the future. I am not belittling their fears but it is interesting that they lacked the fortitude to state the real issue, and that is all to common with respect to Islam today.

The only answer to Muslims requesting accommodations for their religion is NO! If you can't live in our culture go where you feel comfortable but we don't change!

As discussed earlier, *dhimmitude* is not something to be taken lightly but it is slowly evolving with the growth of the Muslim populations in the West. *Dhimmitude* becomes more and more difficult to stop once the door is opened and the percentage of the Muslim population grows within a particular nation. Europe is tragically experiencing the destruction of its very cultural fabric at the present time.

Pim Fortuyn, a Dutch politician whose book *Against the Islamitization of Our Culture* took a position arguing that "the rise of an illiberal Muslim subculture threaten democratic values and that the Netherlands was doomed unless it seriously addressed this threat."

The renowned Historian and Princeton professor Bernard Lewis speaking at his 90th birthday party in 2006 stated:

> "The very composition of society is at stake. The rate of immigration from parts of the Muslim world is altering the way in which society is run. And the Muslim populations of the EU, many of whom started out as quite moderate in their native lands, seem to be indoctrinated by some of the worst elements of their own co-religionists. Central to this is the oil money of Saudi Arabia, funding extreme Wahhabite doctrines."

At the opposite end of the spectrum Oxford professor and Islamic apologist Timothy Garton Ash writes in *Free World*, Europe needs "more cross-cultural knowledge . . . How many non-Muslims know when or what Eid-ul-

Fitr (a Muslim holiday) is?" Since when does the host country need to learn or adopt the ways of the immigrant? How often do Jews or Christians say: "you must learn our ways" to the population at large? Perhaps Professor Ash should suggest that the Muslims learn the language and ways of the countries they now live in.

Here is one last story of fear-induced cowardice.

Ali Ayaan Hirsi is the author of a book that is strongly critical of Islam's treatment of women, *The Caged Virgin.* As a result of this book, her collaboration with Theo Van Gogh (the murdered film maker), her out spoken support of women's issues as well as her strong critique of radical Islam and the European policies that help it grow she is under constant death threats from Islamic killers. Ms Hirsi was also a member of the Dutch Parliament, a third world émigré and a black woman. She is also a moral giant! (Imagine a member-of-Parliament being under death threat for what she believes, says and writes. This is against every principle of western culture, law and society.) Because of the death threats the Dutch government kept her as a virtual prisoner, which in turn made it impossible for her to do her job as an elected representative. Eventually the authorities found her an apartment in a protected building. She still attended parliament but by guarded autos and constant bodyguards. Her neighbors in the secure enclave apartments filed suit and complained that her presence exposed them to risk. Because a court upheld the suit even though the buildings were the most secure in Holland. Since Ms Hirsi was now required to vacate the apartment she would be in mortal danger. Adding injury to this insult the Dutch government suddenly found a mistake in her application for asylum that was filled out many years before (they had to be looking real hard to discover this issue years later) and ruled that she was not a citizen and would be asked to leave the country. She therefore was forced to resign from parliament and seek asylum in the U.S. where she now lives and works. (In mid 2006 the Dutch government reversed their position on Hirsi having to leave the country, but it was too little too late)

The events surrounding the Hirsi incident are a tragedy on two levels. The first is the obvious one, i.e., the injustice that Ali Hirsi was subjected to, but it is the second level that is truly tragic in a broader sense.

The fact that a country that has been, for generations, a bulwark of free speech and freedom of human behavior and tolerance has just succumbed to a segment of their population that would normally be prohibited from impinging on another citizen's freedom of speech, opinion and movement is truly tragic. The Muslims effectively drove Ms Hirsi out of Parliament, her home and her country and the Dutch did nothing. This is a reversal of the very foundation of what their society stood for. How can such an extreme and dramatic change occur in one generation? The answer lies in the fact that the ***philosophical and moral context*** of an entire generation was altered dramatically in such a way that it changed the very belief system of the culture. It is this change in beliefs that allowed them to accept the set of events surrounding the Hirsi story and to do nothing. The discussion of the philosophical, moral and contextual changes that are permitting this impingement on Western culture will be covered in detail in Chapter 27 *Multiculturalism*.

As the *Ten Steps* show, there is a constant pressure emanating from the local Islamic groups and population for the West to learn and to accommodate their ways. And there seems always to be an underlying threat of violence if accommodation is not achieved. This is the road to *dhimminitude*.

16 A Different War—Terrorism

TERRORISM AND THE CREATION OF FEAR

The origins of the modern "terrorist movement" as we know it today took form almost thirty years ago. It was the outgrowth of the radical views put forth by Ayman al-Zawahiri, a physician, author, poet and former head of the Egyptian Islamic Jihad–a group he later merged with al-Qaeda. Al-Zawahiri is also a supporter of Takfir wal-Hijra an Islamic extremist group dedicated to violence. In his early years al-Zawahiri envisioned the way *jihad* could be used to unify Islam and undermine the West. Since then he has become a fanatic with a deep belief in *jihad* and devoted to furthering the ways it is used.

The central issue, with respect to the West, for a fanatic like al-Zawahiri, and more recently Osama bin Laden is that all things outside of Islam (essentially Western culture, i.e., freedom, individualism, etc.) are a threat to the traditional ways of life as defined by the *Qur'an* and the *Hadiths* and therefore must be destroyed. A classic military frontal attack was obviously impossible and al-Zawahiri understood this but he also understood the potential power of fear as a weapon and the way to use terror to induce that fear within societies. He believed a continuing and escalating fear would undermine these societies thereby causing chaos and weakness. And *jihad* was the perfect means to instigate extensive terrorism.

Certainly Zawahiri understood the nature of Western societies and how internally fragile they are when confronted with the constant threat of explosive violence. Retrospectively this is easy to see. The infrastructure of civilized countries is a sophisticated and complex mechanism that is meant to serve the needs of the population effectively, seamlessly and safely. Introduce into these mechanisms the potential for death and destruction and the very convenience and ease of use become a source of concern for one's life. Transportation is a perfect target. It is, along with communications, an essential element of a complex society. Prior to the potential of a terrorist attack air travel was safe, swift and easy to utilize. Look at the nightmare it has become. One attack has the ability to sustain fear and cause enormous out lays of capital to prevent another attack. The security elements put in place to prevent another attack stay in place; they become part of the eroding quality of life and a reminder of the danger we live with.

Carry this to the next step of creating the same level of fear with respect to train travel. Then the subsequent step of making it questionable if you will return from shopping or a restaurant because of a potential suicide bomber attack, as is the case in Israel and the many places in the Middle East. And it is easy to see the way life under these conditions becomes strained and exhausting. It is this ability to create a constant sense of fear and the necessary reactionary expenditures of human and financial capital that is draining on a country's wealth and will. Furthermore it creates within the country a degree (and after time an extreme) of political divisiveness unseen before. And these conditions are exactly the goals of terrorism.

The Islamic objective was achieved when, as an example, Spain precipitously broke off all support for the U.S. in the Iraq war as a direct result of the Madrid train bombing.

The Madrid terrorist attack caused many deaths and destroyed much property. However, the greatest loss to Spain was its independence. As a result of the terrorist attack there was a political backlash against Spain's involvement in the Iraq war that caused an underdog, left wing anti war candidate (Jose Luis Zapatero) to upset and win the presidential election (from Jose Maria Aznar). Before the election Zapatero announced that he would pull Spain's troops out of Iraq if elected and he did so immediately upon assuming office. A huge win for the terrorists was achieved by comparatively little effort. The fact that Spain pulled out of Iraq is, in a fundamental sense, immaterial to either Spain or the Iraq war but it is very material to enforcing the efficacy of terrorism. What is interesting about the Madrid terrorist attack is its timing. It was perfect in terms of being just a few weeks before the national election that pitted an anti-war candidate against a pro-war candidate. Does anyone wonder if that was only a coincident? Does Spain really think it won a battle?

Another victim of the "wearing out" effect of years of terrorism and conflict is Israel. The way Israel abandoned Gaza shows a degree of policy-by-exhaustion rather than clear, purposeful strategy of self-interest. In all of Israel's history this "escaping mentality" has not been seen before. The governments that fall victim to this Islamic tactic never admit that they are giving in to the implied "blackmail" or pressure but it is transparently obvious that it is a major factor in the new decisions that seem to contradict long established firm policies. Certainly this has also proven to be true in Europe but in the context of Islamic accommodations and political alignment with Islamic policies.

Another aspect and dimension of the effectiveness of terrorism is its economic impact.

There are distinct types of terrorism: narrowly focused and broadly devastating. The individual suicide bomber attack is narrow in scope. The bomber incident is a terrible thing but it is an event with terrible but local consequences. Its economic impact is difficult to gauge and is most likely in the form of loss of revenue in particular venues, i.e., restaurants, theaters, etc. If event frequency increases the economic impact would certainly increase dramatically (e.g., in Israel). A second class of attack is on infrastructure and is by its nature more difficult to achieve but yields greater "terror," death and destruction; but still it is generally perceived as only locally disruptive. However the economic impact to prevent incidents of this type is quite substantial. The money spent on concrete barriers in front of buildings in Manhattan and in many major cities, increased building screening and surveillance both in equipment and personnel is quite considerable and of course costs are always eventually passed on to consumers in one form or another, which translates into a direct loss of purchase power and therefore a decrease in standard of living.

The big terrorist prize is the destruction of air travel (almost an ongoing process) or the release of a biological agent or a nuclear agent (all intelligence experts say that these events are being planned for).

Air attacks can take four forms:

Using the planes as a huge missile as was the case on 9/11 and the WTC

Firing missiles at passenger-planes such as the attack on an Israeli plane taking off from Mombassa in Kenya in 2005. There have been other attacks of this type.

Planting explosives on the plane in its cargo compartment as was the case with the Pan-Am plane that blew up over Lockerbie, Scotland

Carry-on explosives in the plane's passenger compartment, as was the case with the shoe-bomber (or by other means).

The most recent (mid 2006) example of the carry-on category is the spoiled plot to blow up a large number of planes traveling from London to the U.S. using undetectable chemicals brought on board in personal hygiene products.

The complexity of air attacks (all four categories) clearly demonstrates a degree of coordination, training, support, logistics, money and technical knowledge far beyond that which is needed for the individual suicide bomber. The combination of the intent to cause mass destruction and death and the resources behind the attack are in a very real sense a definite "declaration of war." Further to this point it is clear that the objective of attacks of this nature go beyond the obvious destruction and death and actually strike at the heart of commerce of the Western world. Air travel is as essential to the global economy as any of its other major elements. Without air travel many economies will slow and the current trend to globalization will also slow. This is a very definite objective of the Islamists. It would not take many incidents to achieve this goal.

The West tends to think of victims of terrorism and does not focus on the enormous economic implications of successful terrorist attacks. And this is the way in which the West normally thinks, i.e., in a context of the sacredness of human life, and that is part of the greatness and superiority of Western culture. But in fact the economic consequences of a successful major terrorist attacks can be absolutely devastating.

> "Even a backward and impoverished nation like Afghanistan under the Taliban had shown it could pose a serious threat to American security through its support of terrorists. Estimates of the economic damage done by 9/11 range as high as $600 billion; whole industries–airlines and travel in particular–were threatened with bankruptcy. If 9/11 had been followed up by similar terrorist attacks in the United States and Europe, the possibility of global economic instability with its attendant civil and political disruption was a real and daunting prospect." (1)

The aftermath of 9/11 has been an outlay of billions of dollars spent on airport security in the U.S and more billions spent by other Western countries. And we have not come close to closing all of the potential avenues of attack against air travel. In addition we have not begun to address port security, containers and rail security. It is a task that is truly daunting and capable of destroying Western economies if taken to an extreme. It is the fear that is driving us. It is of course valid but it is important to name the driving factor–fear. Fear is the perfect creation of terrorism. And Islam is intent on bringing that "perfection" to the entire non-Muslim world.

Emotional exhaustion is pernicious and debilitating and from Islam's perspective very effective. The recognition by Islam of the long-term negative effects of terrorism on Western society has led to the development of a vast and sophisticated network support system for terrorism and its practitioners.

A WEB OF TERROR

The terrorist web of today is global and it is connected. Specific cells do not necessarily know of other cells but at appropriate levels of terrorist organizations the interconnectivity is known, actively used, managed and above all always changing. In communicating, the terrorists effectively use the "connected" world - the Internet, cell phones and the real time fund transfer systems to plan, execute and fund the acts of terrorism. (This is the principle reason that so many Islamic organizations in America are so opposed to *The Patriot Act* and other surveillance programs aimed at identifying these activities. You can be sure that constitutional rights are the furthest things from their mind as a reason for protest.)

Money flows from various factions and countries throughout the Middle East (Saudi Arabia, Iran, etc.) to endless Islamic "charities" and from these to mosques and front organizations and eventually into the hands of terrorists. Communications for organizing, planning and the dissemination of training literature and instructions flow over the communications networks throughout the world to the terrorist cells. The single specific act of terrorism belies the complexity of the network that operates in support of the terrorists. However the sophistication and complexity of the network becomes clear when one understands that the same method and network support terrorist activities in dozens of countries often simultaneously.

Most recently a number of terrorist plots have been uncovered that have given the West a clear view of the nature of the operation of the local cells and the international structure that supports them. The support takes the form of logistics, material, training, personnel, target selection and reconnaissance.

The network operates both globally and in country and often in response to Western actions deemed not acceptable to Islam.

By way of example the aborted Toronto terrorist case is most illustrative.

On Friday June 2, 2006, in Toronto, Canada, 17 suspected Islamist terrorists, mostly from the Toronto area were arrested. It is alleged that they were planning multiple attacks on targets in southern Ontario. According to the Canadian Security Intelligence Service (CSIS, Canada's CIA), the group intended to blow up government buildings, including the CSIS and the Royal Canadian Mounted Police (RCMP) headquarters in Toronto, in retaliation for Canada's support of America in the War on Terror. The group had acquired three tons of the fertilizer used in the manufacture of explosive devices. (The Oklahoma City bomb blast that destroyed the Federal Building used only one ton.) They also had a cell phone detonator and military equipment used in training.

What led to the Toronto arrests was a long chain of events that are still unfolding. However, enough information has now been made public so that a clearer picture of the trail to Toronto and the nature of the *web* that exists among terrorists are emerging. (Of course the authorities have been aware of this for a long time but it has become so obvious that it is now entering the realm of common knowledge.) Scotland Yard arrested Younis Tsouli (alias Irhabi 007 - Irahbi means terrorist in Arabic) in London on October 22, 2005. The charge was planning a terrorist attack and other related activities. It was this arrest and the information obtained from Tsouli that ultimately led to the breakup of the Toronto plot.

During the raid on Tsouli's home Scotland Yard found a PowerPoint presentation that demonstrated in great detail how to make a car bomb. Also seized were various bomb-making manuals and a digital video clip of various Washington monuments. (These were turned over to U.S. authorities.) U.S. Federal law-enforcement officials now say that the digital movie, believed to be a surveillance video, was taken by one of two suspected Atlanta terrorists, Syed Haris Ahmed and Ehsanul Islam (who were arrested and charged in March 2006 in a separate operation). Both of these terrorists suspects are U.S. citizens who grew up in the Atlanta area, and according to FBI Special Agent Richard Kolko there may have been a connection between them, the Canadian suspects, a Georgia Tech student and another un-named American who had traveled to Canada to meet with Islamic extremists to discuss locations for a terrorist strike. The FBI would not comment further. However seeing where the videotape wound up (in Tsouli's possession) there is little doubt as to the relationship between these two and the groups they worked with.

In parallel to the London investigation the Federal Bureau of Investigation (FBI) had been engaged for months in a shadow war with Tsouli because of his alleged close ties to the commander of al-Qaeda's operations in ***Iraq***, Abu-Musab al Zarqawi (killed by U.S. troops in Iraq in mid 2006). In addition to his terrorist activities Tsouli is a particularly adept computer hacker and Web designer. He used these skills in support of a vast Internet operation that distributed *jihadist* propaganda as well as the broadcasting, by al-Qaeda and other *jihadist* groups, of video tapes, among them the tape showing the gruesome beheading of American and other foreign hostages in Iraq by Zarqawi. In addition to these activities Tsouli was the "intellectual" inspiration that encouraged the American and Canadian Muslim youths to plan attacks in the U.S. and Canada.

The network that educated, drove and controlled the Toronto group went from Iraq to London to Toronto and included Atlanta. The Web is organic and constantly changing while ensnaring more Muslim youth in its message of hatred. (2)

The Canadian plot is a typical manifestation of the continually changing *web of terror* and its broad based support structure, i.e., where terrorist groups clandestinely move funds and material and logistic support across the West and Middle East in support of terrorists' activities generally aimed at other countries.

Up until now, Canadian based terrorists, many of them Canadian citizens, have mostly acted following this model, i.e., using Canada to raise money, find recruits and plan attacks in ***other*** countries. However we now have the situation where these domestic groups are actively plotting to carry out terrorist attacks in their own country as well. And this coincides perfectly with aspects of the Ten Step program aimed at developing in-country Islamic resources over time and subsequently using these resources to create chaos within the country, thereby destabilizing it. It is one thing to have a foreign national enter a country for the purpose of terrorist attack. It is a far more unsettling prospect to have the seemingly law biding middle class citizens of one's own county execute the attack. It is also more difficult to screen for and prevent.

In keeping with this thought the profile of the terrorists that the West is now encountering is quite different then one expects. Whenever they are caught the response is the same shock, surprise and incredulity. Most neighbors claim the youths to be quiet respectful, good people, etc. They are never delinquent types. They are educated, employed or university students and middle class citizens of the country within which they are operating. Yet they are part of the new wave Muslim terrorists appearing in the West. The Canadians and Americans involved in the above incidents are strikingly similar to the British subway bombers. They are all second and third generation Muslims that have never lived in an Islamic country, at least for any length of time, and have never attended an al-Qaeda training camp, but are inspired either by Osama bin Laden or the message of Islamic fundamentalism, i.e., the hatred for the West. At the center of these Muslim's "education" and conversion to terrorism is the Mosque.

THE MOSQUE

In all the cases of terrorist incidents in the West there is always one entity that is seen as a major support factor and an integral part of the *web of terror*. It is the mosque.

Mosques act as hubs in the *web of terror*, a "switching point" of sorts. They supply aid in the form of introductions into the Islamic community of the terrorists; they help find housing, supply communications, fund raising and transfer of funds, etc. and worst of all they act as indoctrination centers for potential terrorists. (With all of these activities in support of terror occurring within many mosques one can only wonder where there is time for enlightenment and spirituality.) Most of these mosques also happen to be Saudi supported and all preach the Wahhabi form of Islam, the most extremist form that preaches the destruction of the West through the achievement of *dar al-Islam*.

The following is a brief survey of some known centers of terrorist support. It is not at all a comprehensive list, but only illustrative.

The *ADAMS Center* (All Dulles Area Muslim Society) - Ahmad Totonji serves as a director of the mosque. Totonji is also a key member in the Saudi funded Safa group now under federal investigation for terror-related transactions. The headquarters was raided after 9/11. A Pakistani member of the mosque confided that "there will be suicide bombers blowing up buses in this country, just like in Israel," - rhetoric or prediction?

The *Bridgeview Mosque* (Chicago) has been under investigation for some time for channeling funds to terrorist groups. Among the beneficiaries of this largess are The Benevolence International Foundation (tied to al-Qaeda), The Global Relief Foundation (al-Qaeda), and The Holy Land Foundation (Hamas). The mosque also employs members of all three terrorist groups. It has been alleged by investigators that the Muslim Brotherhood (an Egyptian terrorist organization) has influence over the mosque. It is this organization that originally formed Hamas.

The *Islamic Center of San Diego* has been found to give aid to two of the Saudi 9/11 hijackers Khalid al-Mihdhar and Nawaf al-Hazmi. It was also found that the mosque used al-Hazmi's bank account to receive funds from an al-Qaeda operative working in Dubai. The imam of the mosque is a close friend and associate of a known member of the Muslim Brotherhood that was connected to Zacarias Moussaoui (the twentieth hijacker). Another attendee at the mosque was a Saudi intelligence officer who acted as the advance man for the 9/11 hijackers.

Dar al-Arqam Islamic Center - it has been discovered that after the 9/11 attack eleven members (all American citizens) of a would be terrorist organization named the Virginia *jihad* network attended lectures, in this Washington area mosque, given by the imam Ali al-Timimi wherein he stated that America is the "greatest enemy of Muslims." When Timimi was arrested the FBI found photographs of Washington monuments, terrorist handbook, instructions for using explosives and chemical weapons. The same imam is quoted as saying: "Our enemy until the Day of Judgment is the Christians, what we call westerners or Europeans." Timimi was indicted last year on charges of aiding and abetting terrorists.

Ayah Dawah Prayer Center was one more center that gave aid to the 9/11 hijackers. The morning before the 9/11 attack one of the hijackers left a duffel bag at the mosque with a note on it that read: "FOR THE BROTHERS." Many members of the radical mosque have been questioned since the 9/11 attack. I imagine the message was saying that his martyrdom and 9/11 was for his Islamic brothers. (3)

The above examples are just a sample of the many mosques that are involved in rhetoric of this type and in supplying extensive aid and support to terrorists; they are all extremely anti- American.

The Pakistani from the ADAMS Center stated that if America tried to curtail any of the mosques or Muslims' right to freely worship (that is a strange use of the word given the above context) Washington and other American cities would erupt into the kind of violence seen in the streets of Baghdad. It is an interesting and very revealing statement. No one has ever said anything about curtailing a Muslim's right to worship yet that is exactly what the speaker would do if the situation were reversed. It is also interesting how given the nature of the conversation he was involved in he could have the gall to talk about worship.

There is always the veiled threat of violence when dealing with Islam.

Terrorist activities are constant and spreading in every country in Europe and in America, in Afghanistan, India, China, Kashmir, Chechnya, Ossetia, Thailand, Bali, the Philippines, Bosnia, Kosovo, Palestine, Lebanon, Egypt, Algeria, Morocco, even in Saudi Arabia and now Hugo Chavez of Venezuela has been found to be collaborating with al-Qaeda and building diplomatic and economic "common interests" with Iran.

When the traditional terrorists activities are not enough or when the Islamists require some diversion or an opportunity to weaken the West further they begin incursive incidents into or wars with Israel or provoke the U.S. with politically charged situations such as the nuclear acquisition in Iran. With events like these it is hoped that a wedge is placed between allies in the West and in fact the objective has been very productive to that end.

Terrorism only wins when countries that fall victim to terrorism succumb to the fear (of course it is near to impossible not to). Without the influence of fear terrorism can be seen for what it is: a morally bankrupt reprehensible act of murder executed by people who have been dehumanized by an equally bankrupt culture. As true as this may be the tragedy is that at the current time the West seems not to be able to state this fact with any degree of moral certainty, i.e., the bankruptcy of current Islamic culture. Compounding this moral failing is the fact that the West is stuck in a purely defensive battle against an implacable enemy and narrowly focused tactics cannot defeat terrorism. Incidents can be prevented and terrorist rings can be destroyed but all of this will have little effect on the long-term cessation of terrorism. It will take a strategic thrust (based on unequivocal moral certainty) at the underlying support mechanisms of terrorism to destroy it.

Beyond terrorism the battle has a very different character. The battlefield moves from fear, bullets and bombs to politics but always with the same central theme - driving Islam forward to world domination.

17 A Different War—Subversion

Islam cannot win the battle for supremacy by military means. Technologically and militarily the West, particularly America, is vastly stronger and more capable then all of the Islamic countries combined. Therefore alternate means must be pursued. Islam's main weapon in the battle has become infiltration and subversion of non-Islamic countries, organizations and cultures. And terrorism is infiltration's handmaiden fostering destabilization.

The dramatic impact of Islam on Western societies is just now becoming apparent, most notably in Europe but also in the U.S. to a lesser extent. The impact is by way of affecting changes to the norms of the society. The changes are small and subtle to begin with but if examined can easily be seen to change some fundamental norms of the society. Over time there is an empowering cumulative effect of the changes that in turn generate new "requested" changes of a more dramatic nature. (This is already true in Europe.) By causing basic changes to the way of life and accepted behavior that is traditional and vital to the fabric of a particular society, the society is undermined without its population initially being aware of the "incursion." The eventual result is a culture at war with itself, two competing cultures in one country.

Free societies do evolve over time as new norms are slowly insinuated into the culture by each new generation. In addition immigrants often bring with them, as they did to the shores of America, the best of their country of origin and this best often finds its way into much of the culture. And then from America the styles and ways of this evolving culture often find their way to other Western and even Eastern countries in an endless give and take. It has been like this for 200 years and one can hope that it will continue, for it enriches our country and our lives and often enriches other countries as well. The changes I speak of, in a real sense, are benign to the foundation values and principles that made America great. There is no threat either implicit in the evolution of our culture in this way or is there any explicitly intended threat by the people involved in the process. However change that is radically opposed to the core values and norms of the indigenous culture is destructive to the host society. The West is on the verge of being inundated by this type of change.

The following items are "a word picture" of a culture under attack in every aspect of its essence: institutions, laws, norms, dress, education, style, freedoms and of course religion, all are under pressure to change, to accommodate Islam.

Denmark

There is growing fear amongst politicians that the immigrant environment in the Nørrebro area in Copenhagen, which has been unofficially declared an "Islamic State" by some of its residents, is developing into a parallel society where Islamic traditions threaten Danish law. Professor of Islamic studies Mehdi Mozaffari tells of how he and thousands of others have fled *burqas, Shari'a*, blood money, *muftis* and *Islamism* in the Middle East, only to witness the same repressive Islamic elements be realized in Europe. Mr. Mozaffari warns of the consequences: "Historical experience has shown that those whom people ***fear*** (emphasis added), will win eventually. We saw this in Nazi Germany. There were too many Nazis, and people were scared. I fear that this is where we are heading, once more."

Flemming Rose, the culture editor of the Danish newspaper Jyllands-Posten, is planning a move to America, at the urging of friends and security contacts. He set off a global storm by publishing the now infamous twelve cartoons of the prophet Muhammad. The twelve Danish cartoonists who drew the caricatures are staying out of public entirely for fear of attack.

Norway

In 2005 Stortinget, the Norwegian Parliament passed a new Discrimination Act. The act states in clear words that in cases of suspected direct or indirect discrimination based on religion or ethnicity, native Norwegians are ***guilty until proven otherwise***. This was precipitated by Islamic pressure.

France

France a very long time traditional Christian country is having its social norms pressured to an extensive degree. As an example, a Catholic farmer was ordered to remove the cross he kept in his own cornfield, because "the sight of that religious symbol caused tension with the Muslims." It never created tensions for other religions.

In another French case at the Collége Edgard Quinet, where 95 per cent of students are Muslim, a "fifteen year-old non-Muslim girl was savagely beaten by her classmates and thrown into a garbage-bin because she was wearing blue jeans." The school Principal rescued the girl as her fellow students were about to set fire to her. He was stabbed twice.

In France there exist many swimming pools exclusively for women. "A swimming pool off-limits to men, with an exclusively female staff, and smoked windows. It's not in Saudi Arabia but in France, in the fine town of Lille." More interesting yet, this swimming pool is not a private concern but one of only four sponsored by the Lille municipality. As a private enterprise there would be nothing wrong with a pool of this nature. Customarily in the West private groups normally provide solutions addressing unique religious requirements. However to have a pool like this paid for by taxpayers and sanctioned by an official entity of the government is where capitulation occurs. No group should be permitted special treatment at the expense of the citizens of the country. Certainly no other group has extended to it the level of exceptions that Muslins ***demand***.

Germany

In Germany the courts have ordered that Muslim instruction be offered in public schools. Currently Christian education is being offered. There have been protests against this because the "brand" of Islam that is taught is Wahhabism, the radical fundamentalist brand. (Turkey, an Islamic state so far resists teaching this form of Islam and prefers to teach a secularized version. In Germany Wahhabism is what the imams and mullahs want to teach.) What Germany has approved will further polarize the population since another generation of Islamic radicals will emerge from school. (This is a good reminder of why the American model of keeping religious instruction out of ***public schools*** helps to facilitate assimilation at least within the student community.)

Several researchers, journalists and members of Parliament working on Islamic issues receive police protection because of threats by radical Muslims.

Hans-Peter Raddatz, an Islamic-studies expert lived for an extended period under police protection, finally moved to the U.S.

England

Hindus and Jews were banned from being selected as jurors hearing a criminal case against an Islamist in Great Britain.

In England the recognition of polygamous marriages for tax purposes is allowed even though polygamy is illegal.

In England authorities banned the use of piggybanks, the symbol of frugality, in their advertising because it might upset Muslims.

Holland

Dutch police say politicians reported 121 death threats last year from Islamists. The number this year will likely be much higher.

Geert Wilders, a right-wing member of parliament who also lives in a high-security apartment owned by the state, says he has received over a hundred menacing emails and letters since January (2006). One of the latest reads: "Oh you cursed *infidels*! Don't think you are safe from our mighty organization. It is our wish to kill you by decapitation. Your *infidel's* blood will flow freely on cursed Dutch streets!"

America

Allows a Muslim prisoner the unheard-of right to avoid strip-searches in New York State.

Prohibit families from sending pork or pork by-products or "Any matter containing religious materials contrary to Islamic faith" to U.S. military personnel serving in the Middle East.

Require that female American soldiers in Saudi Arabia wear U.S. government-issued abayas (head dress).

The ID photograph for a female drivers license is taken while she is wearing a burqa in some states. Who is really under that all covering garment?

Women only classes were created to accommodate Muslims at Virginia Tech. "This is the way they teach their courses over there, and this is the way they wish their courses to be taught over here," said Tech spokesman Larry Hincker. The university chose to respect the Saudi culture "rather than impress our culture on them."

The selling of ***publicly held land at discount prices*** for a Muslim Center and Mosque. "At the groundbreaking in November 2002, local politicians hailed the planned construction of an Islamic Center by the Islamic Society of Boston as a bridge between Islam and Boston's other religions, the Boston Herald recounted yesterday in the first of a major two-part investigative series. Mayor Thomas M. Menino hailed the center for 'creating a space for inter-faith dialog,' and thereby bringing 'both the Muslim community and the community at large closer together.' U.S. Rep. Michael Capuano (Democrat) predicted the center would 'help to create a dialogue between Muslims and non-Muslims so we may learn more about each others' traditions.' The Boston Redevelopment Authority, a public agency, was no less enthusiastic about the project and sold a 1.9-acre lot to the Islamic Society of Boston for $175,000, or well under the property's market value."

> "All this looks pretty dumb a year later, with revelations in the Herald that the Islamic Society of Boston is closely associated with Yusuf Abdullah al-Qaradawi, the Egyptian Islamist whose outspoken backing for Hamas led the Department of State to bar him from entering the United States in 1999; and Abdurahman Alamoudi, the American Islamist recently arrested on terrorism-related charges (see "United States of America v. Abdurahman Muhammad Alamoudi") who in the past has publicly supported Hamas, Hezbullah, and other terrorist organizations." (1)

And in American Education:

> "Become a Muslim warrior during the crusades or during an ancient *jihad*." Thus read the instructions for seventh graders in *Islam: A Simulation of Islamic History and Culture, 610-1100*, a three-week curriculum produced by Interaction Publishers, Inc. In classrooms across the United States, students who follow its directions find themselves fighting mock battles of *jihad* against 'Christian crusaders' and other assorted '*infidels*.' Upon gaining victory, our mock-Muslim warriors 'Praise Allah.' There has been a legal action taken to stop this 'game.'" (2)

Does any reader wonder if this game, "from the crusaders perspective", would be allowed in a Muslim country or even in the U.S.?

Australia

In 2000, gangs of Lebanese Muslims in Sydney hunted down young Australian girls on the basis of their ethnicity and raped and tortured them while calling them "sluts" and "Aussie pigs". One of the convicted rapists, Bilal Skaf, sent a text message on his mobile phone, "When you are feeling down…bash a Christian or Catholic and lift up." The very nature of this outrageous act should have caused a furor in the press. However, the mainstream media described the crimes as standard rapes. They then proceeded to eliminate any reference to ethnicity from the crime. When the Premier of New South Wales (the province where the crime was committed) publicly acknowledged the ethnic background of the rapists, the *politically correct* thundered their objections through editorials, etc.

The numbers of exceptions for Muslims living in the West, the existence of ghettoized enclaves of Muslims evolving almost autonomous states within the host country, the aberrational behavior of groups of Muslims following Islamic norms in complete defiance of local laws and customs is a growing problem throughout the West.

Although some exceptions and situations are serious many may seem to be trivial. The objectionable point and danger isn't the "degree of the extreme" of the concession itself but the fact that we are conceding aspects of our culture and our way of life. (In that sense we are not even fighting the war.) We have never conceded any of these exceptions to any group or religion in the past nor would we now. Then why do we grant exceptions to Muslims? Is it fear? Is it weakness on our part? Have we forgotten what it is to stand up for our way of life? In the U.S., the Supreme Court would not allow a statue of the Ten Commandments (a pillar of our Judeo-Christian society and heritage) to be displayed in front of a courthouse yet we concede any number of exceptions to Muslims. If the concessions were challenged in court many of the concessions would be struck down, but there appears to be a lack of will to even fight the concessions on a legal basis. And there is a second danger in this lack of will and that is the issue of "critical mass." At what point have we changed so much of our principles and culture in the process of accommodation that the original society is no longer recognizable?

The pressures for accommodation occur in each country where there is even a small Islamic population but these pressures needed immigration to begin the process and that takes time. Long before the Muslim "infiltration" through population expansion began in earnest, Islam was at war with the West using economic weapons. In addition to the on going large economic expenditures for security the West is also a victim of OPEC's economic attack through oil.

During the Israeli-Egypt-Syrian war of 1973 the Islamic countries of the Middle East issued a number of demands that were both public and unequivocal:

> The withdrawal of Israel from the occupied territories. (It was thought that Israel's economic partners would pressure Israel.)
> The recognition of the Palestinians,
> The presence of the PLO at the peace negotiations.

These demands were then followed by economic pressure through OPEC:

> The quadrupling of the price of crude oil;
> An embargo against the United States, Denmark, and Holland;
> The progressive reduction of the amount of oil extracted thereby creating price pressure and shortages;
> The effort to extend the embargo to countries that would not accept their conditions;

From 1973 until the current day OPEC has continually used the supply and the price of oil as a very effective weapon for molding supportive opinions for Islamic positions in Europe and to a lesser degree in the U.S. while at the same time creating a huge exchange of wealth from the West to Islam.

The wealth in turn has been used to fund dictatorships and Islamic states in the Middle East, terrorists organizations and terrorism, the spreading of fundamentalist Islamic teachings throughout a vast international mosque system and funded an enormous number of emigrants to Europe. In turn the Islamic organizations in the Western countries have further spread the extremist message and influenced the changing of the norms of the indigenous cultures that welcomed them.

THE NEW WORLD WAR

This then is the form and scope of the *new world war.* Through subversion, infiltration and terrorism Islam expects to fulfill the directive of the *Qur'an* to conquer all lands in the name of Allah.

It is going to be a long war; but it is foremost an ideological war, a clash between two opposing and incompatible views of the world. Only one can win. The unyielding nature of Islam itself is the major element that will make the war endless. They do not yield nor do they stop. Islam's claim to absolute truth violently enforced and focused on world domination will not waiver.

The unyielding nature of Islam is also the reason that there are virtually no significant groups of outspoken moderates within Islam as there are in any other religion or political entity. The ability for moderate Muslims to organize or act in concert is nearly impossible and as a result one rarely hears of Islamic dissension. In the Chapter "The Moderate Muslim" we will encounter exceptions to this premise in the form of both men and women who are real heroes. However there is a big difference between a movement and a handful of heroic dissenters.

The dogmatic acceptance of the *Qur'an* and the Hadiths by Muslims, coupled with the fact that Islam governs both the spiritual life and the secular life (every aspect of secular life) through *Shari'a* (which is the antithesis of modern objective jurisprudence) makes Islam incompatible with an advanced secular society. The West and Islam will always be at war with each other as it stands at this time at this point in history: if Islam yields to the secular society in the West then it violates many of the central commands of the *Qur'an* and the *Hadiths* and this is anathema. If the West accommodates Islam to a significant extent then it will cease to exist as a viable culture within a couple of generations. It is this latter situation that is unfolding all too rapidly in Europe and beginning to evolve elsewhere.

There is only one thing that the West can hope for, work for and fight for and that is Islam's abandonment of the literal interpretation of the *Qur'an* and the subsequent separation of "church and state" as happened in the West centuries ago with Catholicism. It is a very slim hope indeed for it would require an intellectual revolution within Islam of colossal significance that would reverse centuries of dogmatic teaching and practice. In the mean time Islam's quest for world domination marches forward.

18 The Council of American-Islamic Relations

The U.S. is not immune from the encroaching Islamic invasion. An invasion that is led by words and public relations and lobbying are all aimed at furthering the cause of Islam in America.

There exists an Islamic organization in the U.S by the innocuous name of the Council of American-Islamic Relations (CAIR). Ostensibly the organization was formed to promote Islamic/American relations and understanding. However CAIR is in reality, the most powerful Islamic pressure group in Washington and an extremely capable media and public relations (PR) representative for the Islamic world. Certainly not in keeping with its role and charter but more in keeping with its real function the following are a few quotes from some its more infamous members. For reasons we will delve into later these quotes are rarely seen in the mainstream media although they are made quite publicly in interviews and speeches:

> Omar M. Ahmed, a CAIR leader, states: "Islam isn't in America to be equal to any other faith, but to become dominant. The *Qur'an* should be the highest authority in America, and Islam the only accepted religion on earth."
>
> Muzammil H. Wahhaj at a Muslim gathering stated that: "Muslims had the numbers to take control of the United States in a political coup." It should be noted that he said this on the same day that he gave the invocation that opens Congress.
>
> Ghassan Elashi, Bassan K. Kafagi, Ismail Royer and Randall Todd all are senior officials of CAIR that have been convicted on terrorist charges.
>
> Ibrahim Hooper a CAIR senior member states: "I want to see the U.S. become an Islamic nation." On another occasion "I wouldn't want to create the impression that I wouldn't like the government of the United States to be Islamic sometime in the future."
>
> Siraj Wahhaj, a member of CAIR's advisory board, was named by the U.S. attorney as one of the "un-indicted persons who may be alleged as co-conspirators in an attempted terrorist assault."

Not exactly the sentiments of people who are in America to enjoy its freedoms but instead to use them to their own ends.

With declared intentions like this, one would expect the organization to be under intensive scrutiny, and in fact recently several government agencies have begun to look into CAIR's activities; in particular the activities surrounding the funneling of funds to terrorist groups. Yet the government accepts CAIR as being the representative of the Islamic world (well actually it is but not in the way Washington thinks). In fact senior members of CAIR are invited to White House functions while the State department has a web link to CAIR.

CAIR is also involved in "sensitivity training" at various police departments in the U.S. NYC appointed CAIR's general council to represent them on Human Rights Commission 573. CAIR also directs a very strong communications program that defends Islam against any bad press or stereotyping. CAIR's standard response is to always accuse the accuser. And the typical accusation is of *Islamophobia* and bigotry. Keep in mind that CAIR runs a very sizeable nationwide communications and PR organization with which to counter any bad press. CAIR particularly focuses on Hollywood, the media and advertising industries to be sure there are no negative images used when portraying Islam. And they are successful. Fear again is a major ally of CAIR. Here are just some CAIR instigated examples of fear tactics:

> Nike designed a new running shoe that displayed a symbol on the heel. (Many of Nike's shoes use other symbols such as the Nike logo.) CAIR claimed that the symbol was too similar to the Arabic word for Allah and stated that this was blasphemous. CAIR rallied the Muslim community to force Nike to remove the symbol. Not only did Nike remove the symbol but also to placate CAIR it financed the construction of playgrounds at several Muslim schools and mosques and made donations to Muslim charities.

> Mort Zuckerman wrote an editorial for U.S. News and World Report explaining how Mohammad had violated a treaty with the Jews centuries ago. CAIR "went ballistic" and rallied the Islamic "troops" across America and essentially paralyzed the office of the magazine. Zuckerman pleaded for an end to the siege. In response CAIR would not back down until Zuckerman

> published a personal apology. Nihad Awad (one of the founders of CAIR) bragged: " Muslims forced a powerful publisher, for the first time, to issue a clear, unequivocal apology to Muslims."
>
> The national radio personality Paul Harvey stated that Islam "encourages killing" he became a CAIR target. Once again CAIR rallied the Islamic army to inundate Harvey's sponsor General Electric (GE) with demands to cancel its sponsorship of Harvey. Harvey capitulated and on the air stated that Islam: "is a religion of peace."
>
> CAIR was successful in having National Review stop the sale of *The Life and Religion of Mohammed* by J. L. Menezes because CAIR states that in the book The Prophet Mohammad was portrayed as licentious and bloodthirsty. The fact that in the process of pressuring National Review they never once stated that the author's assertions were inaccurate. (1)

CAIR even looks out for Islamic radicals on fictional television.

> Kiefer Sutherland, plays a counterterrorism agent on the TV series "24." Recently at the insistence of CAIR, Mr. Sutherland had to read a disclaimer before a particular show that featured Muslim terrorists. CAIR felt that the show could "cast a shadow of suspicion over ordinary American Muslims and would increase *Islamophobic* stereotyping and bias."

In February 2003 CAIR joined with the American Muslim Council and the American Muslim Alliance in forming an Islamic coalition to repeal or amend the Patriot Act. The group was quite outspoken in criticizing American policies but never mentioned the terrorists the Patriot Act is meant to stop.

While CAIR is busy "jumping" all over American companies, commentators and policies they are also shamelessly making apologies for radical Islam. After the 9/11 attacks, CAIR representatives refused to blame Osama bin Laden because it would "simplify the situation." Furthermore CAIR members have been found to actively support terrorists. Ghassan Elashi, the founder of the Texas chapter of CAIR was convicted of supporting Hamas in 2005.

Nihad Awad boasts: "CAIR has become the primary contact for most of the major national and international media outlets seeking an American Muslim perspective for news stories." Imagine asking the Nazi party for their view on issues pertaining to the war during WW II. It might have been an interesting approach but it wouldn't hold much weight in the realm of reality. From this, a reasonable person can easily surmise that the news with respect to Islamic issues is largely–well let's say not exactly "investigative reporting."

While shams of this type are on going Congress and federal agencies most recently began to investigate CAIR. According to Senator Charles Grassley–Republican, the Chairman of The Finance Committee, CAIR is being investigated as part of a group of twenty-five tax-exempt organizations that "finance terrorism and perpetuate violence." The audit is attempting to define the extent of cross-fertilization within America's terror-support network. Leaders of the Holy Land Foundation, a close ally of CAIR, were charged with funneling millions of dollars to Hamas. Those found guilty and jailed included Ghassan Elashi, a founding CAIR board member, headed the Holy Land Foundation. He also helped run the CAIR web site through his company InfoCom Corp. that also illegally shipped high-tech equipment to Syria (a state sponsor of terrorism). InfoCom Corp also had Al-Jazeera as a client until it was closed down. (2) (For the reader that is interested in tracing the endless labyrinth of connections among these self proclaimed "legitimate" groups and terrorists organizations as well as Muslim infiltration in our most cherished and critical organizations, *Infiltration* is a master work of investigative detail and documentation by a noted journalist–Paul Sperry.)

Islamic hypocrisy seems to have no limit. If anything surpasses it, it is the ability to tell the "big lie." One of the three founders of CAIR, Cary D. Hooper, an Islamic convert who changed his name to Ibrahim, stated:

> "I challenge anyone in the eight years of CAIR's existence to find one inflammatory statement that we've ever issued. I mean its just ridiculous."

Well something is ridiculous but its Ibahim's statement that seems to be the most ridiculous thing. There are any numbers of statements made by CAIR members that prove Ibrahim wrong, just review the earlier quotes. Then there are also these:

> "democracy will crumble" Siraj Wahhaj CAIR board member.

> "Oh, Allah, destroy America" prays Abdurahman Alamoudi former

> CAIR board member.
>
> "I want to replace the U.S. Constitution with the *Qur'an*." Ahmad founder of CAIR.
>
> Then Ibriham himself stated the desire to overturn the U.S. system of government in favor of an Islamic state.

If these comments and the previous quotes do not fit Ibriham's meaning of an "inflammatory statement", then we can all be concerned as to what he thinks inflammatory is. I find it incredible, and I hope I am not alone, that these representatives of Islam can take such strong exception to running-shoe logos and radio commentators but can issue the comments they do about their wish for our destruction and then state that they are not inflammatory. And they get away with it.

> "Despite this ugly record, CAIR is still widely accepted in Washington as a mainstream American group. Even leaders in Congress have given it a platform to legitimize militant Islam, conned as they are into buying one of CAIR's biggest lies of all." (3)

And as we have seen from CAIR's current activities it would seem that the CAIR organization is ideally configured and positioned to guide the early and middle stages of the *Ten Step* program. Even if CAIR met its deserved demise the *Ten Steps* would continue.

19 The Euro-Arab Dialog (EAD)

CAIR is not the only Western based organization that is focused on furthering Islamic interests. Moving across the Atlantic we encounter an organization named the Euro-Arab Dialog (EAD) a much older group that is broader in function, and to date more effective in molding political policy on behalf of Islam. From the European perspective the origins of this group did not start out with this intent in mind.

From European history one may recall that Napoleon tried to conquer all of Europe and establish a world governed under French rule. He failed. Then his nephew Napoleon lll attempted to form a French-Arab empire encompassing all Islamic countries from Algiers to Turkey with France at the head. This too failed. The modern French leaders (early 1970s) did not learn much from these failures for it was their desire to once again play a key role on the world power stage. This time France was seeking power in the context of the cold war. To accomplish this, in lieu of close relations with America, France attempted to forge a confederation of the entire Arab world as a protectorate. The assumption was that this federation, which became known as the EAD, would be led by France and would act as an effective counter-balance to U.S. and Soviet power and thereby create a third world power.

> "The Euro-Arab Dialogue (EAD) was conceived initially by the French and the idea was explored in contacts with Libya prior to the outbreak of the 1973 war (The October 1973 Arab-Israeli War). The French leadership, in an attempt to enhance France's prestige and establish a new network of relations between the North and South, showed great faith in the effectiveness of personal contacts, which are well served by diplomatic interactions and dialogue." (1).

Although Frances's main goal was the federation there were secondary reasons that drove French planning and many European countries to accept the French policy and that was a desire to win Arab markets and assure a constant oil supply. Oil, as always, was a very key component. The Europeans had a long memory and they recalled how they had been significantly affected by the energy crises after past Arab-Israeli wars. Another issue that motivated them was, and still is, the security issue. Palestinian terrorists began to strike within Europe itself at the end of the 1960s and they had remained a real threat. The policy therefore was expected to have the added benefit of protecting Europe from the threat of terror. (Once again the motivator of fear was at work albeit as a secondary pressure.) As it came to pass the reality of the EAD was much more than France and its European partners bargained for.

Shortly after the commencement of these initiatives The European Economic Community (EEC) passed a resolution at their November 6, 1973 meeting that met the conditions The Arab League had stated as their requirement for opening a joint dialogue concerning economic "issues." What the EEC adopted was a pro-Arab policy in the context of dealings with Israel. In return the EEC received benefits from the Arab states in the form of an increase in oil supplies and access to Arab markets (primarily for armaments). This was immediately after the defeat of The Arab League in the October 1973 War with Israel. (2)

> "At a meeting on the 26-27 November 1973 between French President Georges Pompidou and West German Chancellor Willy Brandt, the two leaders reaffirmed European intentions to engage in a dialogue with the Arabs. In Cairo, Abdul-Salam Jalloud, the Libyan premier actively enlisted support for a dialogue with the Europeans." (3)

This was the beginning of what was to be a long-term relationship and for the Muslims a very effective one in furthering their goals.

> Note: From the European perspective an additional reason for joining in the formation of the EAD was the development of a continent-wide foreign policy joined with the "Mediterranean countries" (essentially Islamic countries) to become an alternative to American power. What is so interesting about this counter balance to American power is that the concept of an Arab-Europe "integration" was first proposed by Adolph Hitler on October 25, 1941 in a meeting with the Italian Foreign Minister. Hitler said that in a battle against America: "the common interests of a unified Europe within an economic zone (would be) completed by the African colonies." (4)

On November 28, 1973 *The Sixth Summit of the Arab Conference* met and addressed the heads of the EEC. The countries noted "the first manifestations of a better understanding of the Arab cause by the states of Western Europe." The specific conditions that were to be met by the Europeans in return for The Arab States cooperation with the EEC were:

> "Europe would support Arab claims to Jerusalem and the occupied 'territories,'
>
> European states would recognize an autonomous Palestinian people."

The result was to give the Arab states a propaganda weapon against Israel. Prior to this agreement, U.N. resolution 242 referred to the "refugees" when discussing the now named Palestinians. Therefore by designating the "refugees" as the "Palestinian people" the agreement between the EEC and the Arab states effectively blocked the settlement of the "refugees" in the surrounding Arab countries of Egypt and particularly Jordan. Which, as we shall see, is where a good many of them came from.

Through the evolving Euro-Arab Dialog the Europeans were developing a much closer relationship with the Arab and other Muslim states while at the same time beginning to distance themselves from Israel. Following this agreement the Arab Declaration of Algiers requested France to initiate a meeting of the EEC for the purpose of establishing further cooperation with the Arab League. The meeting was held on December 15, 1973 where the Arab states presented their conditions for establishing an accord with the EEC. The issues discussed became known two months later.

On February 24, 1974 The Second Islamic Conference met. A central objective was to resolve an extensive set of points and objectives. However, three points that were resolved clearly defined the Muslim countries policy toward Israel.

> Full and effective support should be given to the Arab countries to recover, by all means available, all their occupied lands,
>
> The restitution of the full national rights of the Palestinian people in their homeland is the essential and fundamental condition for a solution to the Middle East problem and the establishment of lasting peace on the basis of justice,
>
> The constructive efforts undertaken by the Christian Churches, all over the world and in Arab countries,–Lebanon, Egypt,

> Jordan and Syria, to explain the Palestinian question to the international public opinion and to the world religious conference and to solicit their support for Arab sovereignty over Jerusalem and other holy places in Palestine should be appreciated. (5)

The Damascus Conference of September 14-17, 1974 was the last building block in the creation of a "Palestine" that never existed before. The Arabs set out the political preconditions for Euro-Arab cooperation. These were:

> The unconditional withdrawal of Israel to the 1949 armistice lines,
>
> Arab sovereignty over Old City of Jerusalem,
>
> The participation of the PLO and its leader Yasser Arafat, in any negotiations,
>
> Pressure by the EEC on the United States, to detach itself from Israel and bring its policies closer to those of the Arab states.

These points were absolute preconditions for further economic agreements.

The policy agreements that emerged from these events and conferences directly paralleled the evolution of European antagonism to Israel and a pro Palestinian position.

After the Seventh Arab Conference in October 1974 the Arab heads of state affirmed that the EAD could only go forward within the context of *The Declaration of the Sixth Summit of the Arab Conference* (November 28, 1973). By agreeing to this the Europeans were accepting the Islamic states' position on Israel and Palestine. ***The EAD was then made a permanent organization with 350 working members and headquartered in Paris. The EAD consists of a number of committees that govern various joint activities: industrial, commercial, political, scientific, technical, cultural and social.*** The EAD's birth and formation was not widely known by the European public. The EAD was essentially the creation of a group of "elitist" politicians working with their Islamic counterparts and Islamic leaders.

The EAD was now perfectly structured and positioned to become Islam's mechanism for the implementation of the early stages (1973-1974) of the *Ten Step* program in Europe. The Europeans had no idea what the long-term implications of their agreements would be. Although this was a clear victory for

Arab states, it was not without its difficulties. There was still the problem of public opinion. In fact al-Mani in his *Euro-Arab Dialogues* expresses his disappointment that the European public and the majority of the politicians were reluctant to unconditionally side with the Arab states against Israel. However Euro-Arab cooperation did indeed grow in the succeeding years. It was through the EAD that the Islamic strides in immigration occurred and thereby its ability to establish a cultural beachhead in Europe. The deal was quite lop-sided; Islam got considerably more than the Europeans bargained for.

20 Infiltration

The *Islamization* process is much further ahead in Europe then it is in the States but America is far from unaffected and unfortunately the transition is now accelerating. The process is not radical in the sense that one can see specific major events enfolding and changing the society in a very dramatic way. The process is slow and evolutionary. It is a process that infiltrates every aspect of daily life and brings about changes that are in themselves not necessarily notable. The cumulative effect however is devastating.

> "Twenty years ago Muslims, in this country (America) felt it was important to build mosques. Now we have thousands of mosques all over the country. Fifteen years ago, we wanted to build schools, and now we have hundreds of schools where our youth are being educated. Now, the goal of the Muslim community should be to become politically active." Ashraf Nubani, an attorney for confessed terrorist Abdurahman Alamoudi. (1)

To the host country *infiltration* is one of the most potentially dangerous steps of the *Ten Step* program. It is the "step" that is used to undermine the organizations of the host country that are most essential to their ability to resist Muslim expansion and its constant quest for "exceptions" and "accommodations." The organizations most important are federal and local elected office and key administrative organizations. This is the process that is underway in America. As Nubani said they have the mosques and schools in place all over the country teaching the next generation and guiding the current generation of Muslims. It is time for them to move into and accelerate influence in other of the society's major structures.

CAIR is not alone in its attempts at furthering the *Ten Step* program, an organization by the name of the American Muslim Alliance (AMA) has, as its central goal, encouraging and supporting Muslims to seek and gain political office. Agha Seed, an AMA's executive, has identified 521,000 elective offices in the U.S. Although Muslims hold only a few of these Seed says:

> "they (Muslims) need to be awakened to their full potential in the

> American political system. We need to transform our pent-up frustration, anger, and pain into creative and meaningful steps for self-empowerment."

With the help of the 7000 members of the AMA and Muslim think tanks, of which there are quite a few, Seed expects to get at least 2000 Muslims elected to office in the next decade. He is targeting areas where there are heavy concentrations of Muslim voters (Michigan, Florida, Virginia, Texas, New York.) Using this voting base, the goal is to get a number of Muslims into Congress. This normally is a natural and welcomed evolution in the ***assimilation*** process of a minority group into the U.S. In this case however it is actually quite a scary thought given Islam's lack of desire to assimilate and its self-proclaimed desire to create an Islamic state in the U.S. In addition Congressmen have access to a great deal of secret and classified information. One of the previously described "time bombs" or a member of a "sleeper cell" organization could be one of these elected officials and they could feed information to any Islamic group if they desire to. The more compelling issue is however, the influence the "Muslim delegation" could wield in Congress. This is not the raving of paranoia; the scenario is not so far fetched when examined in the context of the other information presented herein and in the sources quoted throughout the book.

What is also most interesting is how Seed says the Muslims must "transform our pent-up frustration, anger, and pain." It is worth a moment's thought to try to figure out what they are so angry and in pain about. Could it possibly be the fact that they live in a free society? That they are free from persecution? That they can live a life-style most people outside the Western world can only hope for, the fact that they have opportunities presented to them of an incredible range? They even are able to achieve an ever-expanding set of "accommodations" unheard of before. This speculation leads one to believe that the negative emotions they need to be freed from has more to do with the actual nature of a non-Islamic country that they are "forced" to live in. The conclusion might be that they wish to change that country in the most fundamental ways possible.

Understand something. The population of the U.S. is now 300 million people. The number of Muslims is less than 5 million. Has there ever existed a minority group within the U.S. that has had such a tiny percentage of the population yet wielded so much power, influence and quested for even more? Has another minority of this size ever had the gall to state that they expected to take over and to change the country within which they are a minor part of the population? If they weren't so effective and dangerous it would be laughable. Don't laugh they are serious and they are driven.

The issue that continues to haunt Westerners is that they do not know how to cope with this situation in that any response smacks of religious prejudice. The mistake is to think of Islam as only a religion. It is first and foremost an engine for world conquest and a political force. Then it is a religion, but like no other.

Another key target of infiltration is the military. In the past the U.S. military has allowed each religion to form a chaplain corps within the armed forces. Although it would be wrong to deny Muslim military men this service, given that we are at war with Muslin nations, a tight control and overseeing function would not be a out of line. (Of course the *multiculturalists* and *politically correct* advocates would scream at this.) Instead Abdurahman Alamoudi oversaw the creation of the Muslim Chaplain Corps. Remember his quote: - "Oh, Allah, destroy America" (see CAIR). He was the former CAIR board member who allegedly had ties to al-Qaeda and was later convicted of terrorist related activities. Furthermore he was Saudi backed which means Wahhabism was the brand of teaching he spread wherever he could.

The major issue is where will the Muslim soldiers' loyalty lie given the *Qur'an's* stated goal of world conquest and the current political situation vis-à-vis Muslims worldwide. If they are devout Muslims then their adherence to the *Qur'an* and its dictates are absolute. If they are not then at minimum they might be co-opted in critical situations. Perhaps Muslims should be viewed as *conscientious objectors* and not allowed in the military.

One might correctly ask why are the Muslim troops different then say Christians in WW II. In the European war didn't Christian Americans fight and kill Christian Germans? The answer is the Muslims may not be different, however their very religion makes them highly suspect. The *Qur'an* is quite definite about not killing other Muslims while it is actually fine to kill the *infidels*. It is absolutely anathema for a Muslim to kill Muslims fighting for *infidel* armies. The Christian religions, and other major religions, admonish against killing, but it is specifically, or at least more likely, murder that is viewed as a sin. Furthermore there is no differentiation between peoples in other religions, i.e., one should not kill humans - period. War has always been a difficult moral dilemma for all religions however Islam is most emphatic about never under any circumstances (except self defense and the execution of *Shari'an* justice) should a Muslim kill another Muslim? However it is fine to kill *infidels*!

The problem is not so academic. There are numerous incidents where supposedly trustworthy and supportive Muslims (not U.S. Military personnel) have in actuality worked to undercut U.S. operations in the search for bin Laden and in translating captured documents, etc. Both the FBI and Military Intelligence have admitted to being the victim of this.

The same Muslim religious recruiters are active in prisons where there are 200,000 Muslim inmates. In fact the prison system has become the top recruiting grounds for al-Qaeda. However this is a fraction of the problem when one compares it to the potential threat inherent in Muslim immigration.

Viewed on a personal level, Muslim immigration is almost always for the correct and normal reasons one emigrates, such as economic betterment, better environment for jobs and family, education, etc. However there always seems to be a "but" when dealing with Islam. In this case the "but" is the ticking time bomb. The time bomb is realized in the form of "spontaneous" demonstrations against some aspect of the West's activities. Once again the Danish cartoons provide a perfect example. The fact that such a large number of normal hard working people (along with many questionable types) all over Europe "spontaneously" took to the streets protesting the cartoons and demanding that they not be published and that the Danish publishers be punished (for exercising freedom of speech). They burnt cars, flags, effigies, etc. The reaction was "too spontaneous and uniform" not to have been instigated and coordinated. There is nothing stopping this type of "spontaneity from erupting in America except for the comparatively lower number of Muslims in this country. The other alarming issue is Mr. Seed's statement about the "pent-up frustration, anger, and pain" within the Muslim community. How will this be manifested if Muslim population grows to the extent it has in Europe.

The Mosques and their Mullahs provide the necessary catalyst to ignite any situation they deem is in the interests of Islam. It is this ability to unify and direct millions of Muslims across Europe and to direct them in a specific behavior, toward a particular target that essentially creates the sense of a "conspiracy". In fact in a very real way i.e., in a "results context" it is a conspiracy of sorts. Almost daily these types of events are happening in Europe. Similar events have been staged here in America by CAIR; as we have seen and as the Muslim population grows the effectiveness and danger of this type of "spontaneous reaction" can be quite devastating to the society. In America we are seeing enfold the first seven steps of the Ten Step program, albeit in various states of evolution. We are nearing the point of Stage Eight: *Population Expansion and Violence*. The expansion is on going; the violence is in general still minimal and limited to isolated instances but as a potential it is discernable on the horizon merely waiting a critical mass.

How is it that the reactions to events that Muslims view as not in their interests are reacted to spontaneously? Islam may prefer to be viewed as a religion without a specific hierarchy, however that is an illusion. The Mullahs do network and do communicate with "superiors" in the Middle East and with terrorist leaders. The cross-organization communications use the technological mechanisms that are offered by the West and they use them most effectively for our undoing. In addition to the cross-organizational communications, CAIR performs the function of organizing activities (as they did against Nike, et al) and information dissemination.

Daniel Pipes wrote shortly after September 11, 2001: "Individual Islamists may appear law-abiding and reasonable, but they are part of a totalitarian movement, and as such, all must be considered potential killers." Mr. Pipes said recently that "I wrote those words days after September 11, 2001, and have been criticized for them ever since. But an incident on March 3 (2006) at the University of North Carolina in Chapel Hill suggests I did not go far enough." He was speaking in the context of a violent event: "a just-graduated student named Mohammed Reza Taheri-azar, 22, an Iranian immigrant, drove a sport utility vehicle into a crowded pedestrian zone….

> "Until his would-be murderous rampage, Mr. Taheri-azar, a philosophy and psychology major, had a seemingly normal existence and promising future…. In fact, no one who knew him said a bad word about him, which is important, for it signals that he is not

some low-life, not homicidal, not psychotic, but a conscientious student and amiable person....

"In brief, Mr Taheri-azar represents the ultimate Islamist nightmare: a seemingly well-adjusted Muslim whose religion inspires him, out of the blue, to murder non-Muslims." (Daniel Pipes)

The reason for the crime Mr Taheri-azar said was:

"people all over the world are being killed in war and now it is the people in the United States' turn to be killed."

About his trial he added:

"I'm thankful you're here to give me this trial and to learn more about the will of Allah." Later in a television interview Taheri-azar read a written statement: "Allah gives permission in the Koran for the followers of Allah to attack those who have raged war against them, with the expectation of eternal paradise in case of martyrdom and/or living one's life in obedience of all of Allah's commandments found throughout the Koran's 114 chapters...The U.S. government is responsible for the deaths of and the torture of countless followers of Allah, my brothers and sisters. My attack on Americans at UNC-CH (University of North Carolina at Chapel Hill) on March 3rd (2006) was in retaliation for similar attacks orchestrated by the U.S. government on my fellow followers of Allah in Iraq, Afghanistan, Palestine, Saudi Arabia, and other Islamic territories. I did not act out of hatred for Americans, but out of love for Allah instead."

Another "time bomb"

"A 30-year-old Pakistani man, announcing he was a Muslim and angry about Israel, pulled out a gun in the Seattle Jewish Federation today and shot six people, one dead.

"The gunman, identified by law enforcement sources as Naveed Afzal Haq, 30, reportedly lives in Pasco, Washington and has a charge of lewd conduct pending against him in Benton County, Washington. He reportedly is a U.S. citizen.

"According to several witnesses, Haq got through security and announced to staff members: "I'm a Muslim American; I'm angry

> at Israel." He immediately began shooting randomly with a semi-automatic 9-mm handgun at the 18 employees and visitors in the offices." (2)

These particular immigrants were clearly not interested in assimilation into the American culture. Regardless of their reasons for being here they were ticking time bombs. The unfortunate thing for America is that they are not alone. There are many cases of individual violence by Muslims against Westerners as well as individual Muslims joining terrorist activities. All of the perpetrators are normal appearing students and workers.

If the Islamic infiltration through the on going implementation of the *Ten Step* program continues unabated, then after two generations, although still a relative minority (so were the Nazis in Germany), the Muslim power structure will, in the U.S., have the political power, the money and a more than adequate participation in major administrative functions within government to realize significant control of the country and its policies. Countering this is an indigenous population that is now heading toward a state of *dhimmitude* through the irreversible series of "accommodations" that will have been implemented over the intervening fifty to sixty years. Not an effective counter-balance to an Islamic takeover by any means.

At that point there will no longer be the country of our forefathers but in its place a *Shari'a* driven Islamic state. There will also be no one to be accused of *Islamophobia*. If at this time or in the intervening years there is a strong and violent backlash against Islam (an absolute tragedy in its own right), the resulting civil strife could also destroy the fabric of the country. In 2006 it is not too late to address these issues appropriately and within the framework of existing law and norms.

Meanwhile it may already be too late for the Europeans where the fabric of society is being stretched to the breaking point. The forms that this takes are endless. For example: in Europe where the social welfare programs are very liberal and easy to partake of even for immigrants they have acted as a beacon for third world Muslims in ever increasing numbers. This itself creates a critically destabilizing pressure on the resources of the host country.

> In Norway almost half of all children with a non-Western background claim social security benefits. This is ten times the rate

> of the native population.
>
> A Danish commission concluded that Denmark could save 50 billion kroner (an enormous sum for a small country like Denmark) every year by 2040 if it shut the door to third world immigration.
>
> At the same time, population statistics indicate that Scandinavians will become a minority in their own countries within two generations, if the current trend continues. While their politicians insist that immigration is "good for the economy," Scandinavians are in reality funding their own colonization.

Although the cost of welfare is significant, it pales in comparison to the price paid through rapidly declining social harmony and increasing insecurity caused by Muslim immigration. Much of the increase in insecurity is due to terrorist threats and the intimidation of critics of Islam and Muslim immigration.

Mullah Krekar, a Muslim supremacist living in Oslo, informed the Norwegian paper Aftenposten that: "Muslims would change Norway, not the other way around." He added: "Just look at the development within Europe, where the number of Muslims is expanding like mosquitoes," he said. "By 2050, 30 percent of the population in Europe will be Muslim."

The one Muslim country that offered hope to the West for becoming a model "modern Islamic state" was Turkey. Since 1923 Turkey has been a secular state. The religion of Turkey was and is Islam but the secular laws and societal norms took precedence ***over** Shari'a*. This context made Turkey unique in Islam; it practiced a liberal form of western democracy while including women in the work force, free enterprise, liberal social standards, freedom of religion (to an extent), etc. Unfortunately a fundamentalist struggle is currently creating a great deal of turmoil and a politically unsettled situation. An avowed Islamist, named Recep Tayyip Erdogan, in 2002 parlayed a minority of votes into a monopoly of power. Since Erdogen's rise to power a huge amount of petro-dollars have flowed into the country from Saudi-Arabia (always helpful) and are being used to strengthen Erdogan's position. Through fear tactics Erdogean has managed to crush a good deal of criticism from the media. In addition most recently there has been a great deal of propagandizing against the West including notably a spate of wildly popular, virulently anti-American books and movies.

Turkey is poised to join the European Union in 2009. As a strong secular state this might not have been a problem even though it is a Muslim country. However with Turkey's move to a more fundamentalist regime the impact to Europe of an additional 70 million Muslims becoming EU citizens could be devastating. The advent of a EU Islamic state would provide for non Turkish Muslims a clear avenue into the EU countries even if immigration laws pertaining to non-EU countries were tightened. The truth of this lies in the fact that if one holds a EU passport one can enter any EU country. There is little doubt that a more fundamentalist influenced Turkey would allow the entry into Turkey of any Muslims seeking entry and then in turn be able to gain citizenship and an EU passport. From there they could proceed to any country in Europe uninhibited.

The tragedy is that the Europeans are not equipped, either from an intellectual perspective or governmentally, to deal with the magnitude of the problem inherent in the emerging dominant Islamic society they see enfolding before them. Their politicians and statesmen through the offices of the EAD have systematically and intellectually disarmed the European countries. The result is, in principle, alarmingly similar to what Europe did with Hitler prior to the war. Appeasement and minimization of the problem was then, and is now, the order of the day. Furthermore, through the constant and subtle propagandizing of the EAD, the European media, schools, and universities have essentially institutionalized, through a strict *political correctness,* a near universal and reflexive antagonism toward the U.S. and Israel that simultaneously minimizes any criticism of Islam. (To some extent recent terrorist events have mitigated this but it is a drop in the proverbial bucket.)

In *Eurabia* Bat Ye'or (a noted historian) writes:

> "Europeans, have unwittingly endured 'thirty years of constant indoctrination,' and while most of them 'harbor no hate,' a culture of animosity toward America, Jews, and Israel has indeed been thrust upon them and has, despite 'the enormous gap between Eurocrat theorists and the European population,' had a real effect, as manifested, for example, in the massive anti-American demonstrations that have taken place in European cities in recent years."

Ms Ye'or is not exaggerating in the least. One need only follow the daily newspaper editorials of the leading European periodicals to see a constant frontal attack, as well as endless subtle innuendos, all negative and all directed at the U.S or Israel. In fact there is no real basis for this degree of "hatred". The U.S can be perceived as arrogant at times and pedantic and is not always consistent in its foreign policy, however these are by no means its dominant characteristics. The U.S. has also supported Europe through two world wars and a subsequent cold war; they have been incredibly generous in terms of aid and help of every type and in every possible context. America has also offered the Europeans enormous trading opportunities and hard currency from tourism. America and Europe share a common heritage, values, and religions and are very similar cultures. It would not be unreasonable to state that the emotional balance should objectively lie on the positive side for the U.S.

As for Israel, it is hard to find a rational reason for so virulent and constant a hatred. Israel itself is a creation of post war European countries working through the U.N. Also Israeli policies have always focused on pure survival. They have no other agenda on the world stage. Of course Europe has always maintained a degree of anti-Semitism even when Israel did not exist or was not an issue but again this alone cannot explain the virulent expanding anti-Israeli and anti-Semitic sentiment. So what is it about Israel that so alienates the Europeans particularly since by any reasonable measure Israel is a Western country steeped in Western culture? The irrational reason could be bigotry but that alone is not enough to explain the degree of anti-Israeli sentiment. The answer is Islam.

If Islam reaches an accord with Israel tomorrow Europe would tone down the anti-Israeli rhetoric. The major reason for this "hate" is more than a core of anti-Semitism but is the result of the tireless active efforts of the EAD to institutionalize a rigid *political correctness* throughout Europe in all walks of life, i.e., in the media, at all levels of the education system, and in corporate life. Implicit in all of the "teachings" has been a constant and automatic anti-American and anti-Israeli bias that allows virtually no criticism or continuing assessment of Islamic governments or of Islam in general. (It is interesting how *political correctness* never extends to America or Israel.) This process of alienating Israel from Europe has been escalating in its rhetoric, as Bat Ye'or states, "for 30 years since the birth of the EAD."

The EAD at its inception was a potentially perfect vehicle for the implementation of the *Ten Step* program and as part of that process the complete isolation and alienation of Israel. In reality it worked better then Islam could have hoped. One can think of the EAD as an intellectual Trojan Horse whose primary objective was Islamic *infiltration* of European countries and culture, slowly, subtly but constantly moving forward through population growth (waves of immigration and high birth rates) and managed public relations. The near dominant position of Islam in many countries in Europe today and the evolution of a consistently conciliatory position on the part of Europe toward Islam did not occur overnight but it was quite deliberate. There are exceptions but the formation of desired policy and the progression of the *Ten Steps* is a work in progress.

The American Trojan Horse consists of not only CAIR and its allies but of the entire intellectual environment created by the American universities that not only preach *multiculturalism* and *political correctness* as though it were a religion itself; but also consistently, over a period that spanned an entire generation, practically indoctrinated students to the point that critical thought and in depth evaluation of political issues are rare and a *politically correct* knee-jerk reaction is the mode of operation in any situation. Against this background it becomes difficult to understand and realistically evaluate the looming crisis. Worse yet it is fertile ground for the expansion of the concept of accommodations and exceptions that Islam needs as part of its infiltration program. And the folks supporting the accommodations do so happily and with a sense of "goodness" even though the entire accommodation concept and process is against everything that the country stood for, i.e., equality for all not accommodation for one.

From the Islamist's perspective the U.S. presents a perfect environment within which to infiltrate and subvert a culture. Whenever Islam oversteps the bounds of what even the tolerant West can stomach and Westerners protest, Islam screams, "racism, xenophobia, Islamophobia", and the Western mainstream media and intellectuals rally to their support with editorials and excuses and calls for the need for understanding in a *multicultural* society. Then the apologists join the fray and voices raised against Islam that aren't accused of bigotry are certainly relegated to the "lunatic fringe."

The supportive scenario is like a "Greek Chorus." At no time do the mainstream apologists for Islam and apologizers for America's actions ever entertain the notion that there is an evil afoot and that we are actually in real danger. The evidence grows daily as does the denials. Yet the *infiltration* continues at every level of Western Society while the outline of a global ideological struggle continues to emerge. Soon it will be impossible even for the mainstream and left leaning and naive politicos and media to deny it. One can only hope that it won't be too late.

21 Population Growth

The *Ten-Steps* program requires that a reasonable size Muslim population exist in a country before the program can effectively advance. The required population is initially achieved through immigration, secondly through high birth rates and thirdly through religious conversions of the domestic population. The objective is to achieve a population density of 10 to 15%. If this percentage is reached the host country is ready for the middle and advanced stages of the *Ten-Steps*.

Through the EAD and its joint European - Islamic agreements, the first major waves of Muslim migration began to arrive in Europe in the mid 1970s. The Europeans had no idea of the scope of the problem they were creating for themselves. The influx of a great number of immigrants of a completely foreign culture presents an astounding problem of assimilation, however if assimilation is not the goal of the immigrants then the problem becomes one of a potentially greater magnitude.

> "In 1995, the late American novelist Paul Bowles, a longtime resident of Tangiers, said that he could not understand why the French had allowed millions of North African Muslims into their country. Bowles had chosen to live among Muslims for most of his life, yet he obviously considered it highly unlikely that so many of them could be successfully integrated into a modern, secular European state." (1)

It is interesting that in 1968 before the waves of Islamic migration to Europe began a marvelously prescient research work dealt with the very issue of immigrant assimilation in large numbers. In *The Tragedy of the Commons*, the authors Garrett and Hardin (2) discuss, in abstract terms, the problems faced by a society from an immigrant group that does not share the host country's values or a willingness to adopt those values. Basically Garrett and Hardin's premise is that as the group's percentage of the population increases over time the group also gains in the ability to pressure and manipulate the host country for the group's specific purposes. These purposes can consist of any number of societal changes. The leaders of the host society are faced with the dilemma of having to balance the pressures from the immigrant group against those of the existing society. The conflict must, by necessity, grow as the immigrant group and its decedents grow. This is particularly true when the population of the host country is not growing at all (as is the current case in Europe). The losers, in the sense of a cultural lose and even a loss of freedoms, occurs to the indigenous population with every accommodation to the immigrant group. (As we have seen through the many cases of accommodations granted by the West to Muslim populations this process is enfolding at an accelerated rate throughout the Western world as the Muslim populations grow.)

When considering the validity of this premise, in a specific context, one must be very careful not to be influenced either by close mindedness or bigotry. The critical point that must be emphasized is that the changes "demanded" by the immigrant group are fundamentally against the norms, laws and even the morality of the host population. (This statement is not evaluative in the sense of cultural preference; it merely represents a specific phenomenon that creates conflict.)

Recognizing the existence of this enfolding reality and rebelling against it or resenting it is not necessarily bigotry. The changes (accommodations, etc.) are fundamentally abhorrent to, and rub against the moral grain of, the host society. In fairness why should the host society have to change a set of norms and a moral code, and even laws that have governed them for centuries, so as to accommodate a moral code they find both immoral and abhorrent? This is not only the worst form of altruism but it is also cultural suicide.

In *The Tragedy of the Commons Revisited* by Beryl Crowe (1969) (3) the issue of expanding non-compatible populations is discussed. Like Garrett and Hardin before him Crowe was quite prescient in that he exactly describes the difficulties that are currently being experienced by European countries, i.e., unassimilated Muslim populations that are committed to over-breeding and do not share the values of the host society. In some cases these groups actually work toward the overthrow of the host societies and its replacement with *Shari'a* law, norms and governance.

The EAD from the beginning had as a central goal the fostering of Islamic emigration to Europe and they were incredibly successful. And perhaps we will never know (I could not find documentation to attest to this supposition) but it is reasonable to assume that the current emerging crisis of assimilation in Europe was exactly the goal of the EAD's push for Islamic migration.

> "The speed and scale of this operation were unique in history. Even the emigration of Europeans to their Arab colonies during the colonial period took place at a far slower pace. The number of European colonizers and their descendants in Arab countries, even after a century or more, were a fraction of the present-day Muslim immigration in Europe after just three decades." (4)

Within the immigrant Muslim populations there is a considerably greater number of large families compared to the indigenous population. In Europe where the indigenous populations have at best a zero growth rate (many have negative growth rates) the Muslims are having six children per wife. In many cases the male has several wives.

The Muslim minorities in Europe, already at or above the 10 percent benchmark in some countries are on the path to successfully destabilizing the host countries' governments as well as cowing the society and even the law enforcement bodies into non-action. This advancing problem needs to be aggressively worked as early in the immigration process as possible. Through the legal and social systems, everything that can possibly be done to promote assimilation and "deghettoization" must be done before either the backlash point is reached or societal collapse occurs. However without a strong conviction on the part of the indigenous population and their government the "takeover" of their society becomes increasingly difficult to stop. Since the people and governments of Europe seem paralyzed to stop the forward movement of Islam it is quite possible that we are witnessing the realization of Mr. Hardin's thesis. The other major issue of course is quite obvious; are the immigrants willing to participate in a program of assimilation or are they so committed to *Islamization* that they will continue to push the envelop toward the realization of *Shari'a*?

One extreme form of answer to that question is found in Italy. In Mazara del Vallo in Sicily, a Tunisian community obtained permission (in the1970s) to retain its Muslim identity in all respects. This included Tunisian/Muslim schools, teachers recruited from Tunisia, Tunisian laws, etc. In addition, although polygamy is illegal in Italy, it is tolerated in this Sicilian town.

Another form of the answer to the question is found throughout Europe in the form of the "virtual independent Islamic state" following its own cultural dictates with total impunity and independent of local law Muslims open unauthorized schools, but no intervention is made; infibulation is practiced on women, but no one is put on trial; rape victims are punished and rapist go free and nothing is done; an honor killing is perpetrated and no arrests are made. On the whole, this creates an asymmetry among citizens before the law, by virtue of which, some minorities are first protected, but then become privileged. This clearly demonstrates the incompatibility of applied *multiculturalism* with the rule of universal law. It is however quite in keeping with the philosophy and tenets of *Shari'a*.

Aisha Farina, an Italian woman from Milan who converted to Islam and has often publicly expressed her veneration for bin Laden said:

> "Maybe all the Italians will end up converting (to Islam). In any case, we will conquer you peacefully, because our numbers double every generation, but you are at zero growth."

She is absolutely correct with respect to the numbers. How prophetic are her words with respect to Italy? Given the experience of Mazara del Vallo she seems to be on a winning track.

> "First in Europe and now in the United States, Muslim groups have petitioned to establish enclaves in which they can uphold and enforce greater compliance to Islamic law. While the U.S. Constitution enshrines the right to religious freedom and the prohibition against a state religion, when it comes to the rights of religious enclaves to impose communal rules, the dividing line is more nebulous. Can U.S. enclaves, homeowner associations, and other groups enforce Islamic law?" (5)

Some Islamist community leaders in the United States are challenging the principles of assimilation and equality once central to the civil rights movement, seeking instead to live according to a separate but equal philosophy. The Gwynnoaks Muslim Residential Development group, for example, has established an informal enclave in Baltimore because, according to John Yahya Cason, director of the Islamic Education and Community Development Initiative, a Baltimore-based Muslim advocacy group, "there was no community in the U.S. that showed the totality of the essential components of Muslim social, economic, and political structure." (6)

It seems that open and liberal societies become paralyzed when encountering a closed and incompatible civilization in their midst. The first reaction is a lack of understanding of the nature of the problem. The population looks introspectively at the cause, essentially because they cannot believe that anyone would not be content with the culture they offer. The tragedy is that although this demonstrates a generosity of spirit it can be terminally naive.

Throughout these last sections one can see the effect of the *Ten Steps* as they are implemented and progress through the different stages in the different countries. There appears to be no way that the West is equipped, at this point, to counter this seemingly inexorable movement toward becoming an Islamic culture composed of Muslims and *dhimmis*. If you think that this is incorrect or absurd, trace the progress of Islam in the West over the past 30 years and then project its accelerating pace forward into the future some 30 to 50 years. There is quite a surprise waiting for you.

22 Jihad

One of the most widely heard phrases in the West emanating from the world of Islam is *jihad*. By now most Westerners know that *jihad* is associated with violence and is synonymous with terrorism. However it is more than that, it is a powerful religious concept and dictate and is used as the justification for terrorism. This alone makes terrorism an acceptable act in a moral sense to the terrorist. There is no room for conscious to confuse the terrorist, he "knows" that he is doing the will of Allah.

> "I was ordered to fight all men until they say 'There is no god but Allah.'"
>
> —Mohammad's farewell words.

Muslims envision a world dominated by Islam in which all men are Muslims or *dhimmis*. To achieve this end it is essential for all male Muslims to work and struggle "*in the path of Allah*." That "struggle" is called *jihad*. (It is interesting to note that Mein Kampf, Hitler's statement of his beliefs and plans, means "My Struggle." It seems that world conquest is always a struggle.)

Although many Islamic leaders claim that *jihad* is a religious term that calls for an inner struggle, they are being misleading and disingenuous. The term *jihad* does mean struggle but the word is also accurately translated into English as "Holy War." Although there may be a religious inner struggle experienced by Muslims during their lifetime it is most clear that a *jihad* is also a war against *infidels*, all non-believers, and apostates. Armed conflict in defense of Islam is a religious obligation throughout the Muslim world. There are 18 passages in the *Qur'an* and *Hadiths* that justify war and violence against non-believers. (1)

The world of *infidels* (all non Muslims) is considered a single entity, *dar al-harb* the house of war. It is through *jihad* that *dar al-harb* becomes *dar al-Islam*, the House of Islam. *Jihad*, the war against *infidels*, will bring the world to Islam.

Sheikh Tantawi of al-Azhar University teaches that:

> "it is permissible for Muslims to fight non-Muslims in other countries for no greater injury than that the non-Muslims are actively condemning or belittling Muslims or the religion of Islam."

That quote takes in a great deal of territory. To the average Westerner the term *jihad*, for many years, seemed almost silly in that there was an aspect of trivialization to *jihad* since it appeared to be instigated by any cleric for any perceived ill regardless of the accuracy or severity of the perception. In addition most of these "crimes," from the Western perspective did not appear to be anything more than an expression of free speech. Furthermore it was inconceivable that ***any cleric*** could call for a *jihad* unilaterally and at will. There did not appear to be a process or a governing body controlling this mechanism.

To a degree this is all true; however, it is more than a group of random clerics, there was a modern beginning to *jihad*. Its initial implementation was in 1981 and emanated from a call to *jihad* by the *Mecca-Taif Resolution of The Third Islamic Summit Conference* when it decided:

> "to declare holy Jihad , as the duty of every Muslim, man and woman, ordained by *Shari'a* and glorious traditions of Islam; to call upon all Muslims, living inside or outside Islamic countries, to discharge this duty by contributing each according to his capacity in the cause of Allah Almighty, Islamic brotherhood, and righteousness." (2)

On both the philosophical and practical level *jihad* is the ideological embodiment of perpetual war. On a religious level it is an absolute requirement. Therefore it seems logical that there is an equally absolute requirement for constant enemies–the *infidels* (and there will always be non-Muslims). On the pragmatic level in today's world the call for *jihad* institutes continuous *terrorism* against the *infidels* since open warfare is beyond Islam's current capability. (With the acquisition of nuclear weapons this too will change.) The reality is that *jihad* is an umbrella permission and justification to do anything necessary to achieve some Islamic end; but in Islam the overriding and obligatory end is for world domination.

In his early campaigns Mohammad learned to use religious language to assist in achieving his worldly objectives. He stated:

> "Stick to *jihad* and you will be in good health and get sufficient means of livelihood." (3)

Muhammad's father-in-law and successor sought to incite the Arabs to his plans of conquest by a call for *jihad* and a promise of:

> "the booty to be won from the Byzantines." (4)

And Mohammad's son-in-law stated:

> "Sacrifice yourselves! You are under Allah's watchful eye and with the prophet's cousin. Resume your charge and abhor flight, for it will disgrace your descendants and buy you the fire of hell in the Day of Reckoning." (5)

If that wasn't sufficient motivation he added:

> "Before you lie in the great sawad (fertile lands of Iraq) and those large tents."

And in modern times, Abdul Aziz bin Baz, vice chancellor of The Islamic University of Medina states:

> "According to the Koran, the Sunnah, and the consensus of Muslims it is a requirement of Muslims to be hostile to the Jews and Christians and other polytheists." He further stated that various verses in the Koran prove: "with absolute clarity that there is a religious requirement to despise the *infidel* Jews and Christians and other polytheists." (6)

The verification of this command can be found in the *Qur'an* itself. It contains many verses supporting the degree of hatred Abdul Aziz bin Baz is speaking of. (Many of the verses have been quoted herein.) It would be reasonable to doubt that any other religion's scriptures, teachers and holy-men so consistently and almost universally preaches hatred and the requisite actions that should flow from that hatred.

There has never been a prolonged time in history where Islam did not use *jihad* to further its goals and empire.

A partial list of major *Jihad* Campaigns through history (all C.E. dates):

Egypt, Palestine, Tripolitania 640-646
Iraq, Syria
Armenia 642
Cyprus, the Greek Islands and Anatolia 649-654
Cilicia, Cesarea 650
The Indian Subcontinent 711-712
Cappadocia 715-720
Spain and France 793-860

Anatolia, Amorium 838
Armenia 847-861
Sicily and Italy 835-851, 884
Hindu Kingdom of Kabul 870
Thesselonika 904
Ghazni India 977-997
Thanesar India 1018-1019
Mesopotamia 1057
Campaigns in India from 1025 through the 14th centuries
Destruction of Buddhist temples during the same period.
From 1057 through 1499 almost uninterrupted campaigns against lands in North Africa, Soain, Greece, Italy.
In parallel further campaigns throughout the Indian subcontinent until 1565.
Armenia again in 1604.
More campaigns in the 18th and 19th centuries in India.
Massacres in Bulgaria in 1876
Slave trade flourishes from captives during the Sudan *jihad* late 19th century.
Genocide of the Armenians 1894-1896. (7)

The goals of *jihad* are no different today then they were over the past fourteen centuries, i.e., conquest and conversion. However because of the incredible technological advancement of the West over the past two centuries while Islam stagnated, modern *jihad* has, by necessity, not followed the same mode of operation as it historically did. Open warfare and invasion has yielded to terrorism. In fact we are now in the Age of Terrorism. Every single act of terrorism is done in the name of *jihad*. (It is interesting to note, and will be discussed in later chapters, that had the world found an alternative to oil say 50 years ago the modern *jihad* and push of Islam would not only not be possible but would not exist.)

We are all too aware of the endless terrorist attacks, every kind from the magnitude of the World Trade Center's destruction to a tragic but narrowly focused single suicide bomber, the entire purpose of the act is to create terror in the minds of the survivors. It is a truly primitive and immoral weapon but it is part of the religion and this enables the terrorist to act with a sense of innocence and righteousness in their own mind. However it is a completely ineffective weapon in one very real sense, it is a weapon that is the last cry of a bankrupt culture–unless we succumb to the fear it generates. Succumb in this context means to appease.

Let us turn our attention to the newest form of *jihad*, what Daniel Pipes calls "Sudden *Jihad* Syndrome."

> "This is what I have dubbed the Sudden *Jihad* Syndrome, whereby normal-appearing Muslims abruptly become violent. It has the awful but legitimate consequence of casting suspicion on all Muslims. Who knows whence the next *jihadi*? How can one be confident that a law-abiding Muslim will not suddenly erupt in a homicidal rage? Yes, of course, their numbers are very small, but they are disproportionately much higher than among non-Muslims.

As an example of this "syndrome" see the already described case of the Iranian student Mohammed Reza Taheriazar, who drove his rented SUV into a crowd of fellow students at the university of North Carolina, to "punish the American government for their actions around the world." This type of event does not happen often in the U.S. but it does elsewhere. Many of the suicide bombers are of this category. A sudden need to wage *jihad* overtakes them and they become suicide bombers or violent killers.

The normal Muslim response of denouncing these negative views of Islam as bias or "Islamophobic" is baseless in general. The numbers paint too explicit a picture to merely accuse the accuser of bigotry. There were 14,600 deaths attributed to terrorist attacks in 2005. American military deaths (non combat) accounted for only 56. (8) Between September 2000 and July 2004 there were 22,400 terrorist incidents in Israel, the West Bank and The Gaza Strip alone. All of these deaths and incidents are part of some *jihad*. For more details about terrorist incidents see Appendix B.

If better understanding and relations with the West were the goal of Islam then instead of always presenting themselves as victims, Muslims would address the issues of Islamism and aggressively reject, as integral parts of their religion, radical Islam, *jihad*, and the subordination of "*infidels*".

23 Shrai'a

Jesus Christ said over 2000 years ago

> "Render unto Caesar the things which are Caesar's and unto God the things which are Gods." (From Matthew 22:17)

Whether one is a believer or not the statement is brilliant in its clarity. It simply states that the realm of the secular belongs to man and the realm of the spirit belongs to God. One of the cornerstones of Western civilization for centuries has been the separation of church and state and where it has been practiced it has served the evolving culture superlatively well. It has also allowed for many different religions, or none at all, to peacefully co-exist; and for the treatment of all citizens as equals under the law regardless of their religious affiliations. Unfortunately separation of powers within the society is a concept that does not exist in Islam, and in fact represents a violation of a core premise of Islam. And therein lies the problem.

SHARI'A AND JIHAD

Shari'a and *jihad* are two sides of the same coin. *Jihad*'s overriding purpose, no matter what its transactional goal may be, is to convert the world to Allah's law and Allah's divine law is *Shari'a*.

> "*Shari'a* refers to Islamic law. In the Islamic state *Shari'a* governs both public and private lives of those living within the state. *Shari'a* governs many aspects of day-to-day life: politics, economics, banking, business law, contract law, and social issues. The term *Shari'a* refers to the body of Islamic law. Some accept *Shari'a* as the body of precedent and legal theory before the 19th century, while other scholars view *Shari'a* as a changing body, and include reform Islamic legal theory from the contemporary period. (1)

Note: At no time does the application of the above quoted clause - "reform legal theory from the contemporary period" - in any way countermand or conflict with the central dictum(s) of *Shari'a*.

Quite explicit in this definition, but clearly not emphasized, is the fact that there is no independent secular law outside of *Shari'a*. *Shari'a* law derives its rules for governing all aspects of life directly from the *Qur'an* and *Hadiths* as well as years of rulings by mullahs. While the essence of *Shari'a* is religious its application is quite often secular.

> "The connection between law and religion thus established by Mohammed and adopted by his followers persisted throughout all later centuries. Characteristically, all expositions of Muslim law begin with the 'religious duties' or 'acts of worship', such as ablution, prayer, and pilgrimage. As in other Semitic religions, law is thought of, not as a product of human intelligence and adaptation to changing social needs and ideals, but of divine inspiration hence immutable." (2)

The immutability of *Shari'a* in the religious or "spiritual" context, one might argue, is of little significance to the secular world. In this narrow sense it is not dissimilar to the scriptures and dictates of many religions. The problem posed by *Shari'a* is its intrusion into every aspect of the secular and the fact that it emanates from a religion that, in a very pedantic way, allows no exception to its goals and teachings. *Shari'a* is so integral to the world of Islam that it is impossible to separate the religion from the secular. (The one quasi exception, Turkey is slipping back into *Shari'a* as we have seen.)

Shari'a was the only legislation governing all of Islam for almost thirteen centuries, until the nineteenth century when European colonization, influence and the intrinsic pressures of the modern world became too great to resist. In response many aspects of western secularism were utilized in a pragmatic way. However *Shari'a* is still the dominant law of Islam, e.g., Egypt, Iran, Syria, Nigeria, Pakistan, Iraq, etc. Even Afghanistan and Iraq's implementation of a "new constitution" was governed by *Shari'a*; the new constitutions were not allowed to contradict any tenet of *Shari'a*. The fifty-six members of the *Organization of the Islamic Conference* (OIC) accept no law over *Shari'a*, which is the only law that is ultimately binding. *Shari'a* is held to be a higher power than any U.N. resolution or international treaties and covenants. This creates a distinct disadvantage for the West in treaty and relationship development. The World of Islam can agree to anything and with clear conscious in the future "break the deal" if it is not deemed "compatible" with the tenets of *Shari'a*.

In keeping with this thought

> "As a Muslim, I feel more protected by the higher democratic

> principle of the [secular] nation-state than by the *Shari'a*, which is interpreted by the religious authorities as they wish, sometimes according to their moods...*Shari'a* has never been a model of good governance in the Arab world. In any case, it must be separated from the political sphere." (3)

It is out of the scope of this book to include a survey of the actual elements and specific laws of *Shari'a* for they are an extensive set and come with even more extensive supporting discussion and rulings from many mullahs through the centuries. However it is appropriate to include the extensive range of life over which *Shari'a* governs.

> "By a million roots, penetrating every phase of life, all of them with religious significance, it is able to maintain its hold upon the life of Moslem peoples." (4)

> "Bousquet, one of the foremost authorities on Islamic law, distinguishes two aspects of Islam that he considers totalitarian: **Islamic law**, (emphasis mine) and the Islamic notion of jihad that has as its ultimate aim the conquest of the entire world, in order to submit it to one single authority." (5)

Shari'a does not allow freedom of speech on such matters as criticism of The Prophet Muhammad, or the cursing of either The Prophet or Allah.

> "The *Qur'an* says that Allah curses the one who harms the Prophet in this world and He connected harm of Himself to harm of the Prophet. There is no dispute that anyone who curses Allah is killed and that his curse demands that he be categorized as an unbeliever. The judgment of the unbeliever is that he is killed....[T]here is a difference between...harming Allah and His Messenger and harming the believers. Injuring the believers, short of murder, incurs beating and exemplary punishment. The judgment against those who harm Allah and His Prophet is more severe–the death penalty."(6)

Shari'a dictates the following with exacting language: dietary laws defining what one eats and even how it is prepared and eaten, laws on appropriate dress, laws governing every aspect of a woman's life, sex, marriage, adultery, beatings, honor killings, laws against religious conversions–punishable by death, even blasphemy is punishable by death. The intrusive nature of *Shari'a* into every aspect of life is oppressive. To see the extreme form of *Shari'a* in action one only needs to revisit the way of life under the Taliban.

And the punishments in the Islamic world are largely inhuman, e.g., amputation of the right hand for minor theft, amputation of two hands for a second or serious offense, death for a third offense crime. Many other crimes also carry the death penalty. Adultery is punishable by lapidating (stoning). Other crimes carry penalties such as be-heading, flogging, etc.

DECLARATION OF HUMAN RIGHTS AND SHARI'A

Comparing *Shari'a* with the *Declaration of Human Rights* (1948) (DHR) is a most interesting exercise.

> Articles 1 through 4 of the DHR deal with the basic human freedoms, securities and respect for the individual regardless of sex, gender, nationality and religion.

Shari'a violates every aspect of these articles. Women are inferior under Islamic law, non-Muslims are *infidels* and those living in Muslim countries have inferior status. In Saudi Arabia the law follows Muhammad's dictate that "Two religions cannot exist in the country of Arabia." Non-Muslims cannot practice their religion and priests are not even allowed in the country. Furthermore non-believers, particularly atheists, do not have the right to life in Muslim countries let alone freedom. Slavery is recognized as an acceptable practice and exists in many Muslim countries.

> Article 5 of the DHR states that no one should be subjected to cruel or degrading punishment and torture.

In Islamic countries practices of cruel or degrading punishment and torture are quite common. One can rightly say that this travesty of humanity goes on in non-Muslim countries and the tragedy is that you would be correct. The difference is that it happens most often in violation of law and religion and it isn't codified and accepted in law as it is in Islam. Perhaps this is poor solace to a victim of brutality but it is an important issue when judging and comparing legal and moral systems.

> Article 6 of the DHR states that everyone has the right to be recognized as a person, an individual before the law.

The concept of an individual capable of making moral choices and being held responsible for them on an equal basis with all is completely missing from *Shari'a*. The concept of individual choice is foreign to Islam.

> Articles 7 through11 of the DHR deal with rights and treatment of accused persons and the trial they are due.

Under *Shari'a* the concepts of justice, truth, fairness, etc. are subordinated to the demands of *Shari'a*. Revenge killings are legal, non-Muslims cannot testify against a Muslim regardless of the crime, (this certainly makes non-Muslims "fair game"), women can only rarely testify.

> Article 16 of the DHR deals with the rights of men and women under the marriage contract.

Enough has been said about *Shari'a*-sanctioned treatment of women.

> Article 18 of the DHR states that everyone has the right to freedom of thought, conscious and religious choice; and also the right to change their religion. In addition the right to express those religious beliefs and practice them in public should be guaranteed.

Shari'a permits no religion but Islam and death is the result of converting from Islam. If death is not demanded then all property and personal rights are denied the convert. In addition in many Muslim countries public expression of other religions is forbidden.

> Article 19 of the DHR states that everyone has the right to freedom of opinion and expression and the freedom to seek information through any form of media.

These rights have been consistently violated throughout most of the Middle East and many other Islamic countries. In fact the form of the violation of this right can be quite extreme. Amnesty International states " Hundreds of Christians, including women and children have been arrested and detained over the past three years, most without charge or trial, solely for the peaceful expression of their religious beliefs. Scores have been tortured, some by flogging, while in detention." (AINO 62 July/August 1993). Also Shi'a Muslims have also been arrested and treated similarly. These practices continue today.

> Articles 23 and 26 of the DHR deal with the rights to work and receive an education.

Under *Shari'a* women are excluded from obtaining these rights in total. Other segments of Islamic society are also systematically excluded as well.

The number of articles that are incompatible with Islam is quite high and as such constitute a rebuke to Islam and an embarrassment. To counter this in 1981 representatives of various Islamic groups met and drafted an *Islamic Declaration of Human Rights*. The document left out all of the human freedoms that contradict *Shari'a*. This was not enough so the Muslim countries attempted to pressure the U.N into changing some of the original declaration's articles to be more compatible with Islam. The U.N. of course complied at least in part. Article 18 dealing with freedom of religion was changed to be more acceptable to Islam.

> "In summary *Shari'a* is the total collection of theoretical laws that apply in an ideal Muslim community that has surrendered to the will of God. It is based on divine authority that must be accepted without criticism. Islamic law is thus not a product of human intelligence, and in no way reflects a constantly changing or evolving social reality (as does European law)." (6)

The West is not an ideal Muslim community. The West and its system of law is the antithesis of *Shari'a*. For a moment imagine living under such a repressive legal system, one that was developed almost 1400 years ago and has permitted very little change in the accommodation of modernity, tolerance or human rights.

And then remember that the objective of *jihad* is to implement *Shari'a* in the entire world, a world they wish to make *dar al Islam*.

24 Islam and Treaties

When exploring the many facets of *Shari'a* one can easily conclude that the concept of a treaty is actually seen as an expedient not a binding obligation unless it is in perfect keeping with the tenants of *Shari'a* itself and made with other Muslims. To reiterate a previously stated point: the fifty-six members of the OIC stated that they accept no law over *Shari'a*, which to Muslims is the only law that is ultimately binding.

As such *Shari'a* is held to be a higher power than any U.N. resolution or international treaties and covenants. Given a belief system of this nature it would seem that the West is always at a distinct disadvantage when negotiating with Islam. And certainly the past forty years of peace negotiations (the number of years itself should be a clue that this is like a bad dream that we can't awaken from) have yielded absolutely nothing! The truth is that the World of Islam can agree to anything and with clear conscious "break the deal" when it is convenient and deemed "not compatible" with its long-term goals.

> "Political Islam finds a number of examples in the life of Prophet Muhammad that sanction the use of treaties as a tactical necessity. In explaining why he signed the Oslo Accord, Yasser Arafat cited a truce signed by Prophet Muhammad with the Meccan tribe Quraish at Hudaybiyah in 628 C.E. According to the PLO leader, Prophet Muhammad had signed the truce when he was not strong enough to win a war and it was to last for ten years. But when, within two years of the signing, the Muslims felt that they have gained enough strength to defeat the Quraish, they broke the truce, attacked the Quraish and captured Mecca."

> "A prominent Saudi sheikh, 'Abd Al-Muhsin Al-'Obikan, also referred to the same treaty while condemning Hezbollah's actions in Lebanon. He issued the edict against Hezbollah's actions not because he considered them wrong but because in his view Muslims, at the moment, are not strong enough to defeat Israel. He said that since the Muslims have no chance of winning this campaign against the Jews, a temporary solution is necessary - a truce similar to the temporary truce of Hudaybiyya." (1)

When dealing with Islam it is always important to believe the most outlandish statements made by their leaders, representatives and particularly their "madmen". They have invariably proven to be true. It would also seem reasonable to state that it is absolutely critical when negotiating with Islam to truly understand their long-range goals. Since Islam is quite open about what they expect to achieve over time and with knowledge of Islamic history and the *Qur'an* it is easier to understand these elements of the negotiating equation then it might appear at first. The problem with the West in general, and with American Diplomacy specifically, is that it appears to be incredibly naive with respect to Islam's intentions. Certainly this was also true when European diplomats were negotiating with Hitler in the 1930s. What is astounding is that today's diplomats can continue to negotiate with Islam oblivious to the things that Islam says and has done over the past 40 years and also completely ignoring lessons from history.

One would think that "Diplomacy 101" would teach that when negotiating with an enemy, or for that matter anyone, it is essential to have a strategic framework that includes our long term non negotiable requirements and a very real and fundamental understanding of the psychology of the group that sits opposite you at the negotiating table. How can one even think of negotiating without this knowledge? Just realizing the truth of the above quotes (regarding Hudaybiyya) should make it clear that unless we negotiate from a position of overwhelming strength and full knowledge that any agreement will be broken in the future, should dramatically change the West's entire approach to the negotiating process, the contents of any agreement and in fact even if the negotiations should occur at all.

This does not seem to be the case now nor has it been for the past 40 years of fruitless talks with various Islamic groups. The West only seems to understand an immediate transaction not the overriding historical context within which the transaction exists, or the nature of the people sitting opposite us. The West has proven itself completely inept at negotiating with Islam and nothing will change until it understands the mind-set of Islam. The Islamic world does not think as the West does. To Islam any disengagement on the part of the West or pleas for peace talks are seen as a sign of weakness just as Hitler thought at Munich in 1938.

To put it in the vernacular: we fight by Marcus of Queensbury rules and Islam is a street fighter. But we still don't get it after 40 years.

For Islam negotiating is a weapon and a tactic to achieve time or tangible gain not peace. They use the negotiation process to wear down their opponents and keep them hoping for progress (that never comes) while Islam continues to execute their plans and use the time for propaganda gains and military regrouping, rebuilding and foreign infiltration. The Palestinian issue is a perfect example of the use of propaganda and the negotiation process as a method of wearing down the opponent.

25 Palestine

The intricate workings of oil, *jihad*, European fear, propaganda and essentially blackmail have gone to create the current Palestinian situation. Throughout the world the issues surrounding Palestine are always thought of in terms of the Palestinian people, the rights of Palestinians, the restitution of Palestine to its rightful people, etc. This implies that there is now, and always has been, a country by the name of Palestine that belonged to indigenous Palestinian Muslims and that it was stolen by the Jews. This is simply not true and has no historical precedent.

To begin with since the Islamic conquests of the seventh century there never existed the concept of "national rights." The entire region was structured as provinces of multiple succeeding Islamic empires. This construct actually existed under Rome and Byzantine as well. Further, ***when Islam conquered the area (7th century), there were only the indigenous Christians and Jews.*** After the conquests the Muslims settled in the area as well; and the Christians and Jews became *dhimmis*.

Overtime the population did not grow so much as become diverse. Surveys by British historians for the Encyclopedia Britannica found no fewer than fifty languages spoken in the area known as Palestine. There were few Arabs although many Arab speaking people. In fact in the late 19th century there were actually so few people living in the area the early Zionists labeled it "a land without a people for a people without a land".

A Palestinian Mandated area was created after World War l by the League of Nations. (The area of the Mandate referred to as Palestine was considerably larger than what constitutes Palestine today.) The population at that time still consisted of Christians, Jews and Muslims. It is important to note that the Muslims were free to move anywhere in the greater area, i.e., into Egypt, Transjordan (a large area east of the Jordan river) and Arabia; but the Jews particularly, could stay only in the area designated as today's Palestine. After the 1948 war Egypt and Jordan occupied the so-called mandated Palestinian territories until the 1967 war with Israel. ***At no time was there any thought of declaring the area a separate country nor was it objectionable that the area was shared by Egypt and Jordan.***

Before 1967 the "Palestinian people" never had, nor claimed, independence as a people or sovereignty over the land that was soon to be contested. No claim over East Jerusalem was made nor of the territories. Even the *Declaration of Algiers Conference of 1973* spoke of the Arab Nation recovering "its" territories from Israel not recovering a specific area for "the Palestinian people." There was no concept of a nation called Palestine, or a people called "Palestinians'. Not until 1974.

The so-called "Palestinian people" were Arabic Muslims living across a wide area, including the smaller area that is now called Palestine. The people were always referred to as "refugees" since in fact there was no specific country of "Palestine" in existence. (In actuality the "refuges" should have been classified as either Egyptian or Jordanian since both countries occupied the area prior to the 1967 war.) How did these people transition from refugees to the Palestinian people? The UN General Assembly Resolution 3236 for the first time referred to the refugees as "the Palestinian people" rather than "the refugees." (This was a departure from an earlier UN Resolution number 242 that had used the word "refugees.") The Arab League Secretary Chedli Klibi stated in response to a question on how the elimination of the designation of refugees came about.

> "That is where your role as Europeans can be effective. To start with, the concept of *refugees* should be replaced by that of *Palestinian people.* **And the consequences of this theoretical modification should also be realized so that this people would be placed in a position to have their own state.** (Emphasis added.) That is where Europe can play a specific role, a dynamic role, a driving role..." (1)

By referring to the "refugees" as "Palestinians" the implication was that they were "citizens" of a real country named Palestine that never existed but was in reality born out of the statement by the Arab League Secretary Chedli Klibi and subsequently supported by most European countries.

In a broad strategic sense the Palestinian issue is a wedge being used by Islam to first isolate Israel and then to drive it out of existence. At a practical level the Muslims want Israel to return land that was confiscated as the result of a war Israel won but that the Muslims started and lost. (Recall the issue of Islam wanting back what they lost as a result of failed wars was discussed in Chapter 10 "The Hypocrisy of Islamic Leaders".) Islam never gives up; and since from the Israeli perspective, capitulation on this issue is out of the question, the situation is at an impasse.

One might argue that regardless of this statement's voracity the situation does require the formation of an independent Palestinian state so as to address the needs and suffering of the people trapped in an untenable situation. The truth is the problem could be solved by incorporating the now designated Palestinians into Jordan that is where they emanated from to begin with years ago; however lets examine the issue of the formation of an independent Palestinian state.

If a separate and distinct Palestinian state was the objective of the Islamic leaders there were two historical events that could have achieved this end. The first was the historic creation of Jordan in 1922 by Great Britain from the Palestinian Mandated area. The area had a population consisting of Arabs, Turcomans and Muslim settlers that were there since the previous century. The nationality of the settlers consisted of Algerians, Egyptians, Syrians, and Turks. (Gaza at that time was predominately Egyptian.) In addition some Christians had settled there fleeing the massacres in Syria and Iraq after WW 1. The area was 78% of the land that the League of Nations declared earlier as Palestine(the mandated area). In the 1922 stipulation by Great Britain no Jews were allowed in this area. (The remaining 22% of the land, comprised of a narrow sliver of land is where the Jews had to settle.) So it was the Muslims that were occupying the mandated area and it is they that would subsequently be called "Palestinians". In effect they already had their country, however it was named Trans-Jordan. There was no difference in the ethnic or religious make up of all the peoples that occupied the area. There was no issue that a separate "Palestine" needed to be subdivided from the mandated area that had just been created. The declared "need" for a "separate and distinct Palestine" was still fifty years in the future.

Secondly: the objective of a separate state for Palestine could have once again been achieved when President Clinton worked out a peace accord with PLO Chairman Yasser Arafat and Israeli Prime Minister Ehud Barak in July 2000 at Camp David. The agreement gave Arafat almost everything he wanted. Ehud Barak gave Arafat unprecedented concessions but at the signing of the peace accord–the signing that is normally ceremonial—Arafat walked out stating that Israel refused to pay reparations to the Palestinians. Reparations had never been part of the negotiations in that Israel had always declared reparations a non-negotiable item. And reparations were certainly not part of the ***agreed upon settlement***. It has been assumed that Arafat was shocked that he got so much of what he asked for and that since there was no reasonable way for him to decline the agreement (that he really did not want) he did the barbaric thing he was so well equipped to do. In doing so he embarrassed Clinton and Barak while making a mockery of the process. It has been nothing but terrorism and propaganda since that fateful day. The question is why did Arafat walk away form what was ostensibly the objective of the "Palestinian people"?

It is important to understand that the idea of an Arab-Palestinian people distinct from the larger Arab-Islamic nation was not only utterly new, but contrary to two fundamental historic concepts: *umma*, the worldwide Islamic community (all part of *dar al-Islam*), and secondly the concept of the Arab Nation. The Arab Nation was defined within an ideology of pan-Islamism that dated from the 1890s. It promoted a pan-Arab totalitarian nationalism and proclaimed the Arab a superior people. (One can clearly see the similarity of this concept to the Nazi sense of a pan-Europe entity under Germany and the superiority of the Arian race. It is a tragedy of human history that the Jew is always used as a scapegoat.) So by both of these Islamic perspectives the idea of country is subsumed in the idea of the Islamic state.

So what is it about this miniscule sliver of land that has become the alleged "lynchpin of peace" in the Middle East? And why did Arafat walk away from the deal?

There is a critical assumption in that question and that is that peace is the goal of the Islamic and Palestinian leaders and that a Palestinian country is really what is wanted. None of these assumptions could be further from the truth. ***The primary Islamic objective in Arabia is the destruction of Israel*** and one of the weapons to achieve this end is Palestine.

To begin with Israel's destruction is an Islamic obsession because Israel exists on what is viewed by Muslims as Islamic land. "All of the Middle East must be ruled by Islam" is a tenant of their religion, i.e., the dictum of Mohammad stated: "two religions cannot exist in the country of Arabia". (The fact that

Israel existed there for more than three thousand years before Mohammad's birth is immaterial). Israel is therefore a stick in the Islamic collective eye. Israel is also a disaster to Islam from another perspective. It is a viable, thriving, advanced Western state, a non-Muslim state, existing within the "Arab Nation." At the same time out numbered by overwhelming odds, Israel continues to militarily dominate the Middle East (in a self defense context). Both of these things are embarrassing and hateful to Islam.

The Islamic leaders have come to realize that the destruction of Israel can't be achieved by normal force. (Iran's obsession with the acquisition of a nuclear bomb is to a large extent to destroy Israel.) The Arabs tried three times and with disastrous results. Therefore a new non-military approach was needed. The method that evolved was to "isolate" Israel from the rest of the world and then to "erode" Israel away. These two mechanisms work in a pernicious tightening circle.

Isolating Israel would make it economically and politically difficult to run a viable state. To achieve isolation required the changing of world opinion from either a pro Israel or neutral position to a negative perception. Positioning Israel as an aggressor of the poor and down trodden Palestinians and the stealer of their rightful country would erode support for Israel if they could make that issue believable. The tactic would be particularly effective if the pressure on world opinion could be maintained for an extended period. As world sympathy erodes so also will world support for Israel. The result will be to place increasing international political pressure on Israel, and ultimately make, Israel more vulnerable in general. Arafat and the other Islamic leaders understood this point in the past and understand it now (nothing has changed with Arafat's death). As long as the Palestinian situation is kept alive and active, the world's attention will be looking at the drama and the human catastrophe. With time this will only increase sympathy for the "Palestinians." And that is exactly what has happened and is increasingly happening. The Palestine issue has become a perfect propaganda weapon.

If Palestine became a legitimate state the "weapon" would be disarmed. In addition a legitimate Palestinian state would have a difficult time continuing to support the terrorist attacks inside of Israel because the diplomatic community pressures would then reverse and be directed against "Palestine" to stop the terrorists.

The constant strife in Palestine is taking its toll on Israel. It is being worn down. The building of the wall, the unilateral surrender of Gaza, the unsettled internal political situation, all are pointing to an Israel in turmoil both internally and externally. The Muslim perfidy assisted by a supportive European press have achieved a propaganda coup of amazing proportions by positioning Israel as a "Nazi state" and the Palestinian terrorists as its victims.

There was a secondary reason for Arafat turning his back on the Camp David II signing and that was the desire of the Islamic world to undercut and limit America's role in the Arab world and Europe to the extent it could. Particularly since America is still seen as the only remaining ally of Israel. The Islamic block cannot abide this. Also there was the issue of breaking the American near monopoly on the peace process. The Islamic powers knew that better deals could be achieved negotiating through Europe. It appears that the entire Camp David II talks were nothing more than a way of achieving this goal. The Arafat charade in negotiating was actually to prolong the Palestinian issue and keep it on the front page and thereby garnering sympathy and assisting in undermining American efforts. When the negotiations went too well he had to kill them.

The point on undercutting America's role in the Middle East and moving that role to Europe became quite clear in the proceedings of the Parliamentary Association for *Euro-Arab Cooperation* (PAEAC) in Brussels in June 2002.

> "If we consider the fact that Europe has increasingly become aware of the close connection between a stable peace in the M.E. and the future of the Euro-Med partnership in which the Arab World constitutes the cornerstone, it is quite natural then to call Europe to find ways and means to activate its role in the M.E. This would serve our common objectives and would also serve international and regional peace and security." (2)

Had the Camp David II talks actually succeeded, the American influence in the M.E. would have been unquestionably enhanced. The close ties between America and Israel made this potential unacceptable to the Islamic leaders. They could not afford to have the talks bear fruit. Arafat was required to kill them. Given what we have seen developing as a result of the EAD influence makes this proposition seem less preposterous than it would otherwise.

The "Palestinian issue" acts as a catalyst to generate sympathetic public opinion for the "Palestinians," particularly in Europe, and a broad negative opinion of Israel. The objective is to further the goals of the EAD while achieving the isolation of Israel. The process has been unyielding for nearly forty years and it will not cease until there is no Israel. The real issue is that Israel is merely the first projected "Western" casualty in Islam's march.

Further comments on the issue of Palestine and Islamic expansion:

> In 1972, Palestinian terror chief, George Habash told Italian journalist, Oriana Fallaci, that "**the Palestinian problem was about far more than Israel**. (Emphasis added.) The Arab goal, he told her, was to wage war against Europe and America. 'There would be no peace for the West. The Arabs would advance step-by-step, millimeter by millimeter, year after year, decade after decade. Determined, stubborn, patient. This is our strategy. A strategy we shall expand throughout the whole planet.'"(3)

Time has shown Habash was truthful and correct that the Palestinian issue was and continues to be about more than Israel (of course this does not in any way diminish the Islamic hatred for Israel). In modern times Palestine has always been a pawn in the hands of Islamic leaders. Whenever sympathy for Islamic causes is needed the Islamic leaders roll out the Palestinian issue. Whether it is hunger, lack of a homeland or the "injustice of it all" none of it really matters. The "refugees" are used shamelessly. And that is the terrible human tragedy; that so many innocent people can be so ruthlessly used for the furthering of the Islamic cause, but it is consistent with what we have seen sanctioned by the *Qur'an*. If the world, and particularly the media, focuses on Palestine then they miss the more important issues and events. But this is exactly the Islamic objective.

After a generation of talking about Palestine's "poor refugees" and their need and right for a homeland, and assisted by the superb use of the media, bordering on propaganda (particularly in Europe with instigation by the EAD), the Islamic countries have succeeded in creating a severe refugee problem that never needed to exist. In doing this they also created a caldron of terrorism. The Palestinian terror group Hamas and their brethren have given the

West and its allies a horrific legacy of murder, mayhem and massacres.

London 1971

Germany 1972 Cologne February 6, Hamburg February 8 and 19, Munich September 5 (The 1972 Olympics massacre of Israeli athletes), Frankfurt in October

Brussels May 9, 1972

Israel–Lod Airport June 1, 1972

Trieste, Italy August 4, 1972

Letter bombs in 1972 to London, Paris, Brussels, Geneva, Vienna, Montreal, Ottawa, New York, Buenos Aires

Kinshasa September 20, 1972 and November 13, 1972

Thailand December 28, 1972

Khartoum February 21, 1973. Also two American diplomats were murder as was one Belgium diplomat.

Endless suicide bombings throughout Israel that have continued from the early seventies through today.

It is important to note that between 1973 and 2005 there were no major terrorist attacks in Europe. It is not a coincidence that the period is also the one in which the EAD had its growth and increasing influence. The lack of major attacks is the direct result of the Euro-Arab Dialogs (EAD) and Europe's increasing surrender to Islam's influence and demands. The more recent, 2004-2006, terrorist attacks in Spain, England and France is the result of a more diverse set of issues and influences. Chief among these are the instigation and implementation of the more advanced steps of the *Ten Step* program that is aimed at beginning the destabilization process.

Although the strategic context of the Palestinian issue is by far the most important it must be noted that there are very real human emotions driving and compounding all the elements of this puzzle. In this case the emotion is irrationally based religious hatred. From an historical perspective the Palestinian hatred of Jews is really a continuation of policies prevalent in the Middle East during World War II–see Chapter 6 *The Roots of Hatred*.

There are two transactional issues with respect to the Palestinian people and the area in which they live that have a direct bearing on the formation of a new state of Palestine.

First: The Palestinian cult of the suicide bomber is one of the worst and barbarous applications of a religion in many centuries. The fanatical application of the Islamic belief system and the shameless use of the Muslim people living in the area of Palestine has created a

> "self-destructive mentality that causes the Palestinians to consistently choose destruction, poverty, and death: the "embrace of victim-hood, of martyrdom, of blood and suffering is the Palestinian disease." (4)

How can a nation be formed when the potential citizens of that nation refuse to recognize the right of their closest neighbor to exist? How can citizens expect to build a country when their entire preoccupation is with destruction even at the cost of their own lives? A Palestinian state would not change the mind-set or the intent and until these change no negotiations or agreements will yield peace.

Secondly: Sustaining defeats in Afghanistan and Iraq al-Qaeda lost a great deal of actual and potential land that was being used for terrorist training and basing operations. Furthermore as American author and al-Qaeda investigator Richard Miniter stated:

> "U.S. forces together with the Kenyans and the Ethiopians have pretty much prevented al-Qaeda from basing in Somalia or Darfur. That left only Lebanon with all its problems with its various political factions, overlords and the UN. But then suddenly, like manna from Heaven, Israel simply gave them the greatest gift al-Qaeda ever received when Ariel Sharon decided to give them Gaza."

The unilateral pull out of Gaza by Israel in August 2005 provided al-Qaeda with a new training and terrorist breeding ground next door to Israel and with direct access to the sea and Egypt. With Hamas as the "legitimate government of Palestine" al-Qaeda has found a very centrally located new home.

From the act of "state formation as a propaganda tool" we move to "state take-over," Lebanon, by use of many of the Ten Step program's elements.

26 Lebanon

Lebanon went from the Paris of the Mediterranean to a "third world bomb run" in fifteen years.

On September 1, 1920 the nation of Lebanon was formed along with four Syrian states, two regional and two ethno-religious. Over the next six years Lebanon evolved a constitution and became the Lebanese Republic. During the same period there existed "four distinct countries that now make up Syria." These later merged into the Republic of Syria (which was overwhelmingly Muslim). In Lebanon the population consisted of the Maronites, (a Christian sect), other Christian minorities and Syrians. These people thought of themselves as two distinct people: the Lebanese and the Syrians.

Although all the people of the region were classified as Arabs and spoke Arabic the Lebanese claimed that their heritage was that of ancient Phoenicia, which antedated the Arab heritage by several millennia. In addition they believed that their broader Mediterranean heritage was once shared with Greece and Rome, and which they now shared with Western Europe. In that they were Christian, this latter point made a great deal of cultural sense if not ethnic accuracy. However, the Muslim population did not share the theory.

The Christian majority of Lebanon was resistant to sharing governmental power with the Muslims because they felt that the Muslims were susceptible to cross border Islamic influences. This in turn would create a potential trust problem when Lebanese Muslims had to deal with sensitive political or national issues. Security in this context would be particularly problematic. In addition the Lebanese were concerned over increasing Arab nationalism. The early stages of Islamism were diametrically opposed to Lebanon achieving political success. The influences, both internal and from the surrounding Muslim countries, would keep Lebanon in a constant state of instability.

The Arab nationalist point of view could not abide the French-created Lebanese Republic as a nation-state separate and distinct from Syria. In fact the Syrian Republic itself was not acceptable as the final entity to the Syrians. The Syrians were Arabs and as such they believed they should be part of a greater Arab homeland that would include all of the Arabian Peninsula. Arab (Islamic) nationalism at this time was in the ascendancy. Exacerbating this explosive situation was the nation's changing demographic trends, Christian and Muslim inter-religious strife, and proximity to Syria on its border, the departure of European colonial powers, Arab Socialism in the context of the Cold War, the Arab-Israeli Conflict, Ba'athism, the Iranian Revolution, Palestinian terrorism (the Palestine Liberation Organization -PLO), Black September in Jordan, Islamic fundamentalism, and the Iran-Iraq War. There seemed to be a confluence of Islamic religious and nationalistic forces of extensive proportions surrounding Lebanon (as are Israel).

The forces pressing against Lebanon from without were being met by a set of internal forces of equal destructive potential. The external forces were historically named by the encompassing term of Arabism (now Islamism). The internal forces were labeled Lebanism. The more accurate delineation of these external and internal forces is Islamic and Christian. (Granted this is a bit of a simplification but not by much. The immerging Islamism was very much focused on the forward movement and conquest of the non Islamic countries in the area–including Lebanon, while the Christian population, the majority in Lebanon, were focused on establishing their country.) Within Lebanon the two forces collided on almost every major issue of the day that dealt with its political viability and survival.

For the duration of the French mandate Lebanon was protected against such destabilizing Arab interventions in its affairs. Once the French withdrawal occurred, the artificial stability unraveled quickly. When the explosion came it was significant. "In all, it is estimated that more than 100,000 people were killed, and another 100,000 maimed. Twenty percent of the pre-war resident population, or about 900,000 people, were displaced from their homes, and of these about a quarter of a million people emigrated permanently. These human statistics occurred as the consequence of a civil war that eventually involved many international players and that lasted over many years with the result being the destruction of a country and people and its replacement with first rubble then another Islamic state that doesn't quite work". (1)

There are of course many thoughts in this brief overview of Lebanon. There is certainly the issue of Islam desiring the integration of the entire Arabian Peninsula into an Islamic state. Even removing Israel as a consideration the goal is impossible given the endless divisiveness among Arab countries in the past and continuing to the present day and of course there is the ever-present divisiveness between the Shi'a and Sunnis. There is no way, even under Islam, to achieve this level of integration. (But this has never stopped a fanatical movement in the past.) There are other thoughts that are apparent in the history as well. Although Lebanon was Christian, the average Muslim citizen in Lebanon was far better off than he was after the fall of Christian Lebanon or is today. Lebanon was in fact the Paris of the Mediterranean. Photos of Lebanon, just prior to a recent slow rebirth, show a devastated wasteland. Where once there had been shops, restaurants, hotels and boulevards there is now rubble. (The rubble existed even before the most recent Hezbollah/Israeli war.) The most interesting point however is that this is one more example of the destruction of a society that was populated by a large Islamic minority. Lebanon was a Christian country that could not survive with a common border with Islam nor with the internal Islamic minority.

Israel and Lebanon built oases in the dessert while the Muslims destroyed one and will do anything to destroy the other. In all of the reading and research of European/Middle East and Islamic history in preparation for the writing of this book, I could not find a single instance where a non-Muslim country was able to live in peace with a neighboring Islamic civilization for any length of time.

VI

HOW THE WEST SUPPORTS ISLAMIC EXPANSION

The expansion of Islam in the West cannot be achieved without the help of the West, albeit indirectly and mostly as a secondary consequence of policies thought to be otherwise positive. The help is quite broadly based and emanates from politicians, diplomats, universities and the media. Of course these sources very rarely have as their objective the support of Islamic expansion, nonetheless that is exactly the result. All of the beliefs and activities of these groups are governed by their near religious acceptance of *multiculturalism* and its watchdog *political correctness*. These two constructs bear the greatest responsibility for the on going sacrifice of the best interests of America specifically and Western culture broadly.

27 *Multiculturalism* and *Political Correctness*

One can make the following statement and be relatively sure of being on firm moral ground: in a free country all cultures should be allowed to exist as long as they do not impinge on other cultures' rights to do the same nor on the human rights of the individuals as protected by the laws of the country. However in any given country there is a ***prevailing culture***, including an official written and spoken language, customs, norms and above all, laws ***governing all the citizens*** of the country. Together these are viewed as the CULTURE of the country. It is that culture which dominates and is expected to be the template under which all citizens live. Immigrants living in a host country are normally and historically expected to conform to the culture of the host country. They are further expected to act in a way compatible with the norms and socially acceptable behavior and to abide by the laws of the host country. If this is not acceptable to the immigrant then he should not be in the host country. Over the past two centuries this has always been true of the U.S. - Enter *multiculturalism.*

Many individuals believe that essentially *multiculturalism* merely recognizes the cultural and racial diversity of the people of a country, promotes the full and equitable participation of individuals and communities of all origins and ensures that all individuals receive equal treatment and equal protection under the law, while respecting and valuing their diversity. This is certainly what we think of as freedom and equality as it has traditionally existed in the U.S.; and it has proven to be an excellent platform for absorbing diversity. However that is not what *multiculturalism* means nor is it its intent.

> The doctrine holds that all minority cultures must enjoy equal status with the majority, and that any attempt to impose the majority culture over those of minorities is by definition racist. (1)

Looking at the key phrases of the definition an ominous picture emerges.

First: "*minority cultures must enjoy equal status with the majority.* This puts any primitive culture or even a different modern culture that may be the antithesis of the indigenous culture on the same moral and social plane as the indigenous culture. If this is true how does one develop any degree of cultural homogeneity within a given country? How can a country exist with any number of cultures existing at the same time, particularly when the cultures have opposing values that clash? Remember we are not talking of tolerance for norms of dress, worship, food, etc. We are talking of the essence of moral judgments and acceptable behavior as it pertains to every basic aspect of living life in a complex society.

Secondly: "*any attempt to impose the majority culture over those of minorities is by definition racist.*" This immediately frees any minority from the moral bounds set by the indigenous culture and essentially eliminates any vocal opposition to unacceptable behavior, i.e., opposition equals bigotry. This is a recipe for disaster for the indigenous people and culture.

The underpinnings of *multiculturalism* rest on the logically flawed philosophical foundation of *moral relativism* and *altruism*.

> "*Moral relativism* takes the position that moral or ethical propositions do not reflect absolute and universal moral truths, but instead make claims relative to social, cultural, historical or personal circumstances. Moral relativists hold that no universal standard exists by which to assess an ethical proposition's truth. Relativistic positions often see moral values as applicable only within certain cultural boundaries or in the context of individual preferences." (2)

It seems obvious that if basic behavior and human contexts of interaction cannot be judged by a morality based on absolute standards of objective reality, then there is no basis with which to compare the morality of differing cultures. Yet this is the founding premise upon which *multiculturalism* is built. The result: as the degree of subjectivity increases in the realm of morality in a given culture, the culture will surely tend toward degeneration and chaos. And certainly *multiculturalism* is ushering in exactly this chaos in the cultural arena within the West. This corrupt philosophy in practice has created the exact fertile ground necessary for the unchallenged growth and expansion of Islamic culture in the West.

Multiculturalism could not exist without the philosophy of self-sacrifice - *altruism*. (Do not confuse charity or good deeds with altruistic sacrifice.) *Altruism* implicitly sets the stage for the acceptance of *multiculturalism* by creating the premise that it is a virtue to sacrifice. It is not a virtue to sacrifice the good to the less than good or even the evil. If one is willing to promote a culture that is not in the best interest of the indigenous people and their culture then the level of sacrifice is raised to the level of self destruction and cultural suicide.

Multiculturalism as an academic construct is logically wrong-headed and should be dismissed as devoid of any value with respect to a "society-enhancing" philosophy but when it moves from an academic dialog to a real world program, it is a disaster. In today's world *multiculturalism* has become "politicized" and for many a form of "religion." Different countries in the West implement this "politicized form of *multiculturalism*" to varying degrees but it is always the same underlying premise, i.e., ***all cultures are equal and of equal merit, with none better than the other.*** In fact this premise is blatantly false and has proven to be a dangerous societal cancer.

To be obvious but unfortunately controversial: cultures are not equal AND the host country's culture is always superior to the culture of the immigrants' country.

Let's examine the use of the term "superior" from the perspective of what has worked for the host country. Any country that is the target of extensive immigration is ***a country that has some over-riding set of values that make it desirable to emigrate to. It is the host country's values and culture that is responsible for creating an environment conducive to the success of the country and its continued positive evolution and growth***. Obviously this is not the case with the émigrés' country or they wouldn't be emigrating from it. Of course there are aspects of every culture that one might evaluate as superior or better than a specific characteristic or practice of the host culture but that is not the issue. It is the overriding totality of the culture that is in question.

In addition there is an indigenous population in the host country that has a language, a way of behaving, a moral code, a set of laws, a way of interacting with each other and a way of protecting and governing its citizens. ***No one has the right to come to the host country and attempt to superimpose his or her ways on the indigenous people.***[1] This does not mean that the immigrants can't maintain their preferences in the norms that are personal, and ***that are not in***

1 NOTE: This point is true for the U.S as well. As an example: The imposition of a democratic government in Iraq is inappropriate if it is not what the indigenous population truly desires. If they desire an Islamic state that is their right and their decision.

conflict with the society's laws. There should never be an attempt to override the laws of the land. If this is not acceptable to the immigrant they should not emigrate. Is this harsh? Not really, what is harsh is to say that the indigenous citizens of the country, after generations of successful cultural evolution, need to change or in some fundamental and extensive way accommodate immigrants to the detriment of the host culture. Which brings us to the third major issue with *multiculturalism*.

As *multiculturalism* matures and its influence advances through the indigenous culture it cannot help but undermine the supremacy of the indigenous culture. (And perhaps this is exactly the goal of the intellectuals that are so enamored with the concept.) In turn this must create a cultural vacuum of sorts at least for a period of time, and nature abhors a vacuum. Into the West's cultural vacuum has swept militant Islam, demanding accommodations and in incremental steps insinuating itself in the fabric of the culture as the original indigenous culture begins to collapse. How does this happen on a practical level?

Multiculturalism allows for, and enables the implementation of, an extensive range of behavior that is not part of the general population's norms. Although this may not be obvious early on, or even negative in an immediate practical way in the early stages, the problem later becomes: where does one draw the line, how does one get the genie back into the bottle once changes and accommodations are accepted, where does the society stop the continued growth of accommodations and how does it stop them?

At the center of *multiculturalism* lays a radical egalitarianism by which everyone's culture and lifestyle has equal validity and moral stature. This creates a situation wherein people within the indigenous culture who have accepted the philosophy of *multiculturalism* are increasingly unable to make moral distinctions based on behavior. Where once the understanding of right and wrong and socially acceptable behavior and morality were universally accepted we now have a stale, almost cynical *moral relativism*. This has become increasingly prevalent within the U.S. with the generation of young people leaving college over the past twenty or so years. How can people be expected to accept the equivalence of various cultures that are diametrically opposed to the indigenous culture and not also loose the ability to differentiate the appropriateness or morality of behavior?

A perfect example: returning to the Ali Hirsi story of Chapter 15 *As The Ten Steps Enfold*. It was unconscionable that the current Dutch generation could so reverse their country's illustrative history of freedom and independence and effectively drive Ms Hirsi from Holland. The enabling factor was that the current generation had *multiculturalism* drummed into their psyche through school and polities, through media message and liberal groups, through film and theater through all of the intellectual channels of the society for most of their adult lives. ***At this point they no longer had the intellectual ammunition to resist the Islamic pressures by making a moral judgment.*** The Dutch have implicitly accepted that all cultures are equal to theirs, therefore who can say which one is better or correct, right or wrong. They may not explicitly state that view in this context but it is this epistemological framework that allows them to turn their back on the higher values of their indigenous culture and effectively support a deviant set of beliefs and behaviors. They have lost control of their country whether they realize it or not.

On the practical level *multiculturalism* can be seen as empowering and allowing Islam to insinuate its culture into the West on an equal basis and as the process evolves eventually superceding it. In Europe this is a very mature process. In the U.S. it is in the beginning stages.

Europe has allowed "accommodations" such as: acceptance (tacit and otherwise) of polygamy, honor killing, rape and murder of female adulterers, special considerations in diet to be honored by public institutions, cessation of indigenous peoples' public expression of patriotism, implementation of laws that supercede the indigenous society's laws. We have certainly seen many examples of all of these in previous sections of the book.) The degree of disruption that this causes the indigenous country is extreme. Imagine not being "at home" in YOUR own country! No emigrating group has ever done this nor expected the U.S. or European countries to change to accommodate them, except the Muslims. And this is true in every country Muslims emigrate to.

Those who describe Islam in anything but the most benign terms are often slandered as "racists" and as "Islamophobic" and silenced by lawsuits or by fear of lawsuits but worst of all is the silence and "censorship" imposed by *political correctness*. PC is the handmaiden and protector of *multiculturalism*. If one cannot speak out in the public forum against something one finds inappropriate or wrong about aspects of another group's behavior or another group's lobbying for special considerations at the expense of the greater population because of fear of being labeled a racist or an *Islamophobe* then we have already surrendered a basic tenant of freedom. I would rather suffer a fool or a bigot then loose the freedom that allows his inappropriate speech. The issue of course is when one looses the freedom one also looses the "warning alarm." Insulting or hurtful language is abhorrent but should always be preferred over the lose of so precious and vital a freedom as freedom of speech. We have evolved and conditioned our culture over the past three decades to be so sensitive to any type of criticism of groups such that we are now a nation "stepping on eggs" even when our survival may be at stake.

Let's examine some examples of accommodations.

We'll start with the item that is at the highest point of absurdity on the "accommodation index." It is one of many that could be presented but need not because this one says it all. Following the first items are a number of more typical everyday occurrences in today's strange world of "guarded speech" in the land of free expression.

ITEM: Realms of Absurdity
A high school in California supports girl's basketball. A group of Muslim girls who must wear burqas wish to play basketball. Since that is not reasonable given the nature of the restrictive garment the Islamic girls' representatives successfully petitioned the school to build a wall across the court that the girls play on so they won't have to wear the burqas while playing and boys will not be able to see them. It is forbidden in Islam to have the girls mix with boys. If the reader thinks this is a legitimate accommodation then nothing I say will change their mind. However, from my perspective this is as blatantly absurd as it gets.

A member of the community voiced opposition to this "accommodation" in a most eloquent way. She stated that she is an orthodox Jew and her religion also separates boys and girls in a very strict way but her congregation does so at their cost and does it privately without burdening the community with their religious driven needs. (The freedom to enjoy this private realization of a non-indigenous norm/cultural preference is what is great about this country. The burqa example is a tragic capitulation of the norm to the minority. It will not stop at the burqa accommodation.)

What could possibly be driving the school authorities to approve such madness? Are they so afraid of being labeled as "racists" or of being "insensitive" or heaven forbid *politically incorrect*? Once the "accommodation" floodgate is open it becomes impossible to close.

ITEM: Realms of Absurdity

The first Malaysian astronaut will go into space next year. Since he is Muslim the dilemma for this astronaut is considerable. A satellite moving around the earth at incredible speed (17,000 mph) makes finding "the east" difficult. This matters because a Muslim must pray five times a day facing east. Also since prayers are said at sunrise and sunset and the satellite circles the earth 16 times a day, the implication is that a Muslim astronaut would have to pray 80 times per day. A conference was called to address the issue. Adapting a religion founded in the seventh century to space travel has its problems. 150 delegates considered how to pray in space given the difficulties of locating Mecca and holding the prayer position in zero gravity while the east is shifting by the moment. The issues of diet and washing were also discussed, both extremely important issues for Muslims. Mohammad Sa'ari Mohamad Isa, of the National Technical University College of Malaysia has helped to develop a computer program called *Muslims in Space* to solve these issues. Of course the "accommodation" does not yet have to deal with all of the issues of female astronauts in space with Muslims or if the journey moves out into space as the computer program no longer works in the context of the varying trajectories into space, etc., etc., etc. The religion of a person is their responsibility not the governments. If one can't cope with the exigencies of a situation remove yourself from the situation.

ITEM: Realm of the Tragic

Recently many court decisions have prevented the mentioning of God or the teaching of religion in public schools or even the presence of religious symbols of any kind. Many people may not applaud these decisions but if universally applied they are at least fair. The public school system was never meant to be the place for the presentation of any religious doctrine or symbols particularly since the U.S. has so many diverse groups. If this is the law of the land and in challenge after challenge it has been upheld then why is it that California's 9th Circuit Court of Appeals (a court that has found the use of the word God unconstitutional) now ***endorses Islamic catechism in the public school***! The court recently ruled that it is permissible to allow public-school children to participate in Muslim role-playing exercises. These exercises included:

> Reciting Muslim prayers that begin with "In the name of Allah, Most Gracious, Most Merciful . . . ."
> Putting to memory the Muslim declaration of faith: "Allah is the only true God and Muhammad is his messenger."
> Responding to teachers prompts the children sing out "Praise be to Allah."
> Professing as "true" the Muslim belief that "The Holy *Qur'an* is God's word."
> Giving up candy and TV to demonstrate Ramadan, the Muslim holy month of fasting.
> Designing prayer rugs, taking an Arabic name and essentially "becoming a Muslim" for two full weeks.

Parents of the children sued but the court ruled that it was permissible because it was part of a Word History class and was meant to teach the students about another culture. The parents appealed but the 9th Circuit Court upheld the lower courts ruling.

Even more incredible is the fact that the same course does not teach Christianity on the same level as the Islamic section of the course. It is covered in only two days and focuses on the history of persecutions and atrocities done throughout history. Islam is presented as a religion of peace and *jihad* as an inner struggle. Susan L. Douglass designed the course. Ms Douglass is an education consultant and a devout Muslim activist who happens also to be on the Saudi government payroll!

The following items deal with an issue that is even more dangerous and that is the developing "close mindedness" and ultra PC environment in America's universities, the press and civic life.

ITEM Inquiry Commissions
As a result of the terrorist attack on TWA flight 800 a commission was formed to see what could be done to prevent terrorist attacks like TWA800 and at the same time improve on current security systems. The year was 1996. A recommendation was made to build a screening system, Computer-Assisted Passenger Screening System (CAPPS) that would be capable of identifying potential hijackers, etc. The Chairman of the Commission was Al Gore who had the com-

mission and the system ***exclude national origin, ethnicity, religion and gender from the screening criteria entered into the passenger profiling system.*** CAPPS is still run without this very critical profiling information. What's left to profile is of little real value. Mr. Gore was quite vociferous after 9/11 on how much more should have been done to prevent it. It would appear that we are more afraid of being accused of being *politically incorrect* than of any terrorist acts.

ITEM The Press
The same First Amendment, free speech, and academic rights that seem to work so well for Islamists, do not seem to protect our right to criticize Islamic terrorism or Islamic religious and gender apartheid. Thus, by and large, the First Amendment absolutists of the American media chose not to reprint the Danish cartoons in solidarity with the Danish cartoonists. In fact, only one brave young editor, Harry Siegel of the New York Press, walked off the job when his boss refused to allow him to publish the controversial cartoons. Meanwhile, the bookshop so well known for stocking books by dissidents, San Francisco's City Lights Bookshop, absolutely refuses to stock or sell Oriana Fallaci's work which is quite hard on Islam. They stock any diatribe against any organization but not anything critical of Islam.

ITEM Civic
Members of Cincinnati's Council of American-Islamic Relations (CAIR) managed to shut down a production of a play by Glyn O'Malley about the first female suicide bomber. CAIR did not think it showed Islam in a true light. No comment!

ITEM University
The European Universities may be worse than their cousins in the U.S. if this item is any indication.

The University of England at Middlesex has a course in jurisprudence and that contains the following material:

From the text of Muhaqqiq al-Hilli, a 13th century scholar:

> "The water left over in the container after any type of animal has drunk from it is considered clean and pure apart from the left over of a dog, a pig, and a disbeliever."

> "There are ten types of filth and impurities: urine, feces, semen,

> carrion, blood of carrion, dogs, pigs, disbelievers."
>
> "When a dog, a pig, or a disbeliever touches or comes in contact with the 171 clothes or body [of a Muslim] while he [the disbeliever] is wet, it becomes obligatory- compulsory upon him [the Muslim] to wash and clean that part which came in contact with the disbeliever."

It is astounding that the faculty of the University can allow a text of this nature to be part of a course in Jurisprudence. It is not that the university should ever prevent the teaching of any information but the context within which it is taught is incredibly important. The presentation of such information in a history course or a course in comparative studies, etc. would be quite illuminating but to include it in a modern Jurisprudence course is quite telling in a very different way. The university has a large Muslim student population.

ITEM University
A group of Muslim students at De Paul University managed to get Professor Thomas Klocek permanently "suspended" because he tried to voice his position on the Israel-Palestinian issue. Muslim students have a unanimously hostile position on Israel so they were outraged when Professor Klocek disagreed with their anti-Israeli views. They then reported him as a "racist." Professor Klochek's freedom of speech is not as protected as is that of another De Paul University professor, Norman Finkelstein, a notorious "demonizer" of Israel.

Professor Norman Finkelstein also of De Paul University is allowed to express his position (and that is a good thing–but it should be a two way street) that the Holocaust never happened. He further demonizes Israel in any context that arises. Not only has Professor Finkelstein not been suspended for his outspoken and inflammatory views, but also he is up for tenure. Is there anything wrong with this picture?

ITEM University
Professor Indrek Wichman, a Michigan State University professor in February wrote in an email to the University's Muslim Students Association that stated that the group should stop protesting the cartoons that poked fun at the Prophet Mohammad. The email also referred to "dissatisfied, aggressive, brutal and uncivilized slave-trading Muslims." In closing Wichman

said those uncomfortable with American free speech were free to leave. CAIR immediately responded with the following: "The university needs to take appropriate disciplinary action in this case to demonstrate through its actions that anti-Muslim bigotry will not be tolerated on campus," said Dawud Walid, head of the rights group's Michigan chapter. Furthermore Walid said his group had urged university officials to discipline Wichman, but "they said they didn't feel they could take any tangible disciplinary action." Wichman said his remarks were meant as a defense of free speech. "It's not a call for mass deportation or vigilantism," he said. "I just care deeply about the First Amendment and the right to say what you think." Mr. Wichman's position used to be the American standard.

In this case the university did not capitulate to CAIR's pressures and demands–that's the good news. That CAIR would try to have Wichman disciplined is interesting given CAIR's record as previously detailed and the fact that although one might disagree with Wichman or think his remarks extreme he does have the right to make them, particularly since he was making them ***outside of his teaching venue and duties***. His first amendment rights should not be challenged, as they would not be if the subject were not Islam. Any group "maligned" equally has the right to protest but never to attempt to deny another group their right to their expression. The act of attempting suppression is a common practice when Islam is defamed. The right of free speech is a cornerstone of American democracy and a sacred human right and generally the first right to be suppressed in a country moving away from freedom. It is also bad news because sometime the thing being said, the thing being objected too may have an underlying grain of truth that should be examined. If this is so the country is the better for the event, if the objectionable statement is blatantly wrong or preposterous the people can see this for what it is. In both cases free speech continues unscathed.

ITEM University Administration

Both Duke University and Georgetown University have recently defended the right of the Palestine Solidarity Movement (PSM) to hold its annual conference at their respective campuses. The universities stated that even if the PSM hate speech that railed against Jews, Israel, and America was false and inflammatory, it was still protected by the First Amendment and by academic freedom. Really? And I agree but would the universities allow a speech to defame Islam in any way without it being ruled as inappropriate and insensitive and *politically incorrect* and just not suitable to a university environment? Somehow I doubt it.

ITEM University Administration

"The Taliban Man at Yale" case was astounding. An admitted and known member (Sayed Rahmatullah Hashemi) of the Taliban and an ambassador-at-larger for the Taliban government that is, at the time of this news piece, still at war with the U.S., was granted a scholarship to study at Yale University. Imagine Adolph Eichman's child studying at Yale in 1943 and Yale defending that position.

> "The range of debate on campus is narrower than ever today, and the Taliban incident is a wake-up call that moral relativism is totally unexamined here. The ability of students to even think clearly about patriotism and values is being undermined by faculty members who believe that at heart every problem has a U.S. origin." (3)

The belief system that encompasses *multiculturalism* and *political correctness* is the enabler of the behavior demonstrated by the above events and the thousands like them. It is these types of events in growing numbers that will eventually destroy the essence and fabric of our culture. The overwhelming number of our universities and mainstream media are dominated by proponents of these concepts; and the belief in these concepts is the filter through which all too many news stories are reported and slanted whether intentional or not.

A constant, very active and often virulent opposition to real American interests emanates from a significant portion of America's intellectuals. This includes virtually every humanities professor in academia, and also, to a lesser degree, a large portion of the press corps. This "sameness of opposition" to any opposing ideas, almost a *Greek Chorus*, is very similar to the way in which the EAD "influenced," and then began to change, the direction of Europe's evolution to one more conducive and supportive to the Islamic expansion. The intellectuals in this country with their blind pursuit of *multiculturalism and political correctness* and their almost exclusive judgment of all situations from a *morally relativistic* perspective (along with organizations like CAIR, et al) are helping to empower and embolden the Islamists in the same way the EAD did in Europe. There is occurring a wearing down of our intrinsic values and therefore our culture. At what point will we have yielded so much of our culture, morality and norms that we have become *dhimmi* in what was once our nation? Europe is even further ahead on this trail to cultural self-immolation.

Ms Hirsi blames Europe's immigrant problem on concepts of European tolerance and *multiculturalism* that have gone too far. Until recently, this effort at tolerance led policymakers to ignore the serious problems within some of their Muslim communities, i.e., the preaching of hate and *jihad* to the community and of radical Islamist ideas to children, the repression of women and honor crimes. Ms Hirsi Ali also blames misplaced tolerance for confusing Europeans about how to react to the Danish cartoons that satirized the Prophet Mohammed. For her, the issue is clear: Europeans value free speech and separation of church and state, and immigrants must learn to accept those values if they are to live in the West. That is the line she wants Europeans to draw. It sounds like a line that we should draw in American as well.

Working against this premise is the fact that through the EAD the European governments and diplomats have undercut their own position for arguing the superiority of Western culture. In the beginning of Europe's adventure in *multiculturalism* the recommendations of the EAD included the

> "necessity of cooperation between European and Arab specialists in order to present an objective picture of Arab-Islamic civilization and contemporary Arab issues to students and to the educated public in Europe which could attract Europeans to Arabic studies." (4).

The implementation of this recommendation over the subsequent decade effectively ended critical thought in the European public dialogs with respect to Islam.

> "The European governments and universities adopted the Arab perspective on virtually all relevant issues." (5)

This is exactly what is happening in the U.S. for the same reasons. The requests for "accommodation and understanding" that come from Islamic leaders on a continuing basis fall on the ears of a population made fertile and intellectually receptive through their acceptance of *multiculturalism*. This process is on going and accelerating and is changing the nature of our very cultural existence. And they are doing it without a modicum of awareness on our part. The blind adherence to a flawed philosophy has become more dangerous than any terrorists bomb.

At this time the process in its final phase is even more tragic and undercutting to European culture. The European intelligentsia accepted the Islamic view of Islamic civilization. Islam is "convinced" of their tolerance, humanism and the greatness of Islamic civilization. They even emphasize its position as the spiritual and scientific fountainhead of Europe! The real irony is that if these thoughts were expressed regarding Western civilization the outcry would be deafening and would be labeled as "*politically incorrect* and insensitive." (This is exactly what happened to Silvio Berlesconi, Italy's former Prime Minister, when he publicly expressed the superiority of Western culture over Islamic culture. An outcry ensued and haunted him until he recanted.) ***"The truth is political correctness is opposed to any divergent view from its own orthodoxy."*** The ascendancy of this particular mind set and "philosophy" combined with the endless positive positioning of Islam through the offices of the EAD in Europe and further supported by the university environment governed by a PC view has created a Europe that is not only anti-Semitic and anti-American but is positioned for its own cultural self destruction.

> "And so, in a personal attempt to reveal the march of history, allow me to highlight a few pointers that are leading to our future. In several European countries, the invasion of Arab and Muslim immigrants has been accepted as an almost natural and welcome development of a multi-cultural society. Their advocates insist that they will be a contributing addition to their host countries. This is incorrect. They will contribute only to a change in the established norms and practices, until each country will become submissive to the will of the immigrants, and convert to *Shari'a* law."(6)

Least the extremes of what is enfolding in Europe happen in the U.S. (as it has already begun to) it is essential that we recognize the absolute inappropriateness and illogic of *multiculturalism, political correctness and moral relativism* and that combined they send the message to immigrants that our culture is no better than any other. They therefore have no particular reason to embrace the American experience or to assimilate, as did the many generations that came before. Furthermore immigrants must NOT see themselves first and foremost as members of racial, ethnic or religious groups but as ***individuals*** that wish to become Americans and embrace all that that entails. The problem with the Muslim migration is, however, that the literal acceptance of the tenets of their religion makes it near impossible for them to accept that position. It is interesting how easily Islam asks the West to sacrifice our culture and values but they will yield not an iota. Such is the nature of *altruism* in its applied state.

28 The Direct and Lethal Results of *Political Correctness*

We are at war with a "religion." To ignore this reality in the name of *political correctness* is just insane. However that is not to say that the statement isn't inflammatory in the extreme. It is. The principle of being at war with a religion should scare the hell out of any rational person for it strikes at the heart of everything that is great in the West and that we hold sacred. Freedom of religion is so basic a freedom that it is one of the corner stones of the principles of America's founding. Of course that does not change the stated premise one bit. Unpleasant facts do not go away because we don't like them. We are at war with Islam not a group of terrorists who happen to be Muslims.

The truth of this assertion lies in the fact that Islam is a religion that is ***secular and spiritual***. The state and the religion are ONE they are not separate. It is not analogous to any structure in the West where religion is a private matter of worship; and ***the state is independent of any religion*** and where the state acts for the well being and protection of all; and in doing so, does not delve into the realm of the spiritual. In Islam there is only one. There exists only *dar al-Islam*, the realm of Islam. And that concept is at the heart of our war with Islam. The *Qur'an* is quite clear that the world must be converted to Allah or it must exist in a state of *dhimminitude;* and it is the duty of all Muslims to follow this path through *jihad*. It is in the sense that the "state" of Islam and the religion of Islam are one that we are at war with Islam. It definitely does not mean that we are at war with every Muslim, quite the contrary and this issue will be dealt with at some length in later chapters.

If one views the command of Allah to convert the world to Islam as a religious command to proselytize (as most religions do) and/or to struggle internally to reach a state of grace, it is one thing and remains in the realm of the soul but if the idea is interpreted literally and exists at the core of the religion and of the state simultaneously then it is in fact ***a declaration of war against all who are not part of Islam***. And that is why the realm that is not Islam is called *dar al-Harb*, the realm of war. If you think that extreme then how do you explain that Islam is the only religion that spends billions of dollars on the acquisition of armaments?

In the Western mind the thought of being at war with a religion translates into persecution of the members of that faith. That is absolutely NOT what is meant in this context by the assertion that we are at war with a religion.

Because the thought of being at war with a religion is as *politically incorrect* as any statement can be does not change the fact of it one iota. It is exactly the cultural construct of–*political correctness* - that makes the statement of a declaration of war against Islam a subject that cannot be examined and studied and thought about. However we are living with the reality of the consequences of the "unthinkable" throughout the world but by not stating the reality and obviousness of the situation we doom ourselves to fighting defensive battles not the war and its causes.

The current thinking in most intellectual circles is that Islam has been hijacked by a group of extremist fanatics and that that is the only problem. However the truth is that the religion of Islam itself is extreme in all of its teachings. The fanatics are merely living by, and following, the exact teachings of the religion as clearly laid out in the *Qur'an*. They have not misinterpreted dogma they have accepted it, unfortunately literally. One may argue that a modern interpretation of Islam should not be so literal and that it should, in the context of modernity, recognize and understand the metaphorical and allegorical nature of all religion.

In this context Islam's "militarism" and aggressiveness would become focused on the striving within man to attain perfection of soul not a set of worldly conquests. Unfortunately man is not always so rational and with respect to Islam, its dictates, if followed, are quite deadly to Western society and Western culture. This leaves us with the original premise, i.e., we are at war with Islam. Not recognizing that fact has caused, and will continue to cause, an endless number of incorrect policies and actions that are actually self-damaging or at best achieve minimal results while the war being waged by Islam continues its forward progress. We win some battles; they are winning the war. It cannot be any other way until we recognize the nature of the war that we are involved in. But *political correctness* absolutely will not permit the stating of the fact for fear of–what–hurting feelings, generating hatred, and appearing bigoted? The tragic result of not naming the reality is that it prevents the ability to think in a broad conceptual framework which in turn prevents the development of real solutions to the real issues..

> "One of the many failings of our educational system is that it sends out into the world people who cannot tell rhetoric from reality.

> They have learned no systematic way to analyze ideas, derive their implications and test those implications against hard facts." (1)

If the nature of the war is correctly understood then not only can the correct battles be fought with the correct weapons but the legitimate concerns of "collateral damage" in the form of preventing individual prejudices, etc. could be dealt with. However, not naming the war let alone not fighting the war does not make things better in the long run, as Chamberlain and company found out in 1938, things do get much worse. To understand the premise just expressed requires real thought and the conceptualization of many facts into an integrated whole.

Turning from the realm of the strategic, the actual practice of the dogma of PC has already caused considerable "transactional" damage. An example: the loss of an effective weapon, "profiling" is a tragic mistake. One can only hope that it is used clandestinely but it should be used aggressively and with as much sophistication that our technology allows. When there is a need to profile for reasonable cause, not only is profiling logical it is an essential tool for preventing the abuses (terrorists activities) that are all to easy to implement in a free society. It is the guilty, the PC believers and the citizens of the left that cry the loudest against profiling. And it is the latter groups who complain the most when a terrorist incident occurs. Profiling robs no honest person of a right but it does protect the people that might become the victims of the terrorist that wasn't profiled.

It is currently estimated by the FBI that there are as many as 5000 terrorists operatives living innocuously in the U.S. awaiting the time they are called to perform acts of terrorism. These ticking time bombs are Muslims living in the Muslim communities, just like the 19 hijackers of the World Trade Center attack. And they are essentially protected by *political correctness* run amok. In this context I quote FBI Director Robert S. Mueller: "The bureau is against–has been and will be against–any form of profiling (of Arabs and Muslims)." Is he mad?

Could you imagine the FBI implementing such a ludicrous policy with respect to any of the peoples we were at war with in the past or say the Italian mafia in its hay day? Perhaps he is not aware that the War on Terrorism is being fought entirely against Muslims! Mueller is so *PC* that he initiated sensitivity training sessions (Muslim oriented) in the N.Y. field office. Retired

FBI agent John B. Vincent stated: "they even came to Quantico to lecture new agents on how not to pick on them." And Donald Lavey, a twenty year FBI veteran who led the bureau's counter terrorism section said of Mueller "let's hope the director is leading the charge in this war against terrorism with an equal amount of zeal that he shows for cultural sensitivities."

With Mueller's "nonsense" as a context it is important to understand that Homeland Security lists twenty "terrorist target hot spots" in the U.S. at this time. These hot spots also happen to be the areas that have the highest concentration of Muslim population. Of the twenty there are seven that also appear on a list created for Homeland Security by the Census Bureau (see Appendix C) as having a particularly high ratio of Muslims to non-Muslims. The seven areas each have a population of 10,000 or more with a Muslim population of 1000 or more. These areas represent the largest and most close-knit Muslim communities in America. When the two lists are compared there is a very high correlation between the two. In other words terrorists stay, live or interact in areas where there is a sympathetic population providing a support network. Makes sense to me. I hope it does to Mr. Mueller since the correlated list produces an excellent road map to terrorist cells and breeding grounds for future terrorists if he allows his agents to perceive the threat.

It is a widely known fact that Al-Qaeda sleeper cells use Arab and Muslim communities as cover to blend in and live low profile lives until needed. These ethnic communities are also places to raise cash and recruit sympathetic supporters to help facilitate terrorists like the WTC 19. More recently authorities have detained Middle Eastern suspects performing the following "friendly" tasks:

> Took surveillance photographs of cruise ships in Los Angeles,
> Purchased kayaks near the port of Los Angeles,
> Stole explosive devices from the University of Colorado,
> Applied to drive fuel trucks in the Port Everglades, Florida,
> Took surveillance photographs of bridges and buildings in St. Louis,
> Inquired about ambulance services along the east coast,
> Stole large volumes of potentially dangerous chemicals in Ocala, Florida,
> Tried to purchase a fuel truck in Waverly, Nebraska. (2)

These are the ones that we discovered. Does anyone think we discovered 100% of the planning actions undertaken by terrorists? When events of this type are on going and have such ominous potential it seems that an almost silly preoccupation with *political correctness* borders on criminal.

In August of 2006 the British arrested twenty-four terrorists planning to blow up a dozen or so American commercial planes while they were on their transatlantic flight to the U.S from London. Absolutely nothing that has been done with respect to airline security since 9/11 could have stopped the plot from succeeding. The reason is that the terrorists were planning to use simple chemical bombs that could not be detected and did not look suspicious because the "innocent" base chemicals could be separated and brought on board in deodorant, make-up, etc. containers and then assembled. The terrorist ring was broken and the plot discovered because of excellent police work instigated as a result of ethnic profiling and telephone surveillance. It is estimated that as many as 4000 deaths would have resulted if the plan succeeded. Is the use of profiling and telephone surveillance so terrible as to not be offset by the saving of that many innocent lives?

Since the uncovering of that plot Dame E. Manningham Buller, the head of British internal intelligence (MI5) stated that they were investigating 30 major terror plots involving 200 terrorist cells and 1600 individuals (terrorists and support personnel). The group being tracked was part of an identified "Islamic extremist pool" of 400,000 (that is not a typo it is four hundred thousand) extremist sympathizers. Given an environment as explosive as this the thought of PC is not just silly it is insane. The scope of the problem in the U.S. is not yet as extensive as the one outlined by Dame Buller but all indications are that it is growing daily. How can we not use every means at our disposal to deal with an evolving menace of this scope before it approaches the size of the British problem? It should be noted that similar extensive problems exist throughout European countries. (3)

Perhaps the worst tragedy of *PC* and "absurd sensitivity" was revealed in the now infamous *Phoenix Memo.* The memo, prior to 9/11, proposed that the FBI check all Middle Eastern students in flight schools in the U.S. FBI headquarters shelved the proposal because it would have violated bureau guidelines against racial profiling. Obviously no one can say that if the memo's recommendation had been followed it would have prevented 9/11, but it certainly is a possibility. How much more insanity waits behind the facade of *Political Correctness*?

29 Support From The Left

The *multiculturalism and political correctness* mantras of today's "correct society" have always been a product of the left. Through attaining dominance in our universities and graduating, over the years, a constant stream of same thinking young adults, the left wing or "the liberal establishment" has become the dominant force in the mainstream media.

In turn the mainstream media's news reporting is dominated less by facts and more by rhetoric consisting of PC bromides and spin in support of *multiculturalism* and ultra liberal ideals. Even the selection of the news that is reported emphasizes, or casts a favorable light on the orthodoxy of the left. They believe that they are working toward and supporting the development of "the good society." The media has so automated this method of news coverage that they are largely unaware of the process. The result of the constant stream of slanted coverage is a society that is poorly informed and unable to see the specter of destruction hovering over us.

The problem however, from the left's perspective, is that the "good society" is becoming increasingly transparent and a case of the Emperor's Clothes. More and more of the common man or if you prefer people with common sense are seeing through the absurd façade that has been created. In too many cases the dictates of the flawed philosophy runs afoul of simple logic. The programs of the *politically correct* and its left wing supporters are running into real conflicts and contradictions not only with respect to the needs of the War on Terror but also with respect to Islamic antagonisms to the left's traditional and positive values and issues of freedom of expression, elimination of religion from schools and the public arena, minority rights e.g., homosexuality and women's rights.

In David Horowitz's *Radical Son*, he states that he is

> "appalled by left-wing American academics and activists who claim to support the rights of women and gays but who, since 9/11, have romanticized, whitewashed, and marched alongside Islamic fundamentalists who reject those rights." (It should be noted that Mr. Horowitz was himself once a Marxist.) (1)

Again in *Unholy Alliance*, Mr. Horowitz further states that the partnership between left leaning politics and the Islamic fascists is based on a mutual hatred of America and Capitalism,

> "Both movements (the left and Islamists) are totalitarian in their desire to extend the revolutionary law into the sphere of private life, and both are exacting in the justice they administer and the loyalty they demand." (2)

It is easy to see that given a common philosophy between the left and the Islamists like the one pointed out by Mr. Horowitz, (and that is consistent with numerous writers of the left), why the existence of bedfellows of the left and the Islamists is not so strange. What is strange is how they can continue to claim the moral high road when every action they take is so blatantly antagonistic to the fundamental values of America.

Mr. Horowitz recalls the historical connections between Western totalitarianism and Muslim extremists:

> "During the 1930s and after, Arab nationalism in Palestine, Syria, and Iraq modeled itself on Italian and German fascism. In the 1950s Arab nationalists forged military and diplomatic alliances with the Communist bloc and incorporated the Marxist indictments of the West in their own." (3)

This "alliance of the mind can be seen also after the Iranian revolution when the Ayatollah Khomeini became the poster boy for the leftists "by portraying his movement as a revolution of the oppressed." (4) It is always the same with the left, America is always viewed as an oppressor in every context and every dictator is a liberator.

Support for the enemy can take many forms. The obvious and specific forms are material and logistic support, however the lack of honesty in the evaluation of current and historical events can be equally damaging to American interests as can overt moral support for the enemy. As an example of the lack of intellectual, as well as literal honesty Amnesty International (AI) says the current status of gay and lesbian rights in the Islamic world is unclear. Yet when this statement was made homosexuality in Saddam Hussein's Iraq was punishable by death and still is in much of Islam. Who can take AI serious after a statement that is so blatantly dishonest?

And at a peace rally against the war between Israel and Hezbollah the following occurred in front of the U.N.:

> "Women pushing their children in buggies bearing the familiar symbol of the Campaign for Nuclear Disarmament marched last weekend alongside banners proclaiming 'We are all Hezbollah now' and Muslim extremists chanting 'Oh Jew, the army of Muhammad will return.'

For Linda Grant, the novelist, who says that "feminism" is the one "ism" she has not given up on, it was a shocking sight:

> "What you're seeing is an alliance of what used to be the far left with various Muslim groups and that poses real problems. Saturday's march was not a peace march in the way that the Ban the Bomb marches were. Seeing young and old white women holding Hezbollah placards showed that it's a very different anti-war movement to Greenham. Part of it feels the wrong side is winning." (5)

Now juxtapose this women's demonstration with the following.

In the Chapter 11 *Islam and Women* we saw the substandard to abysmal conditions within which women live in Islamic countries; we saw their lack of rights even to their own body and the extent of abuse they suffer at the hands of too many Islamic men. The only conclusion one can draw from this is that women in Islamic society are viewed as "property" to be dealt with much the way one would deal with a slave or a beast of burden. This is a stark contrast to women in Western society. It would not be an exaggeration to state that the women in Western society were better treated several hundred years ago than Islamic women, in general, are treated today. The image of today's woman in the West is so far advanced in every conceivable way such as to be part of another world than that of the Islamic woman.

Why aren't there demonstrations against the situation Islamic women live under? Is support for Hezbollah more important an issue to these women and if so one must ask what is the motivation of the demonstrators?

Any Westerner must feel outrage at the treatment of a large percentage of roughly one half a billion Muslim women. This should truly be a cause for international feminism, especially one would expect it to be taken up by the Woman's Movement in the U.S. given its political clout and advanced state of development. However it is as though the feminist movement had never heard of Islamic women being treated poorly. There is not only NOT an outcry there isn't even a mild protest. The woman's movement is so mired in past glories and so wedded to the political left wing in the U.S. that it can not bring itself to condemn even the most outrageous treatment and acts perpetrated on women in the Muslim world if there is any chance of being associated with *political incorrectness* or politics not of the left wing.

President Bush speaking on the occasion of International Women's Day - 2006: "Our history was altered because strong women stood up and led," the President further told this gathering. "These women broke down barriers to equality."

Why aren't the feminist leaders of today performing the same feats of moral and physical courage on behalf of Islamic women that their sisters did in the past for all women?

Phyllis Chesler is one of those women. As a feminist for many years she was at the forefront of the push for women's rights. More recently she has been one of the very few feminists that have taken up the cause of Islamic women and has challenged American feminists to "wake up." She has spoken out about the Women's Movement's hypocrisy in remaining mute while the deplorable treatment of women under Islam is so great. At the same time the feminists rail about infinitely lesser issues in the U.S. She believes that the "feminists" in the U.S. have become marginalized and essentially irrelevant in the new century. As she stated they have "failed their own ideals and their mandate to think both clearly and morally." She further states:

> "The plight of Islamic women abused in the name of Allah in the Middle East and in Europe requires an aggressive rebuke from women in the free world, but feminists in the West, and particularly in the United States, are struck dumb in an academic ghetto, stuck with a parochial approach to women's studies and obsessed with their personal 'body rights' and their sexuality.
>
> "Because feminist academics and journalists are now so heavily influenced by left ways of thinking many now believe that speaking

> out against head scarves, face veils, the chador, arranged marriages, polygamy, forced pregnancies or female genital mutilation is either 'imperialist' or 'crusade-ist.'"
>
> "The multicultural feminist canon has not led to independent, tolerant, diverse, or objective ways of thinking. On the contrary, it has led to conformity, totalitarian thinking, and political passivity. Although feminists indulge in considerable nostalgia for the activist 60s and 70s, in some ways they are no different from the rest of the left-leaning academy, which also suffers from the disease of politically correct passivity. (6)

What a difference a thousand more or even a hundred more Phyllis Cheslers would make.

The same thoughts of political alignment, protest and outrage apply to homosexuals. The homosexual community's major preoccupation in the U.S. at this time is with gay marriage. However right their cause is the political alignment of the gay community is solidly left wing, no doubt because of an assumed and often perceived and sometimes correct intolerance towards gays by the right of center. Whether true or not (and I believe this is at least partially true but often overstated) the bigger issue is why aren't the gay organizations of the West and their constituents loudly protesting the execution of homosexuals in Islam? The cause of gay marriage is important to gays and I am not about to dissuade them from that opinion but isn't the death penalty for gays something that should be vehemently fought against. Don't both women and gays have the most to lose if Islam's influence takes serious root in America and in American culture?

30 The Double Standard

One of the worst abuses of the law or of social practice is the application of a double standard. It is obviously unfair and in its extreme form it is clearly immoral. It allows one group or a particular set of individuals to act in a way that is prohibited to other groups in the society. Not only is this a miscarriage of justice but also it is ultimately corrosive to human freedoms and to the society itself. In fact there is a close relationship between PC and the double standard in today's society. It must also be stated that the evolving ***acceptance*** of a double standard is very much a part of the Islamic goal to achieve *dhimminitude* in the West.

During the 1990s, there was a trend in the U.S. to implement "hate crime" laws (as opposed to presumably assaults, rapes and murders motivated by "love"). The obvious goal was to set the precedent that the government can punish people, not just for what they do, but also for what they think while doing it or before doing it. No doubt many will think this statement a stretch but think of it. How can one reasonably, possibly prove beyond a reasonable doubt what was in a person's mind at the time of a crime. And in all logic why does it matter? The victim is hurt no more or less regardless of the motivation of the perpetrator. And the perpetrator should be punished based on the crime.

There is an extreme degree of subjectivity involved in interpreting these "new hate laws" that defies and undercuts and eventually destroys rational objective law. It is this assault on objective law that is the real danger to us all in the long run because it very effectively lays the foundation for an entire set of future non-objective laws. Under non-objective law it becomes increasingly difficult and eventually impossible to know *a priori* that something will be judged illegal. It also places an unprecedented degree of unchecked power in the state since the choice to enforce the law also becomes more subjective; it becomes a tool not for justice but for managing society the way the state deems it should be managed.

The next step after "hate crimes" is to outlaw "hate speech"—a step many European nations have already taken. This has become *political correctness* enforced by prison time.

"Especially since the 1970s, Western Europeans have been pass-

> ing bans on speech that "incites hatred" based on race, religion, ethnicity, national origin, and other criteria.... This is spreading to the European Union level, where a stream of rules now prohibits the broadcast, including online, of any program or ad that incites "hatred based on sex, racial or ethnic origin, religion or belief, disability, age or sexual orientation" or—crucially—is "offensive to religious or political beliefs." (1)

> "The use of "hate speech" laws invoked in the name of tolerance are now being used to enforce demands for censorship by the most notoriously intolerant group of all: Muslims. As this is not bad enough the "hate speeches" of Muslims seem to be given with impunity. Europeans have created the apparatus for enforcing their status as second-class *dhimmi* under the heel of Muslim bigots." (2)

In 2002, the well-known French novelist Michel Houellebecq was charged with inciting racial hatred in a novel and interview in which he referred to Islam as "the stupidest religion." Veteran Italian journalist Oriana Fallaci was motivated by 9/11 to criticize Islam as violent and subversive of traditional European mores. As a result she faced a French attempt in 2002 to ban her book as racist, and in another case she was scheduled to stand trial in Italy in June 2006 for statements "offensive to Islam," she died before the trial could begin. These writers are far from the only ones, they just happen to be more prominent.

The problem with laws of this type, laws governing human expression, are that they are, in the long run, extremely deleterious to the society instigating them and ultimately worse than the problem they are trying to cure. The Europeans thought they were eliminating the use of hate speech but instead they have effectively abandoned free speech.

Why is this a double standard? First: the same identical crime has two different ways of being evaluated and of determining punishments. Secondly: it seems not to apply to Muslims–ever. Has any of the Muslim acts or attempted acts perpetrated in America or Europe ever been evaluated as hate crimes? Not one, yet their sole motivator and purpose is pure undiluted hatred.

Masking from the public many of the issues surrounding the nature of the double standard as it relates to Islam especially is the double standard as found in the media.

The Danish cartoon "fiasco" was in every sense of the word a big story. It was big because it so dramatically revealed the nature of the Islam that we are at war with. It showed so clearly that the use of violence and intimidation is the central mechanism used to enforce the Islamic position throughout the non-Islamic world. The message was clear "print the cartoons and you die." The preceding is not a literal quote but it was the message to be found in the death threats made against the Danish publishers and authors of the cartoons.

This alone should have made the cartoons a really big story. How often does a group tell the Western media that it cannot present a particular story or news item and have the West capitulate? Until now the very thought was preposterous.

What was the West's reaction? After the initial publication by the Danish paper no paper published the cartoons in Europe and in the entire U.S. only three major papers had the courage to print them: The NY Sun, The Philadelphia Inquirer and the Rocky Mountain News. (The cartoons were carried in a number of small local papers.) And of all the networks only Fox had the courage to display them.

The *New York Times*, editorialized against the papers which ran the cartoons and was most self congratulatory over its "sensitivity."

> While CNN did not show the cartoons which represented "negative caricatures of the Prophet Mohammad" because "the network believes its role is to cover the events surrounding the publication of the cartoons while not adding fuel to the controversy itself." Later in their broadcast the network stated: "CNN has chosen to not show the cartoons out of respect for Islam." (3)

Many other mainstream media outlets mirrored CNN and the NYT positions of self-righteousness and "sensitivity". However what we really have here is the worst kind of double standard and hypocrisy. Almost all of these sensitive media giants had no compunctions about publishing any number of outrageous articles and photos of art that disgustingly depicted Christian icons. And they continue to do so today.

For example CNN on March 20, 2000 posted on its Web site both story and displays depicting the Virgin Mary in a degrading work of "art". The "artist," Chris Ofili, used elephant dung and images of female genitalia in his work. There was an outcry against this but of course freedom of the press and expression should not be, could not be interfered with in a free society was the response. I certainly agree with CNN as much as I abhor the so-called art. However why does the media show this ultra sensitivity for Islam and none for Christianity. I do not mean to pick on CNN alone, many of the same periodicals that shied away from publishing or even describing the Danish cartoons displayed or at least discussed the art demeaning the Virgin Mary, the most sacred icon, next to Jesus, in Catholicism.

The cartoons are not an isolated case of the double standard under which the media operates today. It seems that any horror, massacre or terrorist attack by Islamic fanatics is treated as an incident and seems almost to be positioned as an expected or even on occasion an "understandable" event (particularly when it comes to the Palestinians). Yet any infraction by the West is exploded into the "horror of the week." The Abu-Ghraib prison scandal as we have seen "horrified the world" and was the focus of non-stop "drama." As for the media's "sensitivity" and "fear of inflaming passions", these self-proclaimed motivations did not stop the Times, CNN, and many other major media outlets from displaying the inflammatory photos of the abused inmates of the Abu Ghraib prison. And the story didn't stop it ran globally for weeks. The difference of course was that in the Abu Ghraib case the media were inflaming Muslims by trashing the American Military. This was completely acceptable.

Another consistent manifestation of the double standard is the way the press reports the atrocities of the war with terrorists. In June 2006 an explosion on a beach in Palestine killed a family including a number of children. It was initially thought to be an Israeli missile or rocket that was fired to destroy Palestinian rocket launchers aimed at Israel. The outcry was quite extensive and critical of Israel; the typical Israeli perpetrated massacre scenario was the order of the day. However no one asked the question "What kind of people set up rocket launchers on a beach 400 yards away from a family frequented recreation area and on a Muslim Sabbath?" Obviously the Palestinian "army" knows that such an installation would draw fire. The answer to the question the press in general does not ask is: it is an example of the Palestinians' classic and cowardly human-shield tactic. They attack innocent Israeli civilians while hiding behind innocent Palestinian civilians. Where is the outrage? There was none and there rarely is. As it turns out the deaths were not due to an Israeli attack but an errant Palestinian mine. Again there was no outrage or apologies to Israel for falsely accusing them.

One more tale of media "double standard." By 2002 the CIA had concluded that al-Qaeda had re-established an operational network in Somalia after their retreat from Afghanistan. To counter the al-Qaeda network the U.S. stationed 2000 rapid deployment troops in Djibouti, a neighboring country. Subsequently the U.S. launched a covert action program relying on a coalition of secular Somali warlords called the Alliance for the Restoration of Peace and Counter-Terrorism. The alliance has been most successful at disrupting terrorist operations in Somalia and in fact captured a key operative, Suleiman Abdalla Salim Hemed for interrogation. A State Department "tip" to the NYT caused the story to be published with negative consequences to our operation. The exposure of this program's existence not only created problems within Somalia but also compromised our ability to work through proxy allies in fighting terrorism.

So the New York Times sees no issue with possibly endangering national security and perhaps jeopardizing American lives (almost every chance it gets) but it is much too "sensitive" to publish the Danish cartoons.

From these examples I can see no scenario but that of Islam cheering the mainstream media.

The evolution that has placed the European writers and press under an ever-increasing amount of fear-induced censorship is the same that is moving their American counterparts along the same road. The process evolves in this way: *political correctness* as a societal norm leads to *political correctness* by law, which leads to a double standard, which leads to *dhimminitude.* Why does *political correctness* in law lead to a double standard? Because the West seems to be completely unable to apply the same standards of judgment to Muslims as they do Westerners. Since the Muslims in a Western society are "exempt from hate speech" prosecution (by practice) and Westerners are prosecuted at the insistence of stray Muslim clerics, leaders or even mobs we have already slipped into the classic role of *dhimmi* status for *infidels* as dictated by the *Qur'an*.

31 The Media

The predominate percentage of the mainstream media consistently seems to be on the side of issues that either make America look bad or support our enemies. Harsh?

Every time the accusation of media bias is discussed the media has a dramatic and opposite reaction, i.e., that it is not true, that the people that hurl these insults are right-wingers or archconservatives, or the lunatic fringe, etc. The one thing that you can be sure of is how little "objective" reporting is presented to prove the original accusatory point wrong. If the accusation is wrong then there must be another explanation for so many endless presentations of the news positioning America in a bad light. The opposite presentation is certainly not desirable either but balance and objectivity seem to be in short supply. The editorial page has moved to the front page. How else can you explain the media's glee at revealing America's war secrets, its eagerness to feed and amplify enemy propaganda campaigns (such as the Abu Ghraib hysteria), and its bizarre detachment from "George Bush's war", as if they have no stake in America's success or failure, or the endless reporting of anything and everything bad and virtually nothing good. Can they find no good, no progress, and no achievements in any action being undertaken? Can there never be a context in which America is correct and Islam is wrong or violent or perfidious?

It is always interesting how consistently Israeli deaths from terrorism are portrayed as "incidents" and Palestinian deaths by Israeli actions are "massacres" or a "disproportionate reaction." And in Iraq, every terrorist bombing is seen as a gigantic set back but the fact that the numbers show a continuing lowering of incidents (as of early 2006) is not reported. (The current evolving "insurgency" will assuredly change these figures for the worse.) The casualty numbers are constantly presented as though they were overwhelming when in fact they are low by any reasonable measure–compared to other wars, or on a percent of deployed troops basis, etc. Of course any deaths are a tragedy but it's a war and in a war what do we expect? Positive things can be found but not in the NY Times, Washington Post, Boston Globe, Time, Newsweek, CNN, USA Today, network television, etc. almost never.

As just one example of imbalance in reporting, albeit the worst, the media coverage of the Abu-Ghraib incidents bordered on the insane. The treatment of the prisoners wasn't half the degree of torture that the media and the professors on the speaking circuit put the country through. Let me state that I am categorically against torture of any kind regardless of the circumstances but the treatment of the prisoners although completely wrong, in the scheme of things was hardly the equivalent act as those atrocities that the world of Islam perpetrates on humanity daily. That is not an excuse but where is the balance? Where is the outrage and demands for action and inquires at the treatment of women in Islam, the be-headings, the honor killings, the *fatwa*s encouraging murder, the real torture chambers. Abu-Ghraib was not America's finest hour but the circus of anti-Americanism orchestrated by the media, the universities and the left leaning politicos was unconscionable. What was worse was the near joy they took in it. And it went on and on.

On the other hand stories that are clear examples of terror related actions are often "sanitized" or down played. The "Beltway-sniper is a perfect example. When John Allen Muhammad was arrested in 2002, CNN would only refer to him as John Allen Williams the name he was born with. However Muhammad had legally changed his name over a year before and had given his name to the police as John Allen Muhammad when arrested. So why not use his legal name? Further "sanitizing" the acts of murder, CNN as well as many other major media organizations, immediately offered many reasons why Mr. Muhammad had killed ten innocent people. The Los Angeles Times offered that it might have been Muhammad's "stormy relationship" with his family, a need to "exert control" over others, or a "stark realization" of loss and regret that led him to commit these murders. The one reason that was not offered was *jihad*. That is strange particularly since Muhammad and his accomplice Lee Boyd Malvo had a drawing in their possession that contained the words " We will kill them all. Jihad." And a second drawing of a plane about to collide with the burning World Trade Center said: "JIHAD ISLAM UNITE RISE!" Is there any doubt as to the reasons for the murders?

A number of journalists have admitted that the majority of their brethren approach the news from a liberal perspective. During the 2004 presidential campaign, for example, Newsweek's Evan Thomas predicted that sympathetic media coverage would boost Kerry's vote by "maybe 15 points," which he later revised to five points. In 2005, ex-CBS News President Van Gordon Sauter confessed he stopped watching his old network: "The unremitting liberal orientation finally became too much for me."

Compared to their audiences, journalists are far more likely to say that they are Democrats or liberals, and that they espouse liberal positions on a wide variety of issues. A 2004 poll by the Pew Research Center for The People & The Press found five times more journalists described them as "liberal" as said they were "conservative." There is absolutely nothing wrong with this. Because one is a reporter there is no requirement that you do not have opinions beliefs, preferences, etc. These are their Constitutional and human rights, however when reporting the news how much of one's personal beliefs "skew" the news, its content, the stories that are covered and the angle from which the story is viewed. That is the issue. There was a time in journalism when this "personalization" of the news was minimal, it appears that now it is not minimal and has become the norm. It is equally wrong when the right wing performs in a similar vein as they often do. It is just that it seems not to be as extensive from the right and there are so many less of them in the mainstream media. (Outside of the mainstream the same accusations for the most part can be applied to the right wing.) Balance, objectivity and fairness should be the "bible" of any journalist. Let the editorial page scream opinion, that's what it is for but not the front page.

Many journalists continue to deny the liberal bias that taints their profession, Mr. Rather was extreme in his bias yet it seemed that he was truly unaware of it. He had automated his thinking. During the height of the scandal over CBS's forged memo (relating to Bush's military service) during the 2004 campaign, Dan Rather insisted that the problem wasn't due to his personal views; it was the problem of those who criticized him. Mr. Rather said in an interview with USA Today in September 2004 that:

> "People who are so passionately partisan politically or ideologically committed basically say, 'Because he won't report it our way, we're going to hang something bad around his neck and choke him with it, choke him out of existence if we can, if not make him feel great pain.'"

I have no doubt that Mr. Rather is correct for some element of the right wing, however he is also describing his own behavior and that of the illiberal liberal press as almost a matter of policy.

Rather further said in the same interview:

> "They know that I'm fiercely independent and that's what drives them up a wall."

That's why he used a forged memo to denigrate the President? Even after it was proven to CBS and Mr. Rather, that the memo was forged he would not back down. That is not courage it is intellectual arrogance and dishonesty.

Mike Wallace of "60 Minutes" fame is one of the best interviewers in the business. His reputation has been earned over a long and distinguished career in which he has been seen as being astute, probing and aggressive while interviewing the world's leaders. During these interviews he has also demonstrated a complete grasp of the person, the subject matter at hand, an insight into the subtle and interesting points that needed to be made and as always he executed an interview with the highest professional aplomb. One of Mr. Wallace's stylistic hallmarks has always been the appearance of control and knowledge.

In the August 2006 Mr. Wallace aired an interview he conducted with the Iranian President Mahmoud Ahmadinejad. Certainly beforehand this event was looked forward to with great expectations of revealing Ahmadinejad for the fanatic he is, or minimally an opportunity to reveal a great deal of Ahmadinejad's thinking on current matters and Wallace trapping him into admissions, etc. all in Wallace's normal style. The actual interview was truly underwhelming. Here is the list of discussion points that viewers ***did not hear and learned NOTHING about***:

Ahmadinejad's alleged involvement in the American Embassy takeover in 1979 in Tehran and the subsequent hostage crisis,

Iran's connection to the 1992 and 1994 bombings of Jewish targets in Buenos Aires,

Iran's extensive support of, and control over, Hezbollah,

Iran's transshipment of weapons to Hezbollah through Syria,

The fact that Hezbollah has killed more Americans than any other terrorist group (before 9/11),

Why was Hezbollah "permitted" to attack Israel and thereby start the war that Ahmadinejad so loudly decries?

In response to an Ahmadinejad "speech" against Israel Mr. Wallace never mentioned or asked Ahmadinejad what his thoughts were on the fact that

the Jews had claims on the Holy Land going back over 3000 years,
Ahmadinejad was not challenged on his belief and statement that the Holocaust never happened,
The connection between Ahmadinejad's stated goal of destroying Israel and his obsessive acquisition of nuclear weapons,
And not once did the subject of Human Rights come up.

We did hear, at length, all about the suffering of civilians in Lebanon. No comeback about how it could be reasonably viewed that the suffering was Ahmadinejad 's fault since there exists ample evidence linking Iran to the attacks on Israel that started the war. No mention of the suffering of the Israelis as a result of the rocket attacks. Even the discussion about nuclear weapons was so half hearted it almost didn't matter.

The interview received considerable criticism largely because Mr. Wallace looked so taken by Ahmadinejad and so weak in his questioning. So what makes the country's preeminent interviewer look so weak and almost deferential to a man like Ahmadinejad? Only Mr. Wallace can answer for sure but it is clear that a great journalistic moment was lost. One might also add that when it comes to the really hard questions few journalists take on Islam or Islamic leaders.

Saddam Hussein will go down in history as a bloody dictator. He is accused of killing a million people over his career. In 1988 -89 he ordered the gassing of 5000 Kurds and the subsequent slaughter of 100,000 more. In the first Gulf War he killed more than 100,000 Shiites. He implemented amputation of various limbs for most crimes that did not carry the death penalty. He has been accused of using extreme and systematic torture and killing thousands of prisoners, etc. Yet if the *European press* is to be believed millions of Europeans backed Saddam against the U.S. and even "hoped we would get a real beating." Again I must ask: What is in these people's heads?

Another favorite positioning that went the rounds of the mainstream domestic media was the Viet Nam comparison to Iraq. Iraq is NOT Viet Nam, no matter how often the press likes the analogy it just isn't in any way, shape or form like Viet Nam. The press loves the comparison because Viet Nam's nature was a true quagmire and one that provided no gain to U.S. interests regardless of its outcome whereas Iraq clearly does. Also in terms of deaths, Viet Nam was huge compared to Iraq (less than 3000 deaths in Iraq compared to over 55,000 deaths in Viet Nam). But if enough people get the negative association of links and similarities between the wars then the same type of mass demonstrations and objections will begin over Iraq. Iraq is a real war not only because of "weapons of mass destruction" (which should have been its secondary priority at best) but because it was a terrorist stronghold and training grounds, its strategic location in the Middle East, and Saddam's pension for creating chaos. The real problem with Iraq never gets an airing in the mainstream media. The real problem with the war in Iraq is the tragedy of not fighting to win; that would require that we confront Iran. But even in the narrower context of just Iraq we fight in an almost half-hearted fashion and too often defer to the Iraqi leaders (an exaggeration of the term if ever there was one).

A significant part of the insurgent phase of the war would have been avoided if Sadr and his Mahdi militia had been destroyed when they were in a state of "rebellion" in Fallouja in 2005. We had them surrounded and we allowed Sadr and his militia to go free. And now his militia is paying the Iraqi government and us back. Also it is common knowledge that Iran is behind the insurgency but we pretend that it isn't so both in the mainstream media and in Washington. Imagine if the press harped on Iran's support (and Syria is as well) as constantly as they did Abu-Ghraib? If we admitted the extent of Iran's involvement we would have to do something about it and no one wants that. So we down play and minimize and talk about talks.

So why bother with the war? And Bush will pay politically and historically for this timidity. But why isn't the press screaming about this "betrayal" of American troops? Iraq should have been a real and necessary part of the shooting War on Terror but somehow we converted it into the basis of a civil war that we do not belong in and should never have allowed to happen. We should have fought the war to win it, not placate the new Iraqi government, the allies abroad and the partisan politics at home. The mainstream media does not report this perspective on the Iraq tragedy because it does not fit the liberal agenda of defeatism and unilateral pull out that they seem so desirous of.

The press is filled with terrorist incidents. And of course this is news and should be reported, unfortunately the stories are almost always positioned, by the mainstream media, as a reason why Iraq is a failure or why the U.S. must leave Iraq immediately or at least set a timetable for withdrawal, as many politicians think we should. Even when the terrorists' attacks are not in Iraq, Iraq is used as an excuse for their actions. Three things strike me about this coverage and the broader context.

The **first**:
is that modern Islamic terrorism and terrorist attacks have existed for over forty years, long before any U.S. involvement with Islam in almost any context except being friendly toward Israel. Blaming any terrorist action on our involvement in Iraq is absurd.

The **second**:

Terrorists killed more than 14,500 people in 11,000 attacks across the globe in 2005,
Fifty-six of those killed were non-combatant Americans, obviously a small number by comparison or by percent of the whole (still too many),
3000 of the deaths were attributable to 360 suicide bombings,
There were 25,000 people wounded and
35,000 people kidnapped,
There are indications of an increase in suicide bombings
(Source: the U.S. State Department's annual report on terrorism.)

What is so damning to the media is that the enormity of these atrocities and the carnage and human suffering represented by these terror statistics in total seem not to garner anywhere near the coverage and focus as that of a Muslim forced to wear a woman's panties on his head in the notorious Abu Ghraib prison. While the reporting of each incident of terrorism is important, it seems that they are almost exclusively reported as specific incidents without the sense of the enormity of the scope of the problem and its threat to civilization.

The scope of the problem becomes blurred when looking only at specific terrorist attacks. The enormity of the problem as a whole, its real causes and its implications for society are the real story. Responsible, professional and neutral journalism would be presenting this picture. Regardless of a journalist's political inclinations the story of terrorism in its totality, i.e., its impact on Western civilization, global human suffering, global economic life and the destruction of life style and peace of mind and the interactions of these things on the fabric of civilization is rarely reported. That story would go a long way in intensifying the public interest and government focus on the whole of the problem rather than just the war in Iraq as though it were some isolated event.

The **third**:
Why would any country at war with a determined enemy ever announce that it was going to withdraw its troops before the job was completed? Or even announce a timetable for withdrawal? Doesn't anyone promoting this insanity think that a position like this would just cause the enemy to "dig in" until we were gone? Yet this story gets a degree of coverage, breadth and consistency that elevates it to the level of a serious and desirable proposition instead of the blatantly silly and wrong-headed idea it is. I do not mean to say that people against the war should not vocalize their position and that the media should not report it. There are good people and real reasons to be against a war (certainly the ones covered above offer plenty of grounds for objection) but where is the balance in presentation and reporting? Why aren't two positions clearly juxtaposed for the public's information? Why aren't the full implications of a pull out or announced reduction in force explained by the same press that wallows in the negativity of every aspect of America's defeats and problems?

And the constant calls for an Iraq withdrawal or timetable have had a real impact. The "insurgents" have stepped up their activities. Not a surprise. They know that the more pressure the louder the cries for exiting.

Before leaving reporting on Iraq one last word on the Weapons of Mass Destruction (WMD). The infamous "weapons of mass destruction" is another example of imbalance in reporting. The New York Times ran endless stories over a two-year period that the President lied to the American people about the existence of weapons of mass destruction. However the intelligence services of Israel, Britain and America all stated that Saddam did have WDMs. Now perhaps Bush knew more than these intelligence agencies and he did lie but we may never know for sure. However, fairness would indicate that the story be reported with all of the data from these agencies supporting the existence of WMD as well. The fact of the intelligence information that the President acted on was very much under-reported. The slant and bias gets worse.

Senator Rick Santorum and Congressman Peter Hoekstra revealed to the press for the first time (early 2006) that the declassified portion of documents demonstrating that U.S. military had uncovered a minimum of 500 weaponized munitions that could in fact be used to deliver mustard and saran gas. These are classified as WMD. Certainly this volume of WMD is not what was thought to have existed still they are enough to kill over eight million people! Senator Santorum further stated that he had first hand knowledge that some of the weapons were removed from Iraq via outfitted 747 Jumbo and 727 jets and sent to Damascus. (1)

Lieutenant General Moshe Yaalon, former chief of staff of the Israel Defense Force (IDF), the top job in the Israeli military, corroborated Senator Santorum's statement when he said: "He (Saddam) transferred the chemical agents from Iraq to Syria. No one went to Syria to find it." The general's assertions were made to The New York Sun.

Of course we have no immediate way of knowing the voracity of these statements but at the very least one would think that this would be an interesting story. The NYT remained completely silent on the issue the day following the discovery. The Boston Globe committed all of two paragraphs. The Washington Post five. Yet combined these newspapers used thousands of paragraphs with huge, large font headlines to say again and again that the President had lied.

Every indication is that the European media is even more "biased". Bat Ye'or states:

> "A striking and monotonous uniformity pervades the EU media, extinguishing independent thought. European magazines and newspapers prattle on about the arch villains Israel and America, while deploring Palestinian victim hood." She further adds:
> "Much of Europe's media consistently place the alleged crimes of Israel above other human tragedies, whether caused by terrorists, tyranny, gender, and child abuse, or anything else."

However Israel is only a part of the European media's unbalanced focus on the Islamic issues of the day. America is never right in any situation. Saddam massacres, tortures *infidels* and Kuwaitis, etc., endless terrorist incidents occur, real torture chambers are discovered and many are known of but its America that is the demon. Abu-Ghraib transcended any reasonable level of concern and in Europe it was trumpeted worse than in America and for endless weeks. It spent more time on the front pages and on TV screens of the media, both in the U.S and Europe, than any reasonable reporting would require. It was not just the fact of the extreme amount coverage but of the endless accusations hurled at the U.S., the military, President Bush and American foreign policy. And then there was the incredible sympathy poured out over the victims, at least some of who were real terrorists. The story transcends news but it was all played out on the front page. Whenever reporting reaches a hysterical level something is not right. Although true, in basic detail the Abu-Ghraib story was so magnified that it was "metamorphed" into real propaganda.

And another form of propaganda is the "big-lie." Israel has been the victim of this invention of mankind throughout modern history.

> "In our time, the Big Lie (or Big Lies, there are so many) is disseminated everywhere, and not merely by the ignorant, but with malice aforethought by the intellectual classes, the governing elites, the most prestigious elements of the press in all capitals of Europe, and by university professors and diplomats." (2)

The big lie takes many forms beyond the telling of a falsehood. Often it can be found in the more subtle forms of constant distortion and propaganda. It is interesting how dramatically the campaign of hate against Israel increased beginning in 2002 as the Americans uncovered many of the terrorist networks working in the West. The bad press that Islam was receiving by these revelations had to be offset, so the public relations machine of Islam and its sympathizers went into high gear creating a barrage of news and editorials attacking Israeli and American policies in the Middle East. The result was a swelling of anti-American sentiment and a six-fold increase of crimes against Jews. More than 70% of all racist crimes, threats, graffiti, etc. were against Jews in this period. This constituted over 1300 hate crimes. Once again the ugly specter of the "Jewish scapegoat" was rampant across Europe. (3)

The more one focuses on the Jew as villain the less likely one focuses on the issues surrounding the war on terrorism or Islam's role in terrorism, both issues would lead one to form some very harsh opinions about Islam itself. It is always the Jews and "The Great Satan" that are the causes of the world's problems, never the dictators or the State sponsors of terror that have anything to do with it or of the hatred preached in mosques around the world. Islam is always the victim, never the aggressor. And this is largely what can be seen in the Western mainstream press as news coverage although not quite so blatant most of the time.

And in the land down-under: Late in 2005, ten Muslim men were arrested by authorities on alleged terrorism offences. Despite the nature of the crimes, the men were allegedly planning to commit against Australian civilians, two of the country's largest newspapers reported sympathetically. The men, they claimed, were in "solitary confinement, dressed in 'Guantanamo Bay orange' and banned from touching loved ones." Have we become so "gentile" that the style of prisoner's dress is a cause? And why is it "Guantanamo Bay orange', didn't the Australia prison system have orange prison clothes before Guantanomo? Isn't orange quite common in prisons because it is easily seen by guards?

The *Sydney Morning Herald* really went "over-board" for the alleged terrorists. In a story entitled *"Terror Suspects: Christmas in Solitary"* it reported the men were near breaking point because the conditions were hard, and the Muslim prisoners were not permitted to spend Christmas with their families. Is this paper mad? Muslims do not celebrate Christmas they despise it. They petition against crèches in Italy, a Catholic country. Is there no end to the insanity of trying to generate sympathy for terrorists?

It has been reported often how much of the U.S. media reaches the terrorist organizations. Of course they view as much as possible, they aren't stupid, they are just ruthless. The argument is not for "whitewashing" but for real balance. The impact of an overwhelmingly negative positioning of American operations in both the Iraqi war and in general with respect to the War of Terrorism is a direct aid to our enemies and they are influenced by what they read.

> "According to wire reports, soldiers [at the house where Zarqawi was killed] found a few weapons, a skimpy leopard-print nightie, possibly belonging to one of Zarqawi's three wives, and the May 2 issue of the Arabic edition of Newsweek (which featured a cover story on the Iraq war entitled 'No Exit')."—(5)

The article was titled "No Exit" but thanks to the U.S. Military Zarqawi did end up with the ultimate exit; the U.S. Military killed him in Iraq.

In increasing numbers, the viewing and reading audiences recognize the mainstream media's liberal tilt. Gallup polls have consistently found that three times as many see the media as "too liberal" as see a media that is "too conservative." A 2005 survey conducted for the American Journalism Review found nearly two-thirds of the public disagreed with the following statement, "The news media try to report the news without bias," and 42 percent of adults disagreed strongly.

As if bias wasn't bad enough we have some newspapers actions bordering on treason.

The National Security Agency (NSA) collects certain phone information. The disclosure of this fact created a furor in the press and from the "loyal opposition". It went on for days and in some media outlets for weeks. Despite numerous explanations of the extent (limited) of the NSA practice and the position that it was legal the furor continued. But what actually is the issue.

When a call is made the phone company captures the fact of it in the form of the caller's number and the receiver's number and the duration of the call. This info is referred to as LUD (local usage detail).

Law enforcement authorities do not need a warrant to obtain LUDs from the phone company. The reason that it is legal is that LUDs contain no information about what was discussed during the phone conversations. The LUDs are viewed as business records which belong to the telephone company and not to the caller or the person called.

In its 1978 decision in Smith v. Maryland, the Supreme Court said:

> "This Court consistently has held that a person has no legitimate expectation of privacy in information he voluntarily turns over to third parties...When (a caller) used his phone, (he) voluntarily conveyed numerical information to the telephone company and 'exposed' that information to its equipment in the ordinary course of business. In so doing, the (caller) assumed the risk that the company would reveal to police the numbers dialed."

The NSA uses LUDs to determine if there are connections being made between suspected terrorists. If the LUDs reveal a connection, they are then used as part of the basis for obtaining a search warrant for further investigation. It is doubtful that the NSA has a desire to know that I or you called a mother or girlfriend or husband or wife or child or business partner but if we are making and receiving calls to Saudi Arabia or Egypt, etc. or to and from known suspected terrorists this might be of interest to them.

The LUD program is distinct from the program wherein the NSA actually listens in on telephone conversations between suspected operatives of al-Qaeda and other terrorist organizations abroad and people in the United States. If, as a result of the above LUD data analysis program, the NSA determines that you are making and receiving calls from terrorists or their organizations there is a strong likelihood that your next overseas call will be listened to. This action too is covered by statute and is not deemed illegal if performed within specified bounds. And there was no evidence that the NSA violated those bounds.

The facts of these two NSA programs could have been determined by any reporter worth his pay in very little time, yet the on going barrage of headlines and sound bites and misinformation would lead one to believe that we had arrived in the world of George Orwell's "1984". Even some months after the details came out and the furor died down USA Today rehashed the story as though something new had been uncovered. When the press gets a story that "fits its agenda" it does not let go. When a story is counter its agenda it often doesn't bother to report it, as the following example should clearly demonstrate.

> "U.S. commandos captured in April a situation report from an al-Qaeda commander in Baghdad to his superiors. It was translated and posted on CENTCOM's Web site May 3 (2006).

"The document is blunt and pessimistic. Al-Qaeda's numbers in the vicinity of Baghdad are small. They lack military skill. Their discipline is poor, and they're running out of ammunition, the unknown author says. The Iraqi government is growing in strength, and much of the Sunni population is turning against al-Qaeda.

"'The Americans and the Government were able to absorb our painful blows, sustain them, compensate their losses with new replacements, and follow strategic plans which allowed them in the past few years to take control of Baghdad,' the al-Qaeda commander wrote. 'That is why every year is worse than the previous year as far as the Mujahidin's control and influence over Baghdad.'"

"I did Nexis and Google searches. They indicated no U.S. newspaper ran a separate story about the memo, or an Iraqi roundup story highlighting the memo. I doubt this would have been the case had the memo writer said al-Qaeda was winning. (6)

Even if the press thought that the story was a "plant," that would certainly be the kind of "big news" story the media flogs for weeks. The fact that no mention was made anywhere outside the Internet would indicate that the story and its premise, the document, might very well be true.

Note: the information contained in the statement above that is attributed to al-Qaeda should not be confused with the more recent "insurgency" in the Baghdad area. The insurgency is an Iranian sponsored Shiite action aimed at stopping the formation of a stable Iraq. The last thing in the world that Iran wants in its backyard is a stable democracy housing American bases.

The above media examples do not demonstrate balance but certainly they don't demonstrate treason either. But the N.Y. Times was just warming up.

The Times for some inexplicable reason obviously thinks that part of its function is to declassify government secret anti terrorist operations regardless of the consequences. On June 23, 2006 the NYT printed a story revealing the existence of a secret U.S. government operation that involved the monitoring of financial transactions that are routed through the Worldwide Inter-bank

Financial Telecommunication organization (SWIFT). The organization (European based) routes about $6 trillion a day in electronic money transfers around the world. The monitoring of these transactions is conducted by the CIA and supervised by the Treasury Department. In addition members of Congress were aware of this covert operation. Furthermore an independent auditing firm had been hired to assure that only terrorist-related transactions were/are targeted. For very obvious reasons the nature of the operation required the highest degree of secrecy. This very program was credited with locating the mastermind of the 2002 Bali bombing in Thailand and a Brooklyn man convicted on charges of laundering a $200,000 payment to al-Qaeda operatives in Pakistan. And these are only the successes we know about. (The helpfulness of the program was even admitted by the Times reporters.)

Bill Keller, a senior editor of the NTY was asked by the Bush administration to please not print the story since it was of such a sensitive nature and vital to on going investigations. Mr. Keller stated that:

> "We have listened closely to the administration's arguments for withholding this information, and given them the most serious and respectful consideration. We remain convinced that the administration's extraordinary access to this vast repository of international financial data, however carefully targeted use of it may be, is a matter of public interest."

And the public most interested in stories of this type just happens to be terrorists such as al-Qaeda operatives.

In that the operation was completely legal and being overseen by appropriate authorities and no crime or harm was done to anyone but terrorists and it was an ongoing viable operation, there was no possible reasonable explanation for "wanting the public" to know. The Times was not blowing a whistle, this was not a "smoking gun" this was wanton anti Americanism in the name of freedom of the press.

What is most interesting about this incident is the fact that in the past the NYT was the most vociferous voice demanding to know why our intelligence agencies did not know about and prevent 9/11. However since that event every single program, proposed by the Bush administration that can be used to help prevent a future 9/11, including this one, has been criticized by the Times or the secret ones "revealed" to the public. It is clear that the NYT has lost all credibility as a bulwark of ethical journalism.

The chairman of the House Homeland Security Committee, "Rep. Peter T. King (R-NY) said the newspaper compromised national security when it exposed a Treasury Department program that secretly monitored worldwide money transfers to track terrorist financing..."By disclosing this in time of war, they have compromised America's anti-terrorist policies," said King" (7) King further said that he would call on Atty. Gen. Alberto R. Gonzales to begin a criminal investigation of the newspaper. King may not be the most "unbiased" person in Congress but his point is not off base.

As to the legality of what the Times did, it would appear that in fact they did break the law and can be prosecuted.

Section 798 of Title 18, the so-called Comint statute states"

> "Whoever knowingly and willfully communicates, furnishes, transmits, or otherwise makes available to an unauthorized person, or publishes, or uses in any manner prejudicial to the safety or interest of the United States or for the benefit of any foreign government to the detriment of the United States any classified information . . . concerning the communication intelligence activities of the United States . . . shall be fined not more than $10,000 or imprisoned not more than ten years, or both."

The law was passed by Congress in 1950 in direct response to the need to prevent another Pearl Harbor but this time during the Cold War. The law has a history that is highly germane to the present conduct of the Times.

If the information the NYT published was instead placed on a microdot and given to al-Qaeda the person or organization performing the act would be guilty of treason. The times achieved the same exact result but saved the cost of the microdot.

The New York Times is used in several examples because it is thought of as a prestigious national journal and as such sets a certain standard. The methods and approach to reporting that the NYT uses are shared by an enormous number of papers throughout the country. Certainly the broadcast networks are no better. The above examples are illustrative of endless numbers of examples that can be found daily.

One might ask what does all of this have to do with Islam's forward movement in the world. A great deal is the answer. When the public receives editorial positions as news rather than hard facts they are no longer being informed of the reality of situations. It is hard enough to get at the truth without the added disadvantage of bias (from both sides of the political spectrum). The slant places the public at a very great disadvantage when they must make voting decisions or form opinions on events that are of enormous import. If the bias of the media presents events as if terrorism was an aberration of Islam rather than a tactic one opinion is formed. If the reverse is presented then a more aggressive opinion might be formed. Neither case is the job of the media to "push." The media's job is just reporting the facts, and as appropriate, the larger picture so that the public can think and know and the editorialists can opine. It is not in the interest of the country to have a media dramatically bias in either direction.

32 CAIR Revisited

A perusal of the CAIR web site would find (at least as of this writing) that it supports Civil Rights, Political Empowerment, Job Support, etc. There is nothing wrong with these objectives; they are after all what all groups in the country aspire to and work toward for their constituents. A problem with these goals arises only in the context of what will be done when the political empowerment is achieved. Certainly the CAIR quotes in the section *Islamic Methods* reveals a different picture than the above stated goals might indicate. The mindset of the CAIR people is not friendly in the least. Their clearly stated objective is to have America become an Islamic state.

If the web site stated goals are achieved to better the life, opportunities, standard of living and assimilation of Muslims into the American culture, then we have one more appropriate and positive example of a people striving for improvement while becoming American. (For the most part I am sure this is the goal of most of the common Muslim immigrants.) That does not seem to be the overriding goal of the Islamic leaders however. The desire for, and achievement of, political power can be a great danger particularly if the intent is to use the successes to change the system and culture that gave the people the fruits of a free society. CAIR works ceaselessly to achieve what seems like good goals for bad purposes.

Fortunately there also exists an American organization by the name of "Anti-CAIR". It is this organization's position that CAIR is guilty of extremely deleterious behavior when viewed from the American perspective. To advance and prove the validity of their premise, Anti-CAIR published a set of accusations against CAIR.

> "Let their [sic] be no doubt that CAIR is a terrorist supporting front organization that is partially funded by terrorists, and that CAIR wishes nothing more than the implementation of *Shari'a* law in America."

> "CAIR is an "organization founded by Hamas supporters that seek to overthrow Constitutional government in the United States and replace it with an Islamist theocracy using our own Constitution as protection."

> "Anti-CAIR reminds our readers that CAIR was started by Hamas members and is supported by terrorist supporting individuals, groups and countries."

> "Why oppose CAIR? CAIR has proven links to, and was founded by, Islamic terrorists. CAIR is not in the United States to promote the civil rights of Muslims. CAIR is here to make radical Islam the dominant religion in the United States and convert our country into an Islamic theocracy along the lines of Iran. In addition, CAIR has managed, through the adroit manipulation of the popular media, to present itself as the 'moderate' face of Islam in the United States. CAIR succeeded to the point that the majority of its members are not aware that CAIR actively supports terrorists and terrorist supporting groups and nations. In addition, CAIR receives direct funding from Islamic terrorists supporting countries."

> "CAIR is a fundamentalist organization dedicated to the overthrow of the United States Constitution and the installation of an Islamic theocracy in America."

These are potentially libelous accusations. Anti-CAIR must have known that CAIR might possibly sue them for libel; which is exactly what CAIR did.

In preparing for a court hearing regarding discovery, Anti-CAIR's lawyers filed papers in the Virginia Circuit Court in October 2005 and December 2005 in which Anti-CAIR alleged that there existed links between CAIR's organizers and a Hamas control group and other foreign and domestic Islamists. In addition the papers also alleged that:

> "CAIR's lineage goes back to a key Hamas leader (Musa Abu Marzook), and that CAIR has long been connected with, and 'exploited' the 9/11 attacks to raise money for the Holy Land Foundation, a Hamas front group."

> "CAIR is heavily supported, financially and otherwise, by suspected Saudi and UAE-based individuals and groups."

> "CAIR states that the U.S. judicial system has been 'kidnapped by Israeli interests,' and claims that anti-terror law enforcement action against the Holy Land Foundation was 'an anti-Muslim witch hunt' promoted by "the pro-Israel lobby in America."

Unless there exists a substantial body of evidence to prove these allegations Anti-CAIR could be found guilty of libel. What did transpire is more interesting. CAIR refused to respond to the Anti-CAIR discovery requests made in November 2005. Specifically it would not supply:

> The identities of its Saudi donors,
> It declined to answer whether it aims to convert American Christians to Islam,
> It avoided questions about the anti-Semitic and anti-American activities of its founder and executive director, Nihad Awad,
> It refused to supply Awad's communications with Hamas terrorists, speeches supporting suicide bombings, and advocacy of violence against Jews.

A hearing was to be held in March 2006 at which the court would decide if it should compel CAIR to comply with the requests. (It was almost a forgone conclusion that CAIR would have been forced to comply.) It never came to that. The case was settled.

A condition of settlement was that the agreement would remain private so we can only speculate as to what caused the settlement. However, Anti-CAIR notes that they issued no public apology to CAIR, made no retractions or corrections, and left the Anti-CAIR website (www.anti-cair-net.org) unchanged, i.e., containing all of the original allegations that triggered the CAIR suit. What was CAIR afraid of?

Given the degree of known anti-American activities on the part of CAIR, i.e., financial support for terrorist organizations, explicitly stated goals that are contrary to American interests and activities that could be considered even treasonous one might ask why an organization like this is permitted to operate. The answer lies in the fact that Islam is a "religion" and all the activities of subversive Islamic groups, not overtly guilty of plotting terrorist activities, can easily hide behind the protections afforded religions. We seem not to be able to differentiate between legitimate religious groups and organizations that use religion as a protective screen. And of course *political correctness* is once again a weapon used against us as its demands for silence cloak our ability to communicate the truth, i.e., Islam is much more than a religion and as such must be treated differently than pure religious institutions would normally be treated. Anything else constitutes a degree of passive help to an avowed destroyer of our way of life. Islam is a political entity working toward world conquest AND it is a religion. But it is a religion whose purpose is to support the goals of the political entity. By protecting the individual rights of the practitioner of the spiritual aspects of the religion it is critical not to also protect the secular actions and politics of allied organizations.

Is it difficult to achieve this differentiated view and behavior without stressing or worse, damaging the constitutional rights afforded all religions?–absolutely, but not succeeding in achieving the required differentiation between true religious activities and those deleterious actions hiding behind religion are equally dangerous. When we protect or avoid dealing with organizations that are working toward undermining our way of life because they are part of a religion we are not doing ourselves a service. We are not protecting our rights we are aiding an enemy.

33 Cowardice, Hopefulness or Stupidity

It is more than the left wing and the mainstream media that is guilty of helping to create an environment in which militant Islam not only grows but flourishes. All of the governments of the West combined including their administrative, cultural and political institutions have been involved in one form or another in helping the expansion of Islam. Whether through cowardice, stupidity or misguided optimism doesn't matter. To date there is no universal recognition of the nature of the West's enemy or of its quest or the scope and size of the battle required to stop Islam's forward march. We fight on many fronts a fragmented fight with no strategic integration or unanimity of purpose or goal and we suffer endless infighting. From the Catholic Church that faces ultimate destruction or at best a *dhimmi* role under Islam to the European's rudderless leadership and lack of stomach for even identifying the real issue to American politicians that appear clueless. (In all three groups there are certainly exceptions but as of yet they have not been able to sway the majority.)

THE CHURCH

Misguided ecumenism and John Paul II's naïve geopolitical agenda also prevented the Catholic Church from effectively confronting the spreading threat of Islam. Oriana Fallaci excoriated the church in a 2002 editorial in Corriere della Sera. Some excerpts:

> "I find it shameful that the Catholic Church should permit a bishop (Hilarion Capucci), one with lodgings in the Vatican no less, a 'saintly man' who was found in Jerusalem with an arsenal of arms and explosives hidden in the secret compartments of his sacred Mercedes, to...plant himself in front of a microphone to thank in the name of God the suicide bombers who massacre the Jews in pizzerias and supermarkets. To call them 'martyrs who go to their deaths as to a party.'
>
> "I find it shameful that in the name of Jesus Christ (a Jew without whom they would all be unemployed), the priests of our parishes or Social Centers or whatever they are flirt with the assassins of those in Jerusalem who cannot go to eat a pizza or buy some eggs without being blown up [parentheses in original].
>
> "I find it shameful that they are on the side of the very ones who

> inaugurated terrorism, killing us on airplanes, in airports, at the Olympics, and who today entertain themselves by killing western journalists. By shooting them, abducting them, cutting their throats, decapitating them."

Fallaci further points out that:

> "Catholic Church...remains silent even when the crucifix gets insulted derided, expelled from the hospitals. This Catholic Church... never roars against (Muslims') polygamy and wife-repudiation and slavery...." (1) (Talking about Italy in *The Force of Reason*.)

John Paul II had dedicated enormous energies to opening contacts with Islam by meeting with Muslims more than 50 times, a number that, according to experts, surpasses the total number of encounters between Islam and all previous popes combined. The problem of course is that the Pope received nothing from the Muslims. There was still no permission to build churches in Islamic countries or to stop the practice of *dhimmi*. So once again a major Western figure reaches out to Islam, a form of legitimizing a relationship that in fact does not exist, and in return he gets nothing for it.

And at a synod of Bishops in Rome despite a growing uneasiness with Islam's growth the bishops stated that a welcoming reaction to Islam could help shape the future direction of Islam in Europe. However this position was challenged by Archbishop Giuseppe Bernardini, who has lived in Muslim countries for over forty years; he said "the 'dominion' has already begun with the 'petro-dollars,' used not to create work in the poor North African or Middle Eastern countries, but to build mosques and cultural centers in Christian countries with Islamic immigration, including Rome, the center of Christianity," Bernardini's comments came in a written intervention submitted to the synod Oct. 13, 1999.

"History teaches us that peaceful cohabitation between Islam and Christianity is precarious," said Alain Besançon, a member of the Institut de France and a synod participant. He warned: "a church uncertain of its faith is endangered by conversion to Islam."

Bernardini said a Moslem leader once told him: "Thanks to your democratic laws, we will invade you. Thanks to our religious laws, we will dominate you."

In contrast, Belgian Cardinal Godfried Danneels–while acknowledging the challenge of dialogue with fundamentalist forms of Islam–challenged Catholicism to support the positive elements of the Islamic faith. "We have much to learn," Danneels said, such as "the transcendence of God, prayer and fasting, and the impact of religion on social life." (2)

Clearly the dichotomy that exists within the church will serve Islam well.

The new Pope, Pope Benedict has shown signs of a greater grasp of the scope of the problem the church faces with Islam. The political needs of the Catholic Church are however still at odds with its philosophical teachings. But nowhere in the Catholic teachings is suicide required. The Church cannot continue to support the political and secular Islam to its own continued detriment The simplest of things is typical of the "between the rock and the hard place" the church finds itself. The church has supported the building of mosques in Italy specifically and in Christian countries in general yet there has not been a church built anywhere in Islam in generations while at the same time Christians (and of course Jews) are persecuted throughout Islam. The imbalance and illogical self-destructive policies clearly must stop if the Church is to have any chance of retaining a position of influence in the emerging world. (The Catholic Church is driven by the altruism it has preached for centuries and that philosophy is now undermining the Church's very foundations.)

Also in many instances the church has allowed Muslims to use their facilities, churches, etc. where a mosque is not available. Yet another of a continuing set of actions that are not only not reciprocated but not particularly appreciated where it counts, i.e., Islamic tolerance of others.

In response to the Churches kindness to Islam over the past two decades or more, Pope Benedict became the target of an Islamic outpouring of hatred and condemnation because he had the "gall" to quote a 14th Century historian who denounced religiously inspired violence. And the Pope did so in a theological session not as a direct condemnation of Islam. The implication is quite astounding.

> A "world religious leader such as the Pope cannot think aloud about the links between faith and bloodshed without fear is exactly what is wrong about exchanges between the West and the Islamic world." (3)

SETTING THE STAGE

Moving from the religious to the secular reveals the same model of behavior. Islam has been escalating its attacks on the West and particularly America for well over twenty years.

> In November 1979 Iranian extremists seized the U.S. embassy in Iran and held 52 American hostages for 444 days.
>
> In 1982 Hezbollah terrorists began a ten-year reign of terror in Lebanon by kidnapping Americans and Europeans. They also killed William Buckley. Terry Anderson was kidnapped and held for six and half years.
>
> In April 1983: Muslim terrorists bombed the U.S. Embassy in Beirut, killing 16 Americans.
>
> In October 1983: Hezbollah blew up the U.S. Marine barracks at the Beirut airport killing 241 Marines.
>
> In December 1983 terrorists blew up the U.S. Embassy in Kuwait, killing five and injuring 80.
>
> In September 1984 again Hezbollah exploded a truck bomb at the U.S. Embassy annex in Beirut, killing 24 people, including two U.S. servicemen.
>
> In December 1984: terrorists hijacked a Kuwait Airways airplane and flew it to Iran. They demanded the release of the 17 members of al-Dawa, another terrorists group being held for the bombing of the Kuwait Embassy and murdering two Americans.
>
> In June 14, 1985: Hezbollah hijacked TWA Flight 847 originating in Athens and diverted it to Beirut. They took the passengers hostage and demanded the release of 700 terrorists being held by Israel. The demands were rightfully not met but tragically they shot U.S. Navy diver Robert Dean Stethem and dumped his body on the tarmac.
>
> In October 1985: PLO terrorists seized the Italian cruise ship, the Achille Lauro and killed 69-year-old wheel chair bound American Leon Klinghoffer and then threw his body overboard.

> In December 1985: Muslim terrorists bombed airports in Rome and Vienna, killing 20 people, including five Americans.
>
> In April 1986: Muslim terrorists bombed a discotheque frequented by U.S. servicemen in West Berlin. Two U.S. soldiers were killed.
>
> In December 1988 Muslim terrorists bombed Pan Am Flight 103 over Lockerbie, Scotland. This tragedy killed 259 passengers and 11 people on the ground.

Did these events begin to form a definitive picture in the mind of Western diplomats and intelligence services such that political and foreign policy became aggressively centered on wiping out this scourge? Particularly interesting in reviewing the list of terrorist incidents is the fact that most often it is Americans and American interests that are the target of the attacks. For sure international police efforts were continual and to be lauded but that is quite a different thing from an integrated Western campaign against terrorism, its proponents and its supporters.

THE FIRST PRESIDENT—AN ENIGMA

More damaging than the Catholic Church's attempts to reach out to Islam or European myopia and even collusion with Islamic countries is the lack of action taken by the U.S in the early 90s. From early in 1993 to the end of the Clinton administration a number of terrorist attacks occurred that were viewed as "criminal acts" and not acts of international Islamic terrorism. The naming of these attacks as "criminal" caused a very different reaction then would have been the case had they been properly defined for what they were. I am not saying that 9/11 would not have happened but there is certainly a good chance that that is the case. Why this is possible will become clear after a brief discussion of the events themselves.

> On February 26, 1993 the first attack on the Word Trade Center was carried out by al-Qaeda. The explosion of a truck bomb in the underground parking garage was not by any means a minor incident. In the attack six people were killed and a 1,000 plus injured and tens of millions of dollars in damage to the garage as well as smoke damage to the buildings themselves. The fact that the six Muslim terrorists responsible were caught, tried, convicted, and sent to prison for long terms is the good news. The

> fact that it was not viewed as more than just a criminal act is not reasonable given their backgrounds, affiliations and world events at the time. And of course the long list of previous attacks on American interests and personnel.

The fact is that many experts, including the director of the CIA, (at the time R. James Woolsey), believed the attack was the work of an Islamic terror organization headquartered in the Sudan and headed by a terrorist by the name of Osama bin Laden. This belief and the extreme nature of the attack should have started a major intelligence and diplomatic counter offensive. It did not.

> Two months after that WTC attack, an assassination attempt was carried out on former President Bush (senior) while he was visiting in Kuwait. There was proof it was Saddam's Iraq. Two months were spent getting U.N approval for retaliation! We then fired two missiles into a deserted building in Iraq with of course no effect.
>
> In the spring of 1993 Muslim terrorists (al-Gama'a al-Islamiyya, of the Sudanese Islamic Front and one member of Hamas) were arrested before they could execute their plot to blow up the Holland Tunnel, the Lincoln Tunnel and the U.N.
>
> In March 1995 a van belonging to the U.S. consulate in Karachi, Pakistan, was hit by gunfire, killing two American diplomats and injuring a third.
>
> In November 1995, five Americans died when a car bomb exploded in Riyadh, Saudi Arabia, near a building in which a U.S. military advisory group lived.
>
> In June 1996 when another building (the Khobar Towers in Saudi Arabia) in which American military personnel lived was attacked using a truck bomb. Nineteen U.S. airmen were killed, and 240 other Americans were wounded.
>
> In June 1998, grenades were unsuccessfully hurled at the U.S. embassy in Beirut.
>
> Also in June 1998 U.S. embassies in the capitals of Kenya (Nairobi) and Tanzania were struck.
>
> And again in August 1998 car bombs exploded simultaneously in the same embassies, leaving more than 200 people dead, of

whom twelve were Americans. Al Qaeda claimed credit for the coordinated operation.

On October 12, 2000 the USS Cole was docked in Yemen. A team of suicide bombers ran a small boat laden with explosives into the Cole. Although the ship did not sink 17 American sailors were killed and 39 wounded. In addition the ship sustained massive damage.

During all of these years the American reaction was half-hearted and woefully inadequate. Treating such a massive concerted effort to kill Americans and destroy American property required a suitably strong reaction not a "legal action" as was the case. Neither the Directors of the CIA nor the FBI could "get through" to Clinton. According to Dick Morris, then Clinton's political adviser: "The weekly strategy meetings at the White House throughout 1995 and 1996 featured an escalating drumbeat of advice to President Clinton to take decisive steps to crack down on terrorism. The polls gave these ideas a green light. But Clinton hesitated and failed to act, always finding a reason why some other concern was more important."

The tragedy is that the message bin Laden got from this was that America was a "paper tiger".

> "The sheer audacity of what bin Laden went on to do on September 11 was unquestionably a product of his contempt for American power. Our persistent refusal for so long to use that power against him and his terrorist brethren—or to do so effectively whenever we tried—reinforced his conviction that we were a nation on the way down, destined to be defeated by the resurgence of the same Islamic militancy that had once conquered and converted large parts of the world by the sword." (4)

The sad thing is that even now the left wishes to repeat the mistakes of Clinton.

THE SECOND PRESIDENT—CONFUSED OVER ISLAM'S NATURE

President George W. Bush has done a great deal of good in prosecuting the war on terror but little in containing Islamic expansion. He has also been guilty of being inconsistent with Islam itself.

Bush was the first president to mention a mosque in an inaugural address. In fairness this was before 9/11 and I'm sure was meant to represent his presidency as being inclusive of all Americans, however since 9/11 Bush continues to refer to Islam as a religion of peace despite an enormous amount of data to the contrary. In all situations dealing with terrorism Bush is an apologist for Islam saying that terrorists are fundamentalist that hijacked the religion, again against large amounts of data to the contrary. The reason? You can pick your preference from the title of this chapter.

Bush has appointed more Arab and Muslim Americans to positions of authority and prominence in his administration than any other president. Bush also helped the Islamic Institute to achieve its objective of promoting the appointments of Muslims to positions of influence.

Suhail Khan was placed inside the White House as the official gatekeeper for Muslims. (Khan is an associate of Grover Norquist who is both the founder of the Islamic Institute and a "lobbyist" who has had a close relationship to Karl Rove who is Bush's closest adviser and political strategist.) One of Suhail Khan's first tasks was to create a list of eighty-three Muslims activists whom he wanted Karl Rove to invite to White House Outreach events. Before people are allowed access to the White House they must go through a Secret Service screening. The list turned out to contain a large number of hard-line Islamists and Wahhabists and some who are known terrorist sympathizers and supporters under federal investigation.

One Faisal Gill was placed in a post in Homeland security. Today (2006) Gill is the Policy Director of Homeland Security's Intelligence Division "where he has access to top-secret data concerning the vulnerability of America's seaports, refineries, nuclear plants, and other facilities sensitive to terrorists attacks." When Gill applied to the post he managed to leave out of his national security questionnaire (SF86) the fact that he worked for the American Muslim Council (AMC). The council is a Muslim advocacy group that happens to be under investigation for terrorism financing. The founder of the AMC is none other than the confessed and convicted terrorist Abduraham Alamoudi. Gill's appointment has caused a great deal of alarm among security experts. Gill was called into a White House meeting concerning the issue, however he is still in his job. (5) The fact that a Muslim would be appointed to a position of such extreme sensitivity given the on going war on Islamic terrorism is beyond belief. The fact that he still has that position as of early 2006 should be of great concern to authorities. One could posit as a reason the fact that we still don't understand that we are at war with Islam.

At the White House direction the FBI officially certified Abduraham M. Alamoudi's American Muslim Council (AMC) as moderate–"the most mainstream Muslim group in the United states." This certification was made after the AMC advised its members during post 9/11 investigations NOT to cooperate with the FBI. The embarrassment is that subsequently Alamoudi confessed to plotting terrorism. He is now serving time in a federal prison.

Eight months prior to his "certification" Alamoudi shouted out in a speech he gave in public to a gathering of Muslims at an anti Israel rally

> "I have been labeled by the media in New York to be a supporter of Hamas. Anybody support Hamas here? Anybody's (sic) is a supporter of Hamas here? Anybody's (sic) a supporter of Hamas here? [cheers] Hear that Bill Clinton? We are all supporters of Hamas! Allah akbar (Allah is great). I wish to add here that I am also a supporter of Hezbollah! [cheers].." (6)

Sami al-Arian was also cleared for entry to the White House. He was an alleged founder of Palestinian *Jihad* and is currently in jail on related terrorism charges.

John Loftus, a former Justice department official "alleges that Norquist has been providing 'protection' for accused terrorists like Alamoudi and al-Arian by persuading the White House to stonewall investigations, taking advantage of his relationship with Karl Rove and also Bush's loyalty to the Saudis, who are the primary source of funding for Alamoudi's and al-Arian's operations". (7)

It is out of the scope of this book to explore the relationship of President Bush and the Saudis but as the bard said: "Something is rotten in Denmark!" There is not a single book or article you can read about Saudi Arabia that does not clearly name ***it*** as the "fountainhead" of the intellectual ideas and financial support that drive Islamic expansion and terrorism. Wahhabism, the extreme literal form of Islam that originated in Saudi Arabia has spread its message of fundamentalism and hatred of the West. The endless oil wealth of the House of Saud is the source of a huge amount of the funding for the spread of this hatred. Yet we think of them as an ally. As the saying goes "with friends like these we don't need enemies."

THE CONGRESS—A SHAMBLES

Congress is always representative of a wide cross section of American opinion and interests but one would like to think that at no time does this diversity of opinion include the support of programs or people that are deleterious to the well being of the country.

> "There were a few members on the hill that were outraged that we would ask for the help from the Arab-American community. And this outrage was mainly from members who had Arab-American voters in their districts."–Former FBI special agent Robert M. Blitzer. (8)

Defending one's constituency is certainly in the job description of a Congressman but what could possibly be so wrong with the FBI trying to elicit help from a community that is known to have terrorists within it? Where does reasonability and patriotism enter into the equation of balancing the responsibilities of the job?

The FBI has gotten a great deal of criticism for missing the indications of the 9/11 plot however what does not get as much press is the fact that Congress had its share of blame in "helping" the FBI miss the signs. More than a year before 9/11 the FBI had asked Congress to change laws that would make it easier for them to monitor suspected terrorists. Congress refused, they did not want the FBI spying on the Muslim community. On the surface this may not seem to be terribly inappropriate since we clearly do not want our government agencies becoming excessively intrusive or encroaching on our rights and privacy. There is a very big but in this case however.

In 1999 Congress commissioned a study to determine the best ways to fight terrorism. Ambassador L. Paul Bremer headed the panel and the conclusion of the study warned that al-Qaeda, as well as other religiously motivated Islamic groups, is determined to inflict "mass casualties on American soil." The panel made forty recommendations to Congress that would help neutralize the threat. (The report "*Countering the Changing Threat of International Terrorism*," by the National Commission on Terrorism, 5 June 2000.) The details of the report are too extensive to include herein however the report was amazingly prescient in naming the threats and proposing reasonable preventive steps. One of them was exactly the monitoring that the FBI was requesting.

The report got very little media coverage and although it was widely distributed throughout Congress, the Director of the FBI, Louis Freeh, the Director of the CIA, George Tenet and President Clinton ***not a single recommended item was implemented***! Of course there were some members of Congress that wanted to act but they were a minority. The report gathered dust and we got 9/11. As usual all the "scapegoats" received the blame. (No one bothered to point out that the FBI was working under Al Gore's ineffectual CAPPs system and the ignored Phoenix Memo as we have already seen.)

Today most of the special commission's report recommendations exist in The Patriot Act, which of course, many in Congress are trying to kill! There is a point where national security trumps many privacy considerations, especially when the loss of privacy really affects only those trying to destroy the country. Of course there are those that will say: "what stops the government from over stepping the bounds of the intended narrow use of the Patriot Act?" The answer is: that is the reason the act has expiration dates requires renewal and ongoing review and oversight by Congress.

The other piece of legislation that is despised by the Islamic leaders is "The Secret Evidence Act". Briefly this legislation allows suspected terrorists to be deported without making the evidence against them public because of fear of revealing sources and possibly compromising other operations or operatives. There is court overseeing of the use of the act and it has been exceedingly successful in ridding the country of many terrorists. I certainly understand why the Islamic leaders are against this capability but why do a certain group of Congressmen and Congresswomen want it repealed?

The Secret Evidence Act is not alone on the Islamic "hit list." It seems that everyone that Americans should worry about wants the Patriot Act eliminated. Alamoudi the convicted terrorist was also a silent partner of Norquist. Norquist is the chief lobbyist in the Islamic Institute (the major Islamic lobbying concern in Washington.) Norquist and his Islamic Institute are fighting a strenuous campaign to kill the Patriot Act. It turns out that the act has been instrumental in the discovery of, and actions against, terrorists so of course Norquist would be against it. But why is Nancy Pelosi, Democratic Majority Leader of the House of Representatives, so outspoken about the need to kill this law? She is not alone, there are several members in both Houses of Congress, but the one thing they seem to have in common is a knee jerk reaction of fighting every action that helps America in its struggle with Islamic expansion and always in the name of "protecting" our freedoms. It should be noted that Nancy Pelosi receives large contributions from Islamic groups. (9) It would be reasonable to assume that Ms Pelosi is against the act for reasons that are idealistic or partisan and that it is because of her opposition that she gets the contributions. It might also be thought reasonable that given the near state of war that exists with many Islamic countries acceptance of Islamic contributions would be viewed as suspect by her.

The need to balance legislative threats to our freedoms with effective anti-terrorist programs is paramount least we destroy the very thing we are trying to protect, our freedom. Doing this should not require hobbling our law enforcement men and women in the execution of their jobs. The balance of their need, our security and the protection of our freedoms are challenging to achieve but the first step is not the elimination of our best weapons in the middle of the war. So why isn't intelligent alternative legislation forthcoming instead of a vitriolic attacks on the one thing that is working?

Congress needs to understand that a REAL bipartisan effort must be formed in order to effectively fight this war.

EUROPE A MESS

During the same years that Clinton was avoiding the obvious, the Europeans were avoiding the obviousness of their emerging plight. For two decades the EC chose to protect its oil supplies and general economic interests over the tradition of supporting its allies. It continually indicted America and Israel in any contest with the Islamic World, particularly over Palestine. It was a bright day for Islam as this gulf between traditionally close Western allies widened. In parallel with the breakdown of the Western alliance, the integration of Islam in Europe continued at a brisk pace. Immigration and high Muslim birth rates in Europe were increasing the Muslim population percentage throughout Europe. Islam now requested special privileges for their immigrants. These included vocational training, freedom of movement, suitable living accommodations, financial aid, assistance if they should desire to return to their home country, i.e., more financial aid, and of course the endless demands for "religiously essential accommodations". To a large extent over the latter years of the 20th century these "requests" were met. The burden on European finances was considerable, as we have already seen.

From Islam's perspective not a bad fringe benefit. A weak Europe is certainly an easier one to manipulate.

During these same years the Islamic World itself was becoming more and more unstable given the rapid expansion of Islamic fundamentalism and endless and constant terrorist incidents. It is both interesting and important to note that the Islamic countries in the Middle East were (and still are) run by dictators. They are typically more interested in the accumulation and exercise of power than the betterment of their people. The environment that the conjunction of these contexts created was the worst possible environment for the exchange of advanced technology. Despite this Europe entered into an extensive program of scientific exchange (particularly, France provided massive advanced military aid to Saddam's Iraq.) Even if this exchange was fueled by a sincere desire to "westernize" the M.E. it was at best naive and at worse dangerous to long term stability in the region. How could western values and rational and peaceful applications of advanced technology take hold in countries where concepts like freedom of choice, freedom of conscience and religion, gender equality and dignity for all people were completely foreign. In fact the opposite of these values was the norm. The rudiments of Western values may have been non-existent but a plethora of Islamic "values" were and are quite prevalent. *Jihad* was applauded and taught as a positive and honorable endeavor, religious fanaticism was dominant, bigotry was so integral to the religion and its teaching it was a duty and of course there was the almost uninterrupted terrorist incidents, proclamations of hatred of the West and absolute hatred of Israel.

With events like these enfolding and the increasing domestic financial burden, Europe still saw fit to provide the PLO with over 2 billion euros in grants and loans (which will never be paid back) between 1994 and 1998, thereby funding the PLO's greatest period of terrorism against Israel. It began in October 2000. Although through their policies the Europeans seemed to be oblivious to the actions of the PLO and the plight of Israel, the truth is that they fully knew and tacitly supported the PLO's actions. In a speech in December 2003 Ilka Schroder, a German Green activist stated:

> "It is an open secret within the European Parliament and European commission that EU aid to Palestinian Authority has not been spent correctly."

She further stated that the EU had no intention

> "to verify whether European taxpayers' money could have been used to finance anti-Semitic murderous attacks. Unfortunately this fits well with European policy in this area."

Later in her speech she states:

> "The primary goal of the EU is the internationalization of the conflict in order to underline the need for its own mediating role." (10)

Through the influence of the EAD, compounded by greed and even anti Israeli prejudice, many of the countries of Europe and the European Parliaments have been co-opted to support Islamic policy in general, and specifically as it relates to Israel and the Jews.

34 A Matter of Policy

It is one thing to be an innocent victim of a foreign country's "subverting schemes," it is another to be a voluntary participant in your own doom, and that is exactly what the West is doing with respect to its culture and independence. Through opportunism and pragmatism and the complete lack of a long-term strategic plan and context within which to deal with the Islamic world the West has allowed, and unknowingly supported, the expansion and empowering of Islam. The examination of the type of diplomacy that is followed in both Europe and America is illustrative.

Even though the European countries possessed far superior technology, science, wealth, infrastructure, "know how", etc. Its dealings with the Islamic countries were as one "with hat in hand."

Analyzing the formula of the EAD, John Waterbury writes:

> "The eventual bargaining took place in the form of a trade-off: the Arab political demands against the European economic objectives." (1)

The Europeans were almost exclusively oriented to achieving narrowly and pragmatically defined goals of immediate economic gains while the Muslim negotiators were focused on the long-term strategically oriented political development of Islam in Europe, i.e., European support on Middle Eastern issues and immigration of Muslims to Europe.

As an example of the typical "deal" that was concluded without the common knowledge of the European population, the following is most enlightening.

The November 1973 *European Economic Committee* (EEC) meeting in Brussels expressed its intentions to continue the dialog with the Arabs. The *Sixth Summit of the Arab Conference* (also in November 1973 - 2 days after the EEC meeting) raised the issue of the "Palestinian people" as a distinct group of Arabs. (2) The issue of Palestine once again became pivotal in the unfolding events.

The Arabs specified their conditions for cooperating with the EEC (on economic matters), the EEC would defend Arab claims to Jerusalem and the "occupied territories and would recognize the "***autonomous Palestinian people***".

This was a coup for the Arabs. (The reader may recall from the Chapter 25 *Palestine* that the Arabs did not want the "refugees" to be so designated as they had been by UN Resolution 242 - part of the aftermath of the 1967 Arab-Israeli War.) Further the Arabs did not want the "refugees" ***to be subsumed into other neighboring Arab countries such as Jordan***, (which had been formerly part of the Palestine mandate). At this time the Arabs also wanted the Europeans to recognize the PLO but this was not to be. The PLO recognition awaited a future capitulation.

"Although falling (sic) short of achieving formal recognition of the PLO, the EAD did, however, succeed in persuading the Europeans of the need to establish a 'homeland for the Palestinians' and in 'associating' the PLO with future negotiations on the Middle east. Thus the EAD had served certain limited Arab objectives." (3)

By buying into this agreement the Europeans were granted huge Arab markets. It also assisted the Arabs in keeping the Palestinian issue alive and enabling it to become the device with which to bludgeon Israel, as we have seen. The Europeans by this agreement also unwittingly enabled a reign of terror that would flow out of Palestine in the subsequent thirty plus years. Perhaps a good tactical gain for Europe but otherwise a strategic blunder of "Chamberlainesque" proportions. And it still haunts the West today. By siding with the Islamic leaders on the Palestine issue the Europeans helped create and legitimize a disruptive force (the PLO) capable of enormous negative impact on, and wide spread disruption of, any real peace plans or progress in the most sensitive part of the Middle East. The efforts of the PLO were not focused on Israel alone. The PLO played a big part in the subversion of Lebanon and the spread of terrorism throughout the Middle East.

On August 26, 1980 future President-elect of Lebanon, Bashir Gemayel described the PLO's terrorist war in Lebanon and then denounced the influence that the organization had in Europe:

> "This is a recapitulation of the doings of those (Palestinian) people on whose behalf the chancelleries of the civilized world are striving throughout the year, and for whose favors the old nations of Europe are competing." (4)

The Europeans at the 1973 meeting in Brussels should not have capitulated to the Arab demands. Along with the U.S. they should have demanded full and final recognition of Israel and the inclusion of the "Palestinians" in Jordan. (As we have seen the Palestinians were ethnically and religiously the same as the Jordanians and were part of the original Trans-Jordan of the U.N. mandated area.) The PLO should have been forced to disband. The influence of the EAD and the fear of terrorism and a potential shortage of oil through an Arab curtailment of shipments cowed the Europeans into their strategic blunder while further empowering the Islamic leaders in the Middle East. And still policies of this type continue to plague the West. Short-term pragmatic expediencies are continually traded for long-term strategic loss.

After the terrorist attack in the U.S. on September 11, 2001, the EAD once again was instrumental in molding European policy to conform to a more pro-Islamic view while attempting to generate anti-American feelings. This was in reaction to a growth in public sympathy for the U.S. after the 9/11 events. On June 20, 2002 the Euro-Arab Parliamentary Dialog (EAPD) met in Brussels. The meeting consisted of members of sixteen Arab countries' parliaments and thirteen members from the European Commission and European Parliaments. The major issues discussed were:

- Political cooperation
- The Middle East peace process
- Eliminating the embargo against Iraq
- Migrations to Europe from Muslim countries
- The brain drain from the Euro-Arab zone
- Agreements on improving cultural cooperation

Of course most of the proposals and discussion points were aimed at addressing the anti-Israeli obsession of the Arab countries and other Middle East issues. However it was stated that:

> "mutual recognition of the right of the Israelis and the Palestinians to live in peace in definite and recognized borders based on the international law and the **relevant resolutions of the United Nations.**" (Emphasis mine.)

This could indicate a possible softening of the Arab position until you understand that the resolutions of the UN (dominated by Islamic countries and sympathizers) want Israel to relinquish a great deal of the disputed territories. The anti-Israeli bias became clear with the issuance of the first communiqué. It reaffirmed the importance of improving the condition of the Palestinians, the elimination of Israeli political and military measures that fueled frustration, despair and retaliation. Two items clearly demonstrated the real intent of the "cooperation." The EAPD stated that:

> "It is a question of knowing if Israel wants to coexist with its Arab neighbors."

Further language also condemned any attempt to connect terrorism with Islam and Arabs!

The other items that were included in the EAPD's Brussels meeting's Action Plan were:

> To strengthen the Euro-Arab economic and financial ties
> To encourage the respect of social and cultural differences. (This was viewed as crucial for improving the dialog.) (5)

The latter point to encourage respect, etc. was from the Islamic perspective well underway in the offices of the Parliamentary Association for Euro-Arab Cooperation (PAEAC). However, the PAEAC in actuality is a public relations arm of the Islamic world and a powerful Arab lobby within the European Union. In true Hitlerian fashion they have continually acted to position every Islamic aggressive action as a reaction to some attack on Islam, either vocal or armed, while influencing pro-Islamic legislation in the different countries of the EU. And always whenever the opportunity presents itself they attempt to manipulate public opinion against Israel. As a typical example of the kind of manipulation the PAEAC is so competent at: In April 2002 Israel cleared out several well-known and documented Hamas terrorist bases in Jenin. The immediate world reaction, fueled by PAEAC press releases, saw Israel as guilty of "war crimes."

These activities were and continue to be in keeping with a statement from *1969 Cairo International Conference in Support of the Arab People* that ***"information should specifically target public opinion in countries where governments were pro-Israeli."***

As the evolution of the EAD went forward, huge amounts of money were funneled to tyrants and terrorist groups from the EU, while the EAD continued to speak glowingly of Arab culture and Arab regimes. These same regimes were among the most oppressive in the world. To complete the equation of pro Islamic public utterances, the EAD issued strong denunciations of the U.S. and Israel. In parallel the EU supported the in flux of millions of Arab immigrants. And as a matter of public policy there was no counter expression of the true nature of these Islamic regimes.

In reviewing many proceedings of the various Islamic/Arab committees as well as books and documents in researching this subject, one story sticks out as being a symbol of what is tragically wrong with the policies of the West. In ***Damascus, Syria*** on July 11, 1998 the Euro-Arab Parliamentary Dialog convened a meeting of the Arab Inter-Parliamentary Union and PAEAC plus the parliaments of sixteen Arab countries and fourteen European countries. Also in attendance were observers from Canada and the International Committee of the Red Cross (ICRC). The dialog was of the standard variety, i.e., Israel, Palestine, peace, etc. What made this meeting *"a meeting of the callous and the hypocrites"* was two fold. The purpose of the meeting was ostensibly to develop understanding and search for ways to peace. To have a meeting of this nature in a country run by a known terrorist dictator that was at the time occupying and waging war on another country (Lebanon) was unconscionable. And then to issue a communiqué thanking the Syrian people and their leader Hafiz al-Asad for their efforts that contributed to the success of the dialog would be surreal if it wasn't so despicable.

One of the conclusions of the conference with respect to the Middle East Peace Process was that

> "the participants in the conference stressed the close connection between the achievements of peace in the Middle East and security in Europe." (6)

If ever there existed a not so veiled threat that statement is certainly it. And the European representatives and diplomats said nothing and in a very real sense achieved nothing. Once again the pragmatic workings of European policy came up very short in supporting the real security and needs of Europe while handing Islam a resounding policy victory.

The conference and its workings could have been appropriately included in the chapter on Hypocrisy but the key element of the story, hypocrisy aside, is the fact that conferences and meetings like this, where the West enters the meetings with a set of pragmatic goals and concludes by either walking out (good news) or capitulating to some extent (normal, but bad news), is what passes for policy. The West, particularly the EU, seems to always lose in these negotiations. In every case, even if enormous time and effort is expended, nothing of any lasting long-term value is achieved. At the same time the Islamic leaders gain a legitimacy they do not deserve and the further positioning the West in a state of *dhimmitude.*

Turning to the U.S. the picture isn't much better, however the cause of the lack of consistent policies that are focused on national self-interest when dealing with the Islamic world is our internal politics rather than nefarious organizations like the EAD. Neither the liberal nor conservative, neither the Republican nor the Democrat is blameless in an orgy of finger pointing, truth twisting, fear mongering, danger minimizing, self-recrimination, self-flagellation (the "self" being America) and utter lack of an ability to develop positive U.S. centric programs. The U.S. cannot even identify the enemy in any clear agreed upon fashion let alone develop counter measures. Any reasonable review of forty or so years of U.S. history could not help but yield a view of utter chaos and almost total failure with respect to dealing with Islam. Obviously the previous statement as it stands is more editorial than rich in content. The author apologizes. The remainder of this chapter will provide an abundance of detail to prove the point.

One observation that demonstrates the intellectual bankruptcy of Western diplomacy: after forty years of an endless Peace Process in the Middle East the West has even more slaughter and less peace than it did in the beginning. Yet the thought that the process will never work, at least as configured, seems not to enter the heads of Western leaders, not at least as reflected in their policies or utterances. However during this same period, look at the progress that Islam has made: it has spread (actually exploded) throughout the EU, it has had major strides in the U.S., the acquisition of incredible wealth through oil, the wearing down of Israel, acquisition of deadlier weapons in general and now Iran on the verge of a nuclear device. And we still think we can hold more talks to change the situation. At this rate the solution will be achieved but unfortunately it will be by Islam. We'll come back to this issue in the section of the book - *Solutions.*

It is the elevation of "criminals" to the level of diplomats and the honoring of those who wish to preside at our funeral that is the hallmark of Western political policy since before World War II. Treating dictators with all the trappings of leaders of free countries is exactly what the West did with Hitler. And then to yield to their policies as though they were of joint value to both sides of the "negotiations" is despicable and suicidal. The long-term consequences of these recent policies seem to be enfolding exactly like those experienced by the free world in the lead up to the second world war.

The diplomats and professionals that act in this way are not stupid people, so what is there motivation to operate in a mode, that were they to read it in a novel they would be repelled (or tragically, perhaps not) by the characters doing what they do as a matter of policy. Is it fear or greed? Do they actually think that by being inclusive they will be "liked," or perhaps by being inclusive it will cause the "other side" to be more accommodating and receptive to real forward progress? Certainly history has not borne this premise out. Yet they continue to fawn over the most deadly dictators, even to the point of awarding the Nobel Peace Prize to the *father of modern terrorism,* Yassir Arafat. (What a piece of hypocrisy that was.) Thereby giving Arafat a degree of legitimacy beyond any he had a right to expect.

The reasons for these actions they claim are complex but the complexity they suggest only masks their underlying bankrupt philosophy. The mind-set of today's Western diplomats seems to be based on an altruistic self-delusion, in *multiculturalism*, *political correctness* and a cynical elitism–rhetoric or truth? Let's look at some history.

Following the same motivations as the diplomats meeting in Syria (July 11, 1998 the Euro-Arab Parliamentary Dialog), the West, whether consciously or unconsciously, it matters little in terms of results, have followed a path of appeasement and accommodation, to Islam that truly borders on madness. It has been so systematic that it appears to be a matter of policy.

President Bush's policy toward Islam is a complete muddle. As we have seen he continues to say that Islam is a religion of peace while the evidence to the contrary overwhelms him. Then he categorically states (correctly, I might add) that he won't negotiate with terrorists but then he consistently pressures Israel into negotiations with the PLO (one of the worst terrorist organizations) and Hezbollah. The PLO will not even agree to Israel's right to exist. How does one negotiate with someone who won't admit you have a right to exist? Then he fights wars in Afghanistan and Iraq but tells Israel not to fight Hamas. Then he decides to negotiate with Iran on the nuclear issue knowing full well that he will be negotiating with the fountainhead of terrorism. How can we expect to win when we consistently give mixed signals and appear to act from a point of weakness? Then Bush persists in Iraq when he must know full well that he cannot win that battle until he "tackles" the Iranian issue. It is Iran that is successfully fueling the Iraqi insurgency.

And in the Muslim world where we have precious few real allies, President Bush baffled our few moderate Muslim supporters by abandoning demands for democratic reforms and civil societies in places like Saudi Arabia, Egypt, and the Persian Gulf. These demands are not only major intellectual weapons in the fight against terrorism but also more importantly they are what this country is all about. Dropping the demands makes us look at best disingenuous and as callous as so many of the European pragmatists we often criticize. In fact the abandoning of these demands shows that we are not really fighting the battle we should be. In a war it is critical to know who the enemy is and then fight for its destruction at every possible level: strategically, politically, economically and militarily. We are experts at the latter (in big wars) but appear clueless of the former points. In America the President is not reluctant to commit troops (sometimes) to fight and die and perhaps win a tactical battle, but then where it would really count (against Iran) he does nothing. Being consistently inconsistent he cannot focus on the real war nor can he muster the required support for a war aimed at destroying the enemy. Certainly politics is a part of the inconsistency but even here Bush wastes vital political capital on non-essential (to our survival) domestic issues.

Terrorism is a tool not the enemy. The enemy is militant Islam and Islam's forward march. The ideas that fuel this forward march emanate from the intellectual centers of radical Islam, i.e., the Al-Azhar University of Cairo and the Wahhabi Imam Muhammad bin Saud Islamic University in Saudi Arabia. The proselytizing scripts, positions on world events and philosophy move from these centers to the Muslims residing in the West and into the groups around the world that are the tools of fundamentalist Islam. The universities' work is funded by Saudi Arabia through its 20,000 princes and the endless wealth that flows into their coffers from the West's constant and increasing appetite for oil. And the receptivity is grand indeed. Al Qaeda, Islamic *Jihad*, Egypt's Muslim Brotherhood, Hamas, the Chechen Islamic movement, Hezbollah, the Iranian mullahs, and the various Islamic liberation movements throughout Asia, all are energized and actualized by the flow of ideas from these universities and money from the House of Saud. And what do we do in response? We claim Saudi Arabia to be a vital ally in the war on terror!

The Islamic message is consistent, radical and terrible from the West's perspective. And their methods are equally consistent, i.e., ruthless and unyielding. And there is no cohesive unified set of policies and activities attempting to stop them. Worst yet, we enable them. We enable them through our lack of cohesive, intellectually and morally based integrated "war" plans. Not only are we not fighting an offensive battle we aren't even fighting a consistent defensive one. We can't seem to even close the absurd "loopholes" that enable terrorists; and that should be the easy battle. Here are just a few of the types of things that should be easy to correct but which we can't because of divisive politics.

Dozens of terror suspects on federal watch lists were allowed to buy firearms legally in the United States last year, according to a Congressional investigation that points up major vulnerabilities in federal gun laws. People suspected of being members of a terrorist group are not automatically barred from legally buying a gun, and the investigation, conducted by the Government Accounting Office, indicated that people with clear links to terrorist groups had regularly taken advantage of this gap. There are dozens of insane policies of this type that are fertile ground for terrorists to utilize, and they do.

We know that we must ferret out terror plots across the globe and especially plots that have the U.S as target. The *Patriot Act* and *Secret Evidence* are programs that help considerably. Unfortunately they are not without their issues. But do we address the shortcomings with sound, workable and non-bureaucratic overseeing capabilities? No instead the "loyal opposition" wants to scrap them and what ensues is an endless verbal tennis match of squabbling among mental adolescents hell bent on showing the other guy up as an idiot or appeaser or a Fascist, etc.

Then there is the issue of profiling or the lack there of. Not profiling is as stupid and suicidal a policy as one can find. I'm sure that it was dreamed up in Tehran because I can't believe it was a pro American that thought it up. Look only to *political correctness* for the villain.

On a transaction level the case of the terrorist attack on The Khobar Towers and its almost Kafkaesque aftermath is exactly the type of inconsistent policy that causes the U.S. to look weak to our enemies, and thereby emboldens them, inconsistent to our allies, and thereby contributes to the problem of inconsistent support from them.

The following is an editorial written by Louis J. Freeh who was the FBI director from 1993 through 2001.

> "Ten years ago today, acting under direct orders from senior Iranian government leaders, the Saudi Hezbollah detonated a 25,000-pound TNT bomb that killed 19 U.S. airmen in their dormitory at Khobar Towers in Dhahran, Saudi Arabia. The blast wave destroyed Building 131 and grievously wounded hundreds of additional Air Force personnel. It also killed an unknown number of Saudi civilians in a nearby park.
>
> "The 19 Americans murdered were members of the 4404th Wing, who were risking their lives to enforce the no-fly zone over southern Iraq. This was a U.N.-mandated mission after the 1991 Gulf War to stop Saddam Hussein from killing his Shiite people. The Khobar victims, along with the courageous families and friends who mourn them this weekend in Washington, deserve our respect and honor. More importantly, they must be remembered, because American justice has still been denied.
>
> "Although a federal grand jury handed up indictments in June 2001–days before I left as FBI director and a week before some of the charges against 14 of the terrorists would have lapsed because of the statute of limitations–two of the primary leaders of the attack, Ahmed Ibrahim al-Mughassil and Abdel Hussein Mohamed al-Nasser, are living comfortably in Iran with about as much to fear from America as Osama bin Laden had prior to Sept. 11 (to wit, U.S. marshals showing up to serve warrants for their arrests).

"The aftermath of the Khobar bombing is just one example of how successive U.S. governments have mishandled Iran. On June 25, 1996, President Clinton declared that "no stone would be left unturned" to find the bombers and bring them to "justice." Within hours, teams of FBI agents, and forensic and technical personnel, were en route to Khobar. The president told the Saudis and the 19 victims' families that I was responsible for the case. This assignment became very personal and solemn for me, as it meant that I was the one who dealt directly with the victims' survivors. These disciplined military families asked only one thing of me and their country: "Please find out who did this to our sons, husbands, brothers and fathers and bring them to justice."

"It soon became clear that Mr. Clinton and his national security adviser, Sandy Berger, had no interest in confronting the fact that Iran had blown up the towers. This is astounding, considering that the Saudi Security Service had arrested six of the bombers after the attack. As FBI agents sifted through the remains of Building 131 in 115-degree heat, the bombers admitted they had been trained by the Iranian external security service (IRGC) in Lebanon's Beka Valley and received their passports at the Iranian Embassy in Damascus, Syria, along with $250,000 cash for the operation from IRGC Gen. Ahmad Sharifi.

"We later learned that senior members of the Iranian government, including Ministry of Defense, Ministry of Intelligence and Security and the Spiritual Leader's office had selected Khobar as their target and commissioned the Saudi Hezbollah to carry out the operation. The Saudi police told us that FBI agents had to interview the bombers in custody in order to make our case. To make this happen, however, the U.S. president would need to make a personal request to Saudi Crown Prince Abdullah.

"So for 30 months, I wrote and rewrote the same set of simple talking points for the president, Mr. Berger, and others to press the FBI's request to go inside a Saudi prison and interview the Khobar bombers. And for 30 months nothing happened. The Saudis reported back to us that the president and Mr. Berger would either fail to raise the matter with the crown prince or raise it without making any request. On one such occasion, our commander in chief instead hit up Prince Abdullah for a contribution to his library. Mr. Berger never once, in the course of the five-year investigation, which coincided with his tenure, even asked how the investigation was going.

"In their only bungled attempt to support the FBI, a letter from the president intended for Iran's President Mohammad Khatami, asking for "help" on the Khobar case, was sent to the Omanis, who had direct access to Mr Khatami. This was done without advising either the FBI or the Saudis who were exposed in the letter as providing help to the Americans. We only found out about the letter because it was misdelivered to the spiritual leader, Ayatollah Ali Khamenei, who then publicly denounced the U.S. This was an embarrassment for the Saudis who had been fully cooperating with the FBI by providing direct evidence of Iranian involvement. Both Saudi Prince Bandar and Interior Minister Prince Nayef, who had put themselves and their government at great risk to help the FBI, were now undermined by America's president.

"The Clinton administration was set on "improving" relations with what it mistakenly perceived to be a moderate Iranian president. But it also wanted to accrue the political mileage of proclaiming to the world, and to the 19 survivor families, that America was aggressively pursuing the bombers. When I would tell Mr. Berger that we could close the investigation if it compromised the president's foreign policy, the answer was always: "Leave no stone unturned."

"Meanwhile, then-Secretary of State Madeleine Albright and Mr. Clinton ordered the FBI to stop photographing and fingerprinting Iranian wrestlers and cultural delegations entering the U.S. because the Iranians were complaining about the identification procedure. Of course they were complaining. It made it more difficult for their intelligence agents and terrorist coordinators to infiltrate into America. I was overruled by an "angry" president and Mr. Berger who said the FBI was interfering with their rapprochement with Iran.

"Finally, frustrated in my attempts to execute Mr. Clinton's "leave no stone unturned" order, I called former president George H.W.

Bush. I had learned that he was about to meet Crown Prince Abdullah on another matter. After fully briefing Mr. Bush on the impasse and faxing him the talking points that I had now been working on for over two years, he personally asked the crown prince to allow FBI agents to interview the detained bombers.

"After his Saturday meeting with now-King Abdullah, Mr. Bush called me to say that he made the request, and that the Saudis would be calling me. A few hours later, Prince Bandar, then the Saudi ambassador to Washington, asked me to come out to McLean, Va., on Monday to see Crown Prince Abdullah. When I met him with Wyche Fowler, our Saudi ambassador, and FBI counterterrorism chief Dale Watson, the crown prince was holding my talking points. He told me Mr. Bush had made the request for the FBI, which he granted, and told Prince Bandar to instruct Nayef to arrange for FBI agents to interview the prisoners.

"Several weeks later, agents interviewed the co-conspirators. For the first time since the 1996 attack, we obtained direct evidence of Iran's complicity. What Mr. Clinton failed to do for three years was accomplished in minutes by his predecessor. This was the breakthrough we had been waiting for, and the attorney general and I immediately went to Mr. Berger with news of the Saudi prison interviews.

"Upon being advised that our investigation now had proof that Iran blew up Khobar Towers, Mr. Berger's astounding response was: "Who knows about this?" His next, and wrong, comment was: "That's just hearsay." When I explained that under the Rules of Federal Evidence the detainees' comments were indeed more than "hearsay," for the first time ever he became interested–and alarmed–about the case. But this interest translated into nothing more than Washington "damage control" meetings held out of the fear that Congress, and ordinary Americans, would find out that Iran murdered our soldiers. After those meetings, neither the president, nor anyone else in the administration, was heard from again about Khobar.

"Sadly, this fits into a larger pattern of U.S. governments sending the wrong message to Tehran. Almost 13 years before Iran committed

> its terrorist act of war against America at Khobar, it used its surrogates, the Lebanese Hezbollah, to murder 241 Marines in their Beirut barracks. The U.S. response to that 1983 outrage was to pull our military forces out of the region. Such timidity was not lost upon Tehran. As with Beirut, Tehran once again received loud and clear from the U.S. its consistent message that there would be no price to pay for its acts of war against America. As for the 19 dead warriors and their families, their commander in chief had deserted them, leaving only the FBI to carry on the fight.
>
> "The Khobar bombing case eventually led to indictments in 2001, thanks to the personal leadership of President George W. Bush and Condoleezza Rice. But justice has been a long time coming. Only so much can be done, after all, with arrest warrants and judicial process. Bin Laden and his two separate pre-9/11 arrest warrants are a case in point.
>
> "Still, many stones remain unturned. It remains to be seen whether the Khobar case and its fugitives will make it onto the list of America's demands in "talks" with the Iranians. Or will we ultimately ignore justice and buy a separate peace with our enemy?"(7)

The examples of Western governments' inconsistency and long term self-defeating policies in the context of enabling Islamic expansion and accommodations are endless. It is also clear from these examples that in the mind of Western countries there is no connection between domestic leniency, appeasement and accommodation to Islamic populations and the war we are fighting with militant Islam. Every capitulation in a Western community provides an added advantage to Islam in general and to the enabling of local terrorism specifically. It is worthwhile to examine specific examples from the perspective of demonstrating that the one consistency the West demonstrates is an unending ability to deal with Islamic issues in isolation as though each one is a stand alone transaction instead of a cumulative number aimed at a constant wearing down of the West's culture and safety.

Examples:

Italy

The mayor of Colle Val D'Elsa, a small town near Siena, Tuscany, has allowed the construction of a mosque and an Islamic center. The problem is that the mosque is being funded by the Union of the Italian Islamic

Communities (UCOII), which is known to support and work with the Muslim Brotherhood and Hamas. Magdi Allam, the Egyptian-born Italian deputy editor of Il Corriere Della Sera (a major Italian daily newspaper) uncovered the story. Allam himself discovered that most of the mosques and Islamic "cultural" centers preach *Jihadism* to their followers. In that there is extensive evidence to support this discovery why allow the center to be built?

Australia

It has been almost standard practice for many years now for the *Australian Refugee Review Tribunal* to grant asylum to Islamic refugees who claim to be members of the Muslim Brotherhood. *The Australian* (April 08, 2006) reported that Ahmad al-Hamwi–better known to the authorities as, Abu Omar (an alias) had "alleged links to terrorist organizations spanning a good part of the globe." The newspaper further asserted that al-Hamwi was connected to Osama bin Laden and was a "senior al-Qaeda bagman linked to the 1993 World Trade Centre bomber, Ramzi Yousef." There is little doubt about al-Hamwi's terrorist connections. He freely admitted before the *Refugee Tribunal* to playing a key role in the *International Research and Information Centre* (IRIC). According to terrorism expert Zachary Abuza, the IRIC was an Islamic terrorist front that provided funding to "the Moro Islamic Liberation Front, al-Qaeda and Abu Sayyaf, a group that conducted military training with Jemaah Islamiah." Despite this, Australia granted al-Hamwi asylum in 1996. Mr. al-Hamwi is not the only resident terrorist the Australian authorities know about.

Canada

The Toronto terrorist plot to bomb Canadian administrative and police centers (detailed in Chapter 16 "A Different War - A Web of Terror") had a political beginning that not only made the plot possible but also actually enabled its development. How? The Liberals are Canada's party of *multiculturalism*. For 12 years Canada's Liberal party Prime Minister Jean Chretien followed the tenets of *multiculturalism* to the letter. What resulted was the creation of a legal and permissive environment that was (and still is) supportive of Islam. The government developed policies that allowed for appeasement of suspected terrorist groups and an avoidance of enforcing deportation orders (such as the one against Ahmed Ressam–covered in Chapter 16–or the tightening of lax immigration and asylum laws. All for fear of alienating the urban ethnic vote that forms a large part of the Liberal constituency. The result was a very much emboldened and enhanced terror support network operating in Canada.

At one point the PM had the temerity to say that there was no terrorist groups in Canada. In response the CSIS (Canada's CIA) took the dramatic and unprecedented step of going public, via the media, to contradict him. Their official statement said that there were at least 50 terrorist organizations operating on Canadian soil. What could cause such an extreme action, i.e., of an intelligence organization publicly contradicting the Prime Minister?

First: obviously the statement made by the PM was blatantly incorrect; as Prime Minister he had to have known the truth. Secondly: it was the policies of the PM, his accommodation and appeasement of Islamic pressure groups, carried out over a period of the 12 years that frustrated Canadian authorities' abilities to deal with the terrorist issues to such a point that they had no recourse but to contradict the PM. It was the same environment that set the stage for the terrorists' bomb-plot itself.

France

It would be a reasonable statement to say that for many years, actually decades, Saddam Hussein, was a barbarian and a terrorist, a base dictator and a murderer. However the French always seemed to have a close and supportive relationship with him. Always it seemed so as to develop markets. Unfortunately the markets were for sophisticated armaments. The French supplied Saddam with billions of dollars worth of advanced fighter jets, missiles and nuclear reactors and their cores (that Israel fortunately later destroyed). Jacque Chirac, the current French Prime-Minister repeatedly called Saddam "friend" and consistently helped him skirt UN sanctions after the Gulf War. Many subsequent investigations revealed that Chirac, unforgivably, shared with Saddam classified U.S. and UN data right up to the invasion of Iraq. (8) What can a "world leader" expect to achieve from actions and policies that are blatantly illegal and immoral and that undercut the policies and well being of allies?

"French diplomacy today continues to consider Iraq as a cake to be divided and not as a democracy to be constructed." A French diplomat made that statement. (9) Cynicism does not begin to explain the degree of corruption that this statement implies and it is what passes for current French policy.

The Entire West

The war between Hezbollah and Israel should have been the West's finest hour in its war on terrorism instead it was an example of capitulation, cowardice and lost opportunity. Hezbollah (based in Lebanon) secretly infiltrates Israel to kidnap soldiers and kill a number of others while no state of war exists between Lebanon and Israel. Then Hezbollah in response to the Israeli demand for the return of the soldiers rains down hundreds of rockets onto civilian targets killing as many as a couple of hundred Israeli citizens. For once the entire world decries this act of aggression against Israel and states that Israel has every right to defend itself.

Setting the stage for this attack on Israel, the Hezbollah rocket launching locations were installed over a period of six years under the noses of the existing U.N. "peacekeeping" force. In fact one of the rocket batteries was visible by the "naked eye" from a U.N. "look-out" site. The U.N. did nothing and said nothing. (One might ask what were they actually doing for six years or "looking out for".) Further as is normal for terrorist operations the rocket batteries were purposefully set up in civilian populated areas thereby assuring the maximum propaganda return when Israel counter-attacked. Of course the legal Lebanese authorities knew this but did and said nothing also. They were "shocked" later on when there were so many civilian casualties.

Israel invades! The purpose: destroy Hezbollah's ability to launch rockets at Israel. Sounds reasonable to me. The air war is less effective than planned and extensive bombing continues followed by an even more extensive ground force. The world's generosity in the form of recognizing Israel's right to defend itself ends at this point. The condemnation of Israel is overwhelming because Israel used "disproportionate aggression" against Hezbollah. (Only a lunatic could think that when fighting for your life you shouldn't use too much force.)

Compounding the problem Ehud Olmert, perhaps the weakest Israeli PM in history flounders and caves in to the international pressure and his own indecisiveness and diminishes the fighting after hampering the Israeli Defense Force (IDF) from achieving a real victory.

And the ever-inconsistent Mr. Bush buys into the absurd "peace process."

Instead of Israel destroying Hezbollah (a boon to the West and a set back for Iran–Hezbollah's "bank" and major supporter–often through Syria), Israel is in effect pressured into negotiating with Hezbollah. Given the history of negotiations in general and Israel's almost isolated position, at this point Israel could only loose considerably more than it could possibly gain. Perhaps they will get the kidnapped troops back, other than that, does anyone seriously think that Hezbollah will disarm (a part of the agreement). Syria may swear to stop arming Hezbollah if Syria gets the Golan Heights. The Golan is the area from which Syria rained down rockets on Israel in an earlier war. Israel will have to be crazy to give up the Golan. Such is the nature of fighting wars that are not aimed at winning, a current staple in the West's arsenal of suicide tactics. We always lose far more than we ever gain.

How can a peace accord be signed by Israel (and instigated and supported by the West) with an enemy whose position is so clearly stated and constantly reiterated and is so well known by all participants in the process, i.e. Hezbollah's avowed intention to destroy Israel.

> "Either we destroy Israel or Israel destroys us."

So said the most senior cleric for Hezbollah, Husayn Fadlalah.

It is easy to see why Jacque Chirac is supporting this peace negotiating position after all as a demonstration of French "astuteness" the French foreign minister Philippe Douste-Blazy, talking about Iran while in Beirut declared, Iran is "a great country, a great people and a great civilization which is respected and which plays a ***stabilizing role in the region***." (Emphasis added.) (10) This is like saying that in 1938 Nazi Germany was playing a "stabilizing role" in Europe. But why is the President of the U.S. supporting this bogus process? There again is the endless inconsistency of the U.S. government. And if President Bush wasn't supporting it perhaps Olmert wouldn't either. Israel is fighting for its life and the West is " diddling" at self-defeating politics. As of this writing every indication is that this peace agreement will go the way of all the others but even if it sticks it will only be for as long as Hezbollah or other Islamic groups deem it advantageous. Then they will resume hostilities.

If there were a "gong show" for Western Diplomatic stupidity it would be won by the West's practice of "having talks about talks". The development of a nuclear bomb by Iran is the issue. Iran claims they need to develop a nuclear capability for peaceful energy generation. Iran is also the third largest producer of oil in the Middle East with vast reserves but they do not have the ability to refine it. Why not develop oil refineries? You can't blow up Israel with an oil refinery and they have sworn to nuke Israel. Yet we pay credence that Iran won't develop a bomb.

For some reason the West seems to think we have to negotiate with this ultimate terrorist state over this issue; this is bad enough. But then we must first hold talks about what the talks will talk about when we finally talk to Iran. That is carrying diplomacy to the point of insanity. Its as though as long as talks are going on no one will have to face the real issue and deal with it.

Déjà vu! In 1934 the talks between Hitler, Chamberlain and Daladier began. In 1938 they were still talking about what they needed to talk about. Germany in that same period built the world's greatest fighting machine and Britain and France celebrated the peace they achieved by talking.

It may sound like the author is pushing for war with Iran. The answer is not necessarily but the West must get its act together or there will definitely be a war but it will be at Iran's time of choosing.—

And topping the cynicism list is another British intellectual's thoughts on the desirability of terror and chaos so as not to achieve boredom. Timothy Garton Ash writes:

> "even if it were possible for the United Nations to be composed entirely of crypto-Americas [i.e., democracies], this would be deeply undesirable, on grounds of, so to speak, the biodiversity of world politics-not to mention sheer boredom." (11)

Let us not cause Mr. Ash boredom so instead we should strive to keep millions of people living under dictators of endless varieties. As I said before "what is in these people's heads?"

We are faced with an unyielding and ruthless enemy and we meet it with irrational behavior, contradictions, greed, corruption and a total lack of consistency. And this is what passes for policy! Well it is policy but unfortunately it is policy that supports Islam not the West.

35 The Lack of Consistency in Foreign Policy

The U.S. seems to alternate between appeasement in the form of useless negotiations and strong response, either militarily or politically. Europe seems to know only appeasement unless pressured into reluctantly helping the U.S. The one thing we don't have in our foreign policy is consistency. The one thing a country needs more than anything else when fighting a fanatical adversary for survival is consistency. Nothing is achieved in a strategic context without a well thought out and focused strategic policy consistently executed. And we come up short. (A policy defined by consistent focus on a strategic goal does not mean that it cannot be flexible in terms of the exigencies that arise in world politics. It is the goal that cannot change and the driving will to achieve that goal.)

George Habash, a Palestinian terrorist, stated in an interview with Oriana Fallaci over 30 years ago

> "the Arab goal was to wage war against Europe and America and to ensure that henceforth there would be no peace for the West."

He further said:

> "the Arabs would advance step by step, millimeter by millimeter, year after year, decade after decade, determined, stubborn and patient. This is our strategy; a strategy that we shall expand throughout the whole planet."

A little foreshadowing of the *Ten Step* process that was about to begin in the West and a very telling and truthful comment. And they haven't stopped. That is consistency. We just don't believe our enemies. Just as we thought Hitler's Mein Kampf was not serious. Or Bin Laden's position as stated in his Manifesto and speeches are not to be taken at face value. Bin Laden and his allies are serious about what they say and they eventually do what they say. Islam works consistently toward its goal. And History has shown that the forward march of Islam is in fact progressing in exactly the way Habash predicted. Unfortunately the West meets the consistency of its avowed enemy with inconsistency and divisiveness.

A brief review of recent history clearly demonstrates that the current inconsistency of the West is "consistent" over a long period and always with deleterious results. But we seem to learn little from history.

After years of appeasement throughout the 1930s by the Western European's eternal optimists, Hitler was convinced that Western European's failure to stop any of his forward encroachments on independent countries signaled the fact that they would never fight no matter how many countries he invaded.

Similarly with Joseph Stalin. Immediately after World War II he was encouraged by the rapid demobilization of the United States, which to him meant that the U.S. was unprepared and unwilling to resist him with military force. Stalin broke the pledges he had made at Yalta to hold free elections in the countries of Eastern Europe he had occupied at the end of the war. Instead, he consolidated his hold over them. After Stalin's death, his successors continued to sense a weak American resolve with respect to holding them back. This weak resolve took many forms such as an over reliance on the U.N. and the negotiation paralysis we often found ourselves in. But the worst blow to our image as a power came with our withdrawal from Vietnam. We became isolationist and pacifist sentiment seemed to be rising, which in turn resulted in a significant reduction in military spending. Leonid Brezhnev rightly felt safe from our interfering with his plans and as a consequence he invaded Afghanistan in 1979 with merely vocal reaction from the West and U.N.

The same decline of American power, so completely personified by Jimmy Carter, is in essence what emboldened the Ayatollah Khomeini to seize and hold American hostages, with complete impunity. If you don't think that this is true, stop and think for a moment that immediately after Khomeini's sanction of the storming of the American Embassy the Soviet's invaded Afghanistan. As a result there was an immediate swelling of resentment against the Soviets throughout the Islamic world but especially in Iran since it borders Afghanistan. When moves were made against the Soviet embassy the Khomeini regime extended to the embassy total protection. Why?

It is a matter of record that the Islamic fundamentalists in Iran hated the Soviet Union and Communism as much as they hated the U.S. In fact at this point the Soviets came in last in an Islamic popularity contest because they had just invaded an Islamic country, thereby defiling it. The difference in Khomeini's treatment of the two embassies could not be explained by ideological or political factors. What could and did explain it was his fear of Soviet retaliation. Khomeini clearly remembered the Soviet invasion of Hungary and its brutal repression of all the satellite countries. He did not doubt for a moment that the

Soviet's would immediately invade Iran using its compromised embassy as an excuse. As for the U.S. he could thumb his nose as long as he wanted and we would do nothing. And he was correct. It was Ronald Reagan's election to the White House three years later that caused Khomeini to finally free the hostages a month before Reagan took office. Khomeini recognized that Reagan would not hesitate to go to war over the hostage situation.

Although Reagan would have confronted Iran with military action he also proved to be inconsistent over his years in the White House, most notably in Somalia and Lebanon, certainly not Reagan or Americas finest moments. But what Reagan did do was fulfill his promise to rebuild American military power.

In 1990 Saddam Hussein invaded Kuwait in what was widely known as the first step to control the oil fields of the Middle East. The first Bush president, allied with a determined Margaret Thatcher, Prime Minister of England, stated that they would not abide this gross violation of international law. A coalition force was formed and sent to counter Saddam. In retrospect it seems likely that Saddam, always shrewd would have retreated rather than risk a war with the U.S, but he was emboldened by the wave of hysteria in the United States. The hysteria took the normal form of the prediction that tens of thousands of American bodies would be flown home if we actually went to war with Iraq.

Although Saddam was wrong in the beginning given his assumption of our ability or desire to prosecute the war, in the end he was proven correct. After driving him out from Kuwait we "gave-up" because we dreaded the casualties we would suffer if we went into Baghdad. Totally ridiculous given that we had just defeated the Iraqi army on the battlefield and with little real challenge. "We are not about regime change" was the excuse for not pursuing the dictator. Saddam remained in power for us to have to fight again in the future. Did we really think that leaving him in place was not going to come back to haunt us? But the greater impact was the impression that this act of hesitancy said to Osama Bin Laden.

To Bin Laden this was just one more example of America's lack of resolve and proof that in the end we were a paper tiger, as he often stated. He would witness many other examples of the U.S.'s softness in the face of terrorism, particularly from Clinton's lack of response to the many terrorist attacks Bin Laden instigated against the U.S. during Clinton's presidency.

Which brings us to our current pension for demonstrating inconsistency.

In his own mind, Mr. Bush is totally committed to maintaining offensive military operations against the threat of Islamic terrorism. However he is having many on going problems as a direct result of his policies of inconsistency. Bush may always think he is fighting terrorism but he has funny ways of demonstrating it. The following have been achieved with little to no resistance from the U.S.

- From 2003 to 2006 Iran has invaded and infiltrated the Iraqi Shiite political parties and has caused a great deal of dissension and chaos, *Shari'a* has been imposed in Basra,

- The use of improvised Iranian made charges has become a common way to kill American servicemen in the Sunni triangle in Iraq,

- The Israeli withdrawal from Gaza last summer,

- The Hamas electoral victory in the spring of 2006,

- Twice we could have killed Muqtar Sadr the Head of the Mahdi army in Iraq (and core of the Iraqi insurgency) and didn't because of "public opinion" or Iraqi descent, neither a good reason. And now we fight him once again.

- Bush backed Condalizza Rice's decision to lift restrictions on international banking for Hamas in May 2006,

- Mr. Bush's decision to get behind a "Six Powers" deal to ransom America's nuclear security to Iran, (Basically the United States and the rest of Western Civilization has been in full retreat regarding Iran.)

- Iran's instigation and support in the form of personnel, arms and material for the insurgency in Iraq.

- The Iraqi insurgency (invasion by Shiites from Iran) has greatly destabilized the fledgling "democracy" in Iraq.

- The instigation of the Hezbollah attack against Israel with the ensuing war in Lebanon and the U.S.'s joins the world for calls for negotiations instead of encouraging Israel to destroy Hezbollah.

- Iran's successful launching of a large number of long-range missiles capable of reaching Europe.

- The ascendancy of Iran to become the "most powerful nation in the world." This seems to be the case since Iran is able to do what it want as it wants and no one can do a thing but talk some more. Certainly the U.N. won't nor the Europeans and the U.S. can't since Bush has exhausted his political capital and Americans are "weary". Yet the fact remains that more Americans died in 9/11 than in Iraq so the weariness is really the result of the media hype created gloom more than the actual nature of the situation.

The entire Iraq war has been like fighting a boxing match with one hand tied behind your back. Iran has always been known to be the major problem in the Islamic realm not Iraq. The war we should have been fighting is with Iran. Actually Iran, Syria and Iraq were a central caldron of endless terrorist activity. So we decide to fight just Iraq, no doubt the decision was driven by the same back-home hysteria or political partisanship rather than a common goal of destroying terrorists' strongholds and the nations that instigate and support them. The result: Syria supplies the arms and a safe haven for the "insurgents" fighting in Iraq and did so during the actual war itself. This way the insurgents/terrorists live to fight our troops another day. Iran supplied much of the arms and Shiite fighters and a free flow of material between Iraq and Iran.

> "US officials have said Iran, a Shiite nation, has flooded the predominately southern Shiite areas of Iraq with money and political operators to create a 'greater Iran' more sympathetic to Tehran than to the multiethnic Baghdad. Mr. Rumsfeld said in March that elements of the Revolutionary Guards, which enforce adherence to Iran's radical Muslim theocracy, 'are currently putting people into Iraq to do things that are harmful to the future of Iraq.'" (1)

> "We are quite confident that the Iranians, through their covert special operations forces, are providing weapons, [improvised explosive device] technology and training to Shi'a extremist groups

> in Iraq, the training being conducted in Iran and, in some cases, probably in Lebanon through their surrogates." "They are using surrogates to conduct terrorist operations in Iraq." (2)

It would seem from the above brief history that a better model for our strategic geopolitical goals and actions is absolutely required if we are to achieve a lasting success in the conflict with Islam. The same lack of consistency of vision, constancy of action and accuracy in knowing your enemy just keeps contributing to the next disaster. The West's endless ad hoc actions only result in the draining away of resources and energy much like the adage "death from a thousand cuts."

Our fragmented approach to terrorism is the result of our lack of a cohesive vision of the West's true relationship with Islam. If the view of the relationship with Islam is flawed so also will be our ability to develop a cohesive vision and the appropriate plans to realize that vision.

Reality does not abide contradictions. Sooner or later they catch up to you and you must pay reality's price. Since September 11, the US has kept two terrorist movements arbitrarily compartmentalized: terrorists "of global reach," i.e., those who attack the U.S., Europe and Asia and other terrorists, i.e., those who attack Israel. The first group must be tracked down and wiped out; the second group is to be negotiated with, appeased, even showered with international aid. (Ample evidence exists to prove that Iran belongs in the first group but is also quite active in supporting the efforts of the second group.)

In the wake of this insanity Israel has unilaterally abandoned Gaza to the Palestinians after completing their wall. (A wall to keep terrorists out not a wall to keep people in, as was the Berlin Wall.) The problem however is that bin Laden, having lost his bases in Afghanistan and in Libya over the past few years, needs a new base of operations. He can now move into Gaza. It is perfect, a terrorist state in the middle of the Middle East where anarchy reigns supreme and most males over eight are terrorists and many women as well. Under our current policy al-Qaeda can't be attacked inside Gaza. The Iranians have realized the same thing. The result is a new buildup of an "Islamist Axis" against Israel right next door and a new fountainhead of terrorist activity.

And almost immediately the Islamist Axis begins its new work. For the first time Hamas (Palestinian) terrorists were arrested in Jordan while attempting an attack outside of Israel/Palestine. Hamas has always been a local group–you can think of them as "your neighborhood terrorists." With this incursion into Jordan they have taken their first step to becoming not only members of the new axis but a group capable of advancing the global *jihad* and joining al-Qaeda, Hezbollah, Iran and Syria.

> "Adel, who has been operating from Iran since the battle of Tora Bora in November 2001, is reportedly Zarqawi's commander in Iraq and al-Qaida's senior liaison with the Iranian regime. In his manuscript he laid out al-Qaeda's intentions for the third stage of the *jihad*. He explained that the organization needed new bases and was looking for a failed state or states to settle in. Darfur, Somalia, Lebanon and Gaza were all identified as possible options." (3)

However;

> "US forces together with the Kenyans and the Ethiopians have pretty much prevented al-Qaeda from basing in Somalia or Darfur. That left only Lebanon with all its problems with its various political factions, overlords and the UN. But then suddenly, like manna from Heaven, Israel simply gave them the greatest gift al-Qaeda ever received when Ariel Sharon decided to give them Gaza." (4)

Notice how once again we had to fight in Somalia. It always comes around. If we listen to the current group of politicians and activists telling the U.S. to pull out of Iraq we will no doubt be back again in the future. The same man who petitioned for our withdrawal from Somalia and Lebanon is doing it again.

> "The thing that disturbed me and worries me about this whole thing is we can't get them (the second Bush administration) to change direction. And I said over and over in debate, if you listen to any of it, in Beirut President Reagan changed direction, in Somalia President Clinton changed direction, and yet here, with the troops out there every day, suffering from these explosive devices, and being looked at as occupiers—80 percent of the people want us out of there—and yet they continue to say, "We're fighting this thing." We're not fighting this. The troops are fighting this thing. That's who's doing the fighting." (5)

Well Rep Murtha (previous quote) is correct about who is fighting and who ran and who wants to run but as models for what to do in Iraq, Somalia and Lebanon are disasters. The retreat from Somalia came back to haunt the U.S. and the entire world. And we are back in there now doing what we stopped doing in the Clinton years. And because Bush 1 left Iraq undone, Bush 2 is back again.

The act of retreating provides evidence to the *jihadists* that the U.S. has no backbone when there are deaths of U.S. soldiers. In Lebanon a terrorist attack on the Marine barracks caused American deaths. The ensuing political frenzy pressured President Reagan to flee despite the fact that the mission was largely succeeding.

An Al Qaeda backed insurrection began in Mogadishu, Somalia. This caused President Clinton to pull U.S. forces out and to turn control over to the United Nations. As a result we got "Blackhawk Down," al Qaeda got Somalia and as second prize we got to return to Somalia by way of Operation Hope that sent 25,000 troops to that country as well as "clandestine operations" mentioned earlier.

How can anyone point to those two incidents and state that they are models? Yes they are models, models of disaster. If Rep. Murtha is sincere in his admiration for these models, then he certainly has questionable values.

I can't say that the Bush policy is ideal by any means and it is clear that there have been many mistakes, as there always are in complex endeavors but with the unlimited lessons of "where weakness got the West in the past", one would think that the loyal opposition would be loyal by supporting the War on Terrorism efforts or by offering real alternative plans that would have specific ideas and steps for a global victory and not just a proposal for cutting and running and endless bromides. The real shame is that bromides seem to carry the day with too many Americans.

On June 21, 2006 there was a vote on just that subject, i.e., cutting and running. There were 44 Democrats voting for various scenarios of retreat

> "But around noon today Senate Democrats showed that they were, in fact, split in three. First, by 86-13, the Senate rejected John Kerry's cut-and-run proposal, which called on the U.S. to flee Iraq a year from next Saturday. Then, by 60-39, they voted down Carl

> Levin and Jack Reed's resolution, which, in Reuters' description, calls on the president "to start withdrawing troops this year but without setting a deadline for completion." (6)

The fact that no one single plan carried the day is good news since all the plans were as weak a set of alternatives as any that could possibly be found. How can the Democrats say: "we support the troops" when in fact the announcement of a withdrawal would do nothing but reinforce the enemies resolve to stay the course until we left. Which in turn would guarantee more deaths of our troops. It would also demonstrate bin Laden's premise that the U.S retreats when the number of dead American soldiers increases. Put another way America lacks the will.

Neville Chamberlain is synonymous with appeasement. However appeasement is simple while historical blindness is really complex and more dangerous. The West is in a feeding frenzy of historical blindness, lethal pragmatism and cultural suicide. Chamberlain by comparison was a paragon of strength. There is no one more despicable than the vacuous "intellectuals" prattling away the West's freedom. These are the ones who deny that we are in the midst of a cultural, political and existential war with Islam, of which terrorism is the ugliest and most violent weapon, but in the long run the one that is the least important.

The determination of Islam is unquestionable. Its execution of the *Ten Steps* is unrelenting, its single-minded purpose at this point obvious but the thing that is most enabling to Islam is the West itself. To solve any of the myriad issues and problems presented herein we must start with the recognition, on the part of the West, that it cannot continue enabling Islam's expansion and that it must recognize the enormous scope of the problem. Undoubtedly this will require overcoming a great deal of political infighting and partisanship in all Western countries. Unfortunately there is no way around the issue. Without recognizing the scope of the problem we will be doomed to fighting battles as Islam wins the war.

VIII

THE MODERATE MUSLIM

Before analyzing the details of possible solutions to the myriad issues raised throughout the book it would be helpful to review the thinking of a potentially powerful ally in the West's struggle, i.e., the moderate Muslim.

36 The Humanist Muslims

The moderate Muslim surely exists, so why do they seem to be so silent or at best mild in their outrage when confronted by the "extremes" of Islam? The examples are endless: the *fatwas* "authorizing" murder of civilians, the *jihad* against the West, the acts of terrorism, the treatment of women, the extremes of corporal punishment, the undermining of the very societies in the West that have provided a home, a refuge and a place to grow to many Muslims.

The answer is two fold. The easy answer is that of fear. The same fear that keeps Europeans, as we have seen, from speaking out, from taking positive action to save them has affected most of the moderate Muslims as well.

Variation from the teachings of Islam, and this includes dissent or speaking out against any aspect of Islam, is met with strict punishment, ostracism and some times even death. The natural dissent, outrage or questioning on the part of intelligent Muslims when confronted with such a void in civilization is all too often silence.

The second reason is more dangerous in the sense that it stems from the religion itself. The very nature of Islam allows no dissent. It is absolute and demanding of obedience to the *Qur'an's* and Hadith's sayings and teachings, it is unbending and all controlling. However the miracle of independent thought and morality-based action is never lost entirely no matter the degree of repression. From the maelstrom that is today's Islam there are voices of reason that are laying down the ideas that need to be part of the diplomatic and political solution for checking Islam's expansion. Here are just a few.

> "In the beginning, there was Man, and he is mightier and more precious than any other value that he has created, including the religions."

> "In the effort to find an answer to life's knotty questions, a man should not think of turning to religion—which, historically, appeared after [mankind] had already come into existence.... Instead, he should gather all available knowledge, and ponder these questions. He may not find satisfying explanations—but surely it is better for him to have the freedom to inquire and to look into various possibilities than it is for him to restrict himself to [a set of] ready-made answers which, [while they may] satisfy temporarily, will permanently paralyze his mind and his thinking."

> "Whether we be Muslim, Christian, Jew, Buddhist, a member of some other faith, or non-religious, we are [all] responsible for our lives, and we must make these [lives] worthy, as civilized human beings.... We must act according to the humane principles of life, in brotherhood and tolerance, and most importantly—we must not let religion, or political authority, take over our lives and turn us into a blindly following herd." (1)

Dr. Ahmad Al-Baghdadi, a reformist Kuwaiti intellectual and political science lecturer at Kuwait University, states that it is the Muslims themselves that are to blame for the growing resentment and hatred directed at Muslims and not bin Laden. He further states that the Muslims have not repaid in kindness to the countries of the West that have taken them in. Instead they follow the extremism of the Mullahs. He adds that:

> "Muslims in the West must declare that they accept Western values and sever their ties with Muslims in the East, and with the religious clerics."

Pakistani-American philosopher Irfan Khawaja, states that:

> "the Muslim communities of North America and the U.K. are perhaps the most remiss when it comes to confronting the reality of what Islam has become, because they "ought to know better"; He further states that: "religious-studies professors in the West criticize every religion on the face of the earth except Islam."

At age five Irfan Khawaja observed that the *Qur'an* preached:

> "an ideology I did not think anybody could adopt in good conscience."

Ibn Warraq was born and raised a Muslim. In later life he broke with the extreme nature of Islam and its teachings and became a humanist and secularist. In 1995 he wrote a book *Why I Am Not a Muslim.* After the Salman Rushdie *Fatwa*, which he spoke out against he said:

> "it is rare in one's life that one has an opportunity to show on what side of an important life and death issue one stands, the Rushdie issue and the rise of Islam are two such issues and this book is my stand."

He further stated:

> "The horrendous behavior toward women, non-Muslims, heretics, and slaves manifested in Islamic civilization was a direct consequence of the principles laid down in the Koran and developed by the Islamic jurists. Islamic law is a totalitarian theoretical construct, intended to control every aspect of an individual's life from birth to death." (2)

And:

> "Islam is a threat, and it is a threat to thousands of Muslims."

Aayan Hirsi Ali the Somalia-born former member of the Dutch parliament we discussed in earlier chapters always travels with bodyguards because she is under constant death threat. The reason: her strong critique of radical Islam and the European policies that help it grow. Hirsi Ali emphatically says that:

> "In Europe, there is a tendency to appease radical Muslims. We have forgotten how to draw the line." She also says that Muslims must openly debate why their religion has provided justification for acts of terrorism. And Europeans need to debate why they have failed so badly at assimilating immigrant communities, especially those that practice Islam.

From a Saudi journalist:

> "Arab writers and columnists have a tendency to affirm populist notions, whether they're good, bad, factual or false. They write what people want to hear. They write not to educate or challenge the readers' notions, but rather to affirm the readers' preconceived opinions and views. These types of character-driven, pandering scribes care only about elevating themselves and winning the sympathy of their fans.
>
> If a columnist runs out of ideas, there's always one ace in the deck, one thing that is bound to get a cheer from the choir. It's almost too easy. Out of ideas for the day? Simply write an article cursing the United States of America! That's an easy way to earn a day's pay.
>
> Never mind entering the difficult path of hard research and analysis of problems in our society, or in their society, or problems shared by both societies. Forget about it. It's too easy to toss out some hackneyed diatribe against America....
>
> Our society is one that lacks dialogue and rejects the mere concept of criticism...In our society, criticism is a synonym for defamation. (3)

And in a recent work:

> "Today, modern Muslims are attempting to usher a similar reformation of Islam by re-interpreting, not rejecting the Holy Koran

> (many are ready to renounce the Hadith). They call the process "rediscovery", for it is based on the assumption that modern notions of tolerance, liberty and civil rights can be found in the scriptures if searched for by creative minds.
>
> "In this process, one tends to downplay bloody verses as narrowly contextualized, and amplify peaceful verses as central and intentional, even if it means working against the traditional Islamic rules of abrogation (i.e., priority setting)." (4)

There is no point in history that does not have its enlightened thinkers. The Arab philosopher al-Kindi said:

> "We ought not to be ashamed of applauding the truth, nor appropriating the truth from whatever source it may come, even if it be from remote races and nations alien to us. There is nothing that beseems the seeker after truth better than truth itself." (5)

These moderate Muslims expressed different reasons for questioning Islam. The key element for all of them however was the process of thinking that took place for them to arrive at the point at which they formed dissenting positions. One man has taken this thinking one step further and put forth a set of proposals for reforming Islam itself.

37 The 27 Proposals for Reforming Islam

In his book *Manifesto for an Enlightened Islam*, Malek Chebel states that he loves Islam and it is this reason why he believes it is essential that Islam, as it is perceived and practiced by fundamentalists today, must be reformed. The title of his book expresses the concept of an "Enlightened Islam" which to him means that Islam is not against progress. Chebel further asserts that in today's Islamic world there are only two ways the population deals with the phenomena of dictatorship. One of them is to do nothing and this is where the majority can be found. The major reason why this is the response of the majority is because they do not possess the knowledge of the wider world in general and specifically their knowledge of the religion is based solely on what they are told by the imams. The second group turns to Islamism as ***a reaction to the dictatorships***. The social strata of this group cuts across all levels of Muslim society. The tragedy is that once these men turn to Islam as a cause they have bought into the extreme position taken by the fundamentalists, even to the point of being capable of becoming martyrs. (This is clearly one of the strongest practical reasons why the U.S. policy of supporting dictators is at best ill informed and short sighted.)

Although the following points are only a summary of Mr. Chebel's recommended reforms they do provide a reasonable insight and guide to the understanding of Islam as it is practiced today. (1)

1 A New Interpretation of the *Qur'an*:
The modern interpretation of the *Qur'an* must answer the questions regarding Islam that are relevant in a modern advanced civilization. It is only through this means that Islam can be adapted to the needs of the modern world.

2 The Preeminence of Reason over All Forms of Thought and Beliefs:
The Islamic world in general has a tendency to deny science and progress. Religious education must be adapted to the realities of the modern world.

3 Society Must Be Managed by Politics Not Religion:
The secularization (Ilmaniyya) of the society, i.e., the separation of the church and state is critical. Chebel correctly notes that it was

only after the Western world separated secular life from the Catholic Church did the phenomenal progress experienced in the West occur.

4 Investing In Man:
"There is no better way of approaching God than by allowing for the fulfillment of His most beautiful creature, Man," writes Chebel, adding: "Islam will remain forever a religion of the poor if its elite do not strive to place Man at the center of the social apparatuses." Chebel further states: "Investing in Man" also means fighting discrimination based on race or gender, fighting ignorance, and promoting education."

5 The Preeminence of the Individual Over the Community:
In the current world of Islam the community prevails over the individual. This has created a situation where the private sector, both economic life and self-expression, has not had the environment critical to its evolution. Chebel further states: "free choice allows for individual responsibility, which in turn allows for progress."

6 Freedom of Thought and Conscience Must Become a Muslim Virtue:
Islam has placed all Muslims in the identical mold thereby not recognizing differing degrees of religious fervor and individualism. Any manifestation of these qualities is met with accusations of "non believers," an anathema in current Islam. Islam must evolve to a new level of humanism thereby enabling freedom of individual conscience.

7 Respect for the Other:
A retelling of the "do unto to others as you would have others do unto to you." Chebel points out that in today's world of Islam, Muslims demand that the West respect its practices but will not reciprocate in Islamic countries. Mosques are built all over the western world but churches cannot be built in a Muslim country, etc. If the Islamic world is serious about participating in a modern society then it must do so on an equal plane.

8 Declaring Jihad Useless and Obsolete:
Chebel asks: "Is it possible to replace war with peace?" and answers: "*Jihad* should be declared illegitimate since it entails death, which is not a noble thing in the eyes of the Koran, and also because it is used

to justify all kinds of aggression." Further he states: "I believe no other religion spends as much money for its armament, relatively, as does the Islamic world." He adds: "there is no redistribution of wealth, and when there is, it only concerns the construction of mosques." Money is better spent on furthering the needs of peace.

9 Abolishing All Fatwas Calling for Death:
No individual should be allowed nor be capable of issuing a death sentence on another. No individual should be above the courts and law of the land. (Author's note: If the religious and the secular are split then *Shari'a* becomes a religious entity only and therefore not responsible for governing the country as it is today. It would then be illegal for a *fatwa* to be issued concerning anything other than issues of a philosophical and theological nature.)

10 Promoting the Status of Women:
The practices of polygamy, forced marriages, child brides, the killing of rape victims, female genital mutilation, etc. must be banished. Islam has so denigrated women that only the strongest political action can begin to improve the treatment of women, e.g., civil laws need to be changed that recognize a woman's rights.

11 Abolishing Corporal Punishment:
The most barbarous punishments are meted out for many crimes. Stoning, amputations, tongue removal, flogging, etc. do not belong in a civilized society.

12 Banning Genital Mutilation:
Since there is no basis for the practice in the *Qur'an* and very little in the Hadiths the practice should be purged from the religion.

13 Punishment for Honor Killings:
Women should be given freedom of choice including choices in love. There should also be a ban against all so-called honor killings.

14 Modernizing the Civil Law and the Personal Code:
Islamic jurisprudence (fiqh) prevents Islam from being progressive. In turn this hinders any actions involved in promoting peace and

tolerance. Chebel advises the abolition of fiqh, which has become the armed wing of the religious oligarchy, and replacing it with a new set of "laws" tailored to a modern world. His bottom line is that the most barbarous aspects of *Shari'a* must be renounced.

15 An Independent Judiciary:
Most often in the Muslim world the judiciary is subordinate to the political power of the country (which is often the religious power as well). Chebel advises to allow it to be independent. This in turn will promote wider justice for all.

16 Free Access to Sounds and Images:
There is no justification for not allowing free expression and for the free exchange of information, music and art.

17 Fighting the Phenomenon of Political Assassination in an Effort to Promote Democracy:
There is no legitimacy in the *Qur'an* for using political assassination. In the modern Islamic world there have been over 150 such assassinations.

18 Eliminating the Cult of Personality in the Islamic World:
Chebel writes: "The cult of personality (in Islamic countries) is a cancer that blocks political life in most Muslim and Arab countries." The cult of personality is used to serve the anti-democratic regimes. All power, communications, etc. are used to keep the "leader" in power.

19 Firm Sanctions Against Corruption:
There will always be corruption in the absence of accountability mandated by laws. This will be a first step toward democracy.

20 Investing in the Field of World Administration:
Muslims must join the international debate on world administration by reaching solidarity with those countries and promoting an interreligious dialog.

21 Banning of Slavery and All Other Trafficking in Human Beings:
Slavery is still wide spread in the Muslim world declares Chebel and

it must be ended. The organizations that monitor and are against slavery must speak out and demand its end. (Chebel includes in his definition of slavery the caste system in the Tuareg and Sahel regions and in Mauritania.)

22 Promoting a Work Ethic:
Work must be promoted as a positive value. This is not the case now.

23 Ending Usury:
As a result of the exploitation of their people, Muslim leaders realize huge gains.

24 An Active Policy Regarding New Technology:
In fields requiring technical knowledge Muslims depend on the West. Islamic countries invest the least in education. Funding of science and technology and concomitant education is essential if Islam is to join the modern world.

25 Defining a Clear Bioethics Policy:
Issues surrounding abortion, birth control, contraception and euthanasia must be discussed and in a moral context.

26 Protecting the Environment:
Because of their technological backwardness Muslims do not care enough about the environment. Education should instill respect for the environment as well as archeological sites. The tragedy of the destruction of the giant Buddhas at Bamiyan, Afghanistan must never reoccur.

27 Promoting Play:
Recreation in the form of games, playing, sports, theater, artistic creation, etc. is a factor in personal fulfillment. The implicit ban against most of these activities must be lifted. The resulting effect will spur employment as well as aid in the feelings of well being so important to a developing society.

Chebel further states in his book, that the future of Islam will lie with its children. However without reforming the education system their potential cannot be realized. The common values of man must be stressed and the violence of Islam must be a thing of the past.

A closing thought from an Islamic thinker Ibn Warraq from *Why I Am Not A Muslim*:

> "Polemic denunciation of Western "materialism" also blinds Muslims to the spiritual achievements of the West and denies Muslims access to the rich heritage of Europe that should be the patrimony and cause of pride to all mankind, as much as the rich architectural heritage of Islam, for example, is the cause of human pride and wonder. The music of Mozart and Beethoven, the art of the Renaissance should be as much the object of study in Islamic seats of learning as Islamic philosophy. Secularism should open up the intellectual horizons of Muslims who at present, are fed a daily diet of misrepresentation of what the Western culture stands for."

The thought expressed by Warraq and the twenty-seven proposals put forth by Chebel are the tip of the philosophical iceberg that must be used as a "weapon" in this war. The West must, while being inclusive of the moderate Muslims, work toward achieving, through diplomacy, political pressure and proselytizing for the realization of the thoughts expressed in the "27 proposals" and by the moderates.

VIII

SOLUTIONS

38 The Elusive Solution

The entire world is currently engaged in a war of enormous breadth and diversity. We must recognize this fact and recognize that the West's opponent in this war is Islam itself not just some shadowy group of fanatical murderers. The shadowy group–terrorists - is the symptom not the cause. We are fighting an ideology centered on world conquest; a religion determined to engulf the world. The West, Europe and America, and many countries throughout Asia and Africa are struggling to accommodate a culture that is the antithesis of almost everything the Age of Enlightenment has stood for and achieved through the centuries.

Many counter measures and policies dealing with the problem of Islamic expansion and its quest for dominance do exist in ad hoc fashion. These tactical programs are not enough to win the war. The programs must become part of an integrated strategic whole operating at several levels simultaneously and aimed at curtailing the Islamic *Ten Step* program. The battle must be fought on the *philosophical,* the *political,* the *cultural* and the *economic levels* as well as *militarily.* Think of it as a "Five Step Counter Program." These categories must work in concert and form the only context within which the West will build and deploy the specific programs to achieve success. The actual operation of the plan requires discipline and consistency and the support of our societies. It also requires above all else the need to understand that the battle will take generations to win; there are no short cuts.

The most important aspect of the battle ahead will be fought in the realm of ideas - philosophy. All other programs and actions must flow from the beliefs that are defined in that realm. They are the foundation concepts that formed our society and they are the ones that must drive our battle. If the programs do not flow from a constant rational philosophical framework based on the firm belief in, and acceptance of, the Western values of freedom, individualism, and equality for all under the law, rational self-interest and secularism then the victory will not be ours. The second most important battle line is political. We can win only if we have a consistent political context driving the West's international relationships and actions and based on the belief system and values articulated above not based on the pragmatic and often cynical programs of today. The next battle line is in the realm of economics. The economic weapons are essential and important but again they need to operate as a whole and in a rational political framework aimed at driving the West toward energy independence and simultaneously undercutting Islam's expansion. The least important confrontation with Islam, but only on a comparative basis, is the military engagements that undoubtedly will be necessary. These need to be viewed as essential to fight and absolutely vital to win and to win decisively and overwhelmingly. There is no partial victory that is a true victory.

39 Philosophy

IS PHILOSOPHY IMPORTANT?

It seems that the prevailing opinion held today is that formal philosophy is not terribly relevant to the modern world and is more often than not thought to be a game of semantics. Unfortunately the universities do little to dissuade this opinion. It would be truly useful to students to study philosophy in the context of its influence on societal formation by, for example, the creation of real and practical models of societies and life styles based on differing philosophical frameworks. In turn this might demonstrate the efficaciousness of particular philosophical models for evolving successful life sustaining societies. Be that as it may the reality is that philosophy is the essence and foundation of every thought, belief and action a human has and takes in life and as such is at the core of human existence.

The world of Islam offers a compelling example of the incredibly dramatic impact of philosophy on a society over time.

There was a period in history when Europe was in a dark age of ignorance and superstition and Islam was creating a golden age of knowledge and progress. Between the seventh and twelfth centuries Islam had not only created an empire that was greater in scope then Rome at its zenith but was also a great civilization of learning and progress.

> In astronomy they invented the astrolabe that led to a breakthrough in the knowledge of the heavens.
>
> In the field of architecture, the Arabs created some of the most beautiful buildings ever made by man: the Taj Mahal, the Blue Mosque, the Umayyad Mosque in Damascus is thought to be a "jewel of architecture." These architectural achievements stretched from central Arabia through Iran, Tunisia, Egypt, Morocco, Turkey and Afghanistan. The Shrine of Khoja Nasr Parsa in Balkh possesses an "unearthly beauty." Structures of this beauty can still be seen throughout the Islamic world.
>
> In the field of medicine, Islam created the first hospital and developed professional standards for physicians. They even created an encyclopedia of medical information. The first medical textbooks

> were created and later formed the foundation of European medicine and chemistry.
>
> In the field of mathematics the Arabs created the oldest works on arithmetic and algebra. In literature endless stories and poems still enchant the world: The Thousand and One Nights, The Rubaiyat, The Conference of the Birds, endless amounts of poetry. Books on politics, zoology, food, history, humor, there were few subjects that went unaddressed.
>
> Even in the field of music, treatises on music theory were written as well as an extensive body of music.
>
> And most importantly they rescued and kept alive the works of Aristotle and Plato, and many of the finest Greek writers. All of which found their way to Europe over time.

The period was a veritable renaissance. Why? The Islamic society of the day had at its foundation a philosophy of learning and openness. They possessed "unique assimilative powers" says Bernard Lewis. Many of the marvels of the age were contributed to by a wide spectrum of people living in the Islamic empire: Christians, Jews, and many other peoples. It seems that the idea was important not the source. The Muslims combined what they derived from non-Muslims and evolved new things, be it buildings, science, the arts, etc.

> "From its origins, philosophy in Islam, just as in Christendom, strove mightily–and with notable success–to reconcile faith and reason. Islamic philosophy according to Muslim apologists Mohamed Azad and Bibi Amina 'recognized no theoretical limits other than those of human reason itself; and it assumed that the truth found by unaided reason does not disagree with the truth of Islam when both are properly understood.'" (1)
>
> "It is to the eternal glory of medieval Islam that it succeeded for the first time in the history of human thought in harmonizing and reconciling monotheism with Greek philosophy." (2)

The great and lethal problem with this last premise is the fact that the works of reason, logic and the scientific method would, under careful scrutiny, clearly clash with the central concepts of the *Qur'an*. And this is the salient thought; of course if one rationalizes these *Qur'anic* declarations, i.e., places them solely in the realm of the spiritual rather than the temporal one might then balance the *Qur'an* with the philosophies in question. This is however quite a stretch and was never undertaken by Islam and therefore it eventually proved to be Islam's undoing.

The literalists (those in favor of the literal interpretation of the *Qur'an*) in effect "fought back." Many contemporary philosophers argued that the *Qur'an* is the word of Allah and cannot be equivocated. The debate reached its culmination after many years with the advent of *The Incoherence of the Philosophers* by Abu Hamed al-Ghazali. In his work al-Ghazali, an accomplished writer and learned *Qur'anic* scholar argued, using the words of the *Qur'an*, against any "interpretation" of the *Qur'an*. The words of the *Qur'an* must be taken as the literal word of Allah and as such there can be no equivocation or reconciling with other thinkers. Al-Ghazali's work was widely and positively received by the traditionalists and spread its way through the Islamic culture just as all ascendant philosophies do; slowly and inexorably. Over time the reigning philosophy that had made Islam great began to become less and less thought of as a positive model and foundation for an Islamic state and became more and more suspect. Over the next decades the actualization of the literalness espoused in *The Incoherence of the Philosophers* became like a dark cloud covering the sun of reason.

By the eleventh century Islam became fixed in a permanent mindset of anti-intellectualism.

> "The *Qur'an* is a perfect book. What other book do I need? What other books are worth reading?" (3)

Essentially nothing has changed in the intervening millennium. The greatness that was the Islam of that all too brief period was destroyed because the society led by its intellectuals accepted the wrong philosophy and in turn the population of Islam upheld it and lived it. With this as a real life example of how philosophy is in fact a very central and foundational component to a successful society the question becomes how does philosophy become a tactical weapon.

THE PHILOSOPHY—A WEAPON

The question that must often occur to many Westerns, but more specifically to Americans, must be why is it that a large number of Muslims in general and all the "fundamentalist" in particular, hate America so intensely? Many answers are given such as support for Israel and the presence of American troops in Islamic countries being on the top of the list. Both of these are certainly true at some level but neither is the core reason. The essential reason exists in the realm of culture and more importantly in the philosophy that underlies that culture. America's philosophical foundation is the absolute antithesis of Islamic philosophy, America is *individualistic* and Islam is *collectivist;* one is reason based and one is mystic based. Prior to examining these fundamental differences a look at the "pragmatic hatreds" is actually quite revealing.

Near the top of the list of pragmatic reasons to hate America is U.S. imperialism. However as Bernard Lewis points out Russian imperialism, including the Soviet Union's harsh suppression of Islam within its borders has been a far more detrimental factor in the lives of Muslims than anything America has ever done. Yet criticism of Russia by Islamic leaders has never attained the level of vitriol that is reserved for America or Israel. Worse yet many Muslim countries hypocritically refused to condemn the Soviet invasion of Afghanistan and in fact the PLO was quite open in its defense of the invasion. Furthermore in terms of Muslim deaths the Iran-Iraq War caused considerably more death and destruction than all of the Arab-Israel wars and their subsequent on going conflicts combined. And this too received little condemnation. This would seem to indicate that there is something else contributing to the hatred beyond "imperialism."

Since it would seem reasonable to state that imperialism isn't really the basis for such extreme hatred perhaps its support of Israel. And in fact this issue, although not the bulls-eye, does bring us closer to the core reason.

From the Islamic perspective, Israel has no right to exist anywhere in the Middle East - period. A non-Islamic country cannot exist in the "land of Arabia" (from the *Qur'an*). For Islam this is not a point of negotiation. Therefore effectively Islam expects the West to capitulate to the Islamic destruction of Israel justified solely on a seventh century religious statement and thereby ignoring all preceding and intervening history, wars, treaties, U.N. resolutions and basic humanity.

There is no question that the world of Islam hates Israel for the religious reason of Jews being perceived as the dajjal (the equivalent in Islam of the anti-Christ) as well as the historical enmity that has existed against the Jews for centuries. Both of these are true and neither is the fundamental reason that the leaders of the Islamic world truly hate Israel, just as imperialism is not the real reason Islamic leaders hate America. The masses are fed this "party line" continually and believe it but that is not what their leaders care most about. For this we must return to philosophy.

America is a country that is "individual centric." Individual human rights are paramount and the state is meant to be a servant of the people and a guardian of those rights. America is also the most powerful nation in the world and as such poses a potentially significant threat to the expansion of Islam if America ever decided to truly use that power against Islam. America is also still a beacon to all those who cherish freedom, and freedom is not compatible with Islam in any way. Islam is collectivist; the individual has zero status in the Islamic culture, ergo the push for *Shari'a* over any secular system of objective law wherever Islam is found. America is the philosophical opposite pole from Islam and as such from Islam's perspective it is completely incompatible and must be destroyed. Exacerbating the obsession with our destruction is the way so many aspects of our culture are so easily adopted by so many countries around the globe even many people living in the Middle East find American culture magnetic. This is a real and deadly challenge to Islam and they cannot abide it. Coexistence with Islam in its current form is impossible.

In one very real sense Israel is similar to America, certainly in the realm of human rights it is a country that recognizes every aspect of an individual's life as sacred and it supports the individual's expression of that life. For Islam to succeed in its push for dominance it must destroy the very concepts that underlie the development of the West and which are paramount in America and central in Israel. (At one point Europe would have been included in this context but they have so diluted their freedoms and strength in a march toward collectivists beliefs while simultaneously enabling the Islamic insinuation into their culture that they are no longer viewed as a serious threat to Islam. In addition the *Ten Step* program is so far advanced in Europe it is near impossible for the Europeans to stop it at this point.)

Not only is Israel a Western country but it is also positioned in Islam's vital center. Israel cannot be permitted to exist as an example of freedom and human rights in the midst of nations that are dominated by the most repressive religion in existence today. In the world of Islam there is no concept of human rights but there is universal support and acceptance of polygamy, child marriage, the subordination of women, inequitable divorce laws, the death penalty for apostates, the oppression of *infidels,* physical punishment and even slavery. No justification of the validity of these practices need be stated beyond the fact that they are all sanctioned and even exhorted by the *Qur'an*. Islamic scholars throughout the ages, since the end of the Islamic "renaissance" over a thousand years ago, have so said. Islam accepts the *Qur'an* as Allah's given word to be followed not argued with or discussed.

The existence of a society based on individual freedom for all residents, citizens and immigrants alike, in all of their personal choices in every aspect of their life, life style, sexual preferences, marriage choices and beliefs is an effrontery to Islam and everything that is central to Islam's dogma. The Islamic religious and political leaders cannot allow the extremes of these two societies to exist in the minds of its followers without casting the ***non-Islamic society as evil–as infidel***. All the hatred and vitriol heaped upon America and to an extent Israel is to offset the disturbing contrast so obvious between the two worlds and the lives of its respective citizens. And every teaching of the *Qur'an* supports their position.

Perhaps the Islamic intellectuals understand this dramatic difference far better than do the intellectuals in the West, even the ones that are not essentially anti-American. Western intellectuals see the stark contrast of human existence under the West and under *Shari'a* and then fail to extrapolate that the polarization dramatized by that comparison is philosophically based (individualism - free men and capitalism - free markets vs. collectivist–state and mystic domination of man and markets). The Western intellectuals constantly castigate the very philosophical base upon which the Western side of the contrast rests. Thereby creating a climate wherein the very causes of our freedoms come under suspicion from the population. One sees this in every utterance, program and preference coming from the liberal educational and political establishments. So, one might ask what is their motive? Do they really prefer the philosophy of the collectivist Islamic norm of absolute dictatorship of the masses? Or are they so blind to the connection between the philosophical base and the society that evolves from it? The answers could very well run the gamut of both extremes and the many steps between. The end result is the same, a consistent undercutting of the American culture and an enabling support for our enemies.

The next logical question is how can we win against a determined, constant and patient enemy driven by a fanatical set of beliefs if we cannot even abide by the very tenets that made us great? The answer is we can't, not without the same sureness of our morality and the rightness of our cause that were the contextual beliefs and hallmark that built this country and saw it through a century of war. We are being defeated from within. This too is a philosophical defeat just as was the victory of Islam's absolutist philosophy over the ideas of the Islamic renaissance over a millennium ago.

As for the economics, the standard of living and the wealth in a nation are the result of its economic system that in turn is based on its foundational philosophy. Without the philosophy that evolved from The Age of Enlightenment - the principles of individualism, human rights and freedoms, etc.- the economic miracle that was achieved would never have been. It is the free mind of man working in a realm of freedom that created the miracle of today's Western World. There is no greater morality than that achievement. Why morality? Because to create a system that provides the greatest good for the greatest number of people, more than has ever been achieved in history, to extend the human life span, to improve the health and well being of hundreds of millions of people represents a greater moral value than any and all of what Islam has ever achieved since its inception.

We in the West often seem to have forgotten it and some have never known it. Not only should we not forget it we should not allow the world of Islam to think that we will abandon it.

In feigned total ignorance of this very premise the new Islamic intellectuals have a mission to obfuscate the greatness and the efficaciousness of Western Culture and individualism by preaching the morality, wonders and peacefulness of Islam, of course as a contrast to the immorality of America. Two American Muslim intellectuals that have personified this thinking are Imam Zaid Shakir and Sheik Hamza Yusuf. They are brilliant at twisting concepts and words to show that Islam is not what it really seems to be. (Step Two of *The Ten Step* program is *Advertise*. Show the enemy how nice Islam is and its compatibility with the West.)

It is important to understand and remember that *Shari'a* subsumes all secular law under the "guidance" of its dictums. With this in mind it is interesting to examine the case of Imams Shakir and Yusuf. These two American born converts to Islam spent extensive time in the Middle East learning from several mullahs and respected Muslim intellectuals. During this process they also became extremely fluent in Arabic and in fact it has been noted that they speak the language at its purest level with appropriate *Qur'anic* grammar and flawless accents. Since they are native born and raised Americans they are as familiar with current pop culture as with Islamic culture. They are enormously charismatic and are excellent public speakers. As such they have developed a great deal of influence and a great following among young Muslims in the U.S.

While leading a mosque in Connecticut, Shakir wrote a pamphlet that cautioned Muslims not to be co-opted by American politics. He said:

> "Islam presents an absolutist political agenda, or one which doesn't lend itself to compromise, nor to coalition building." He also pointed out the effectiveness of "extra-systemic political action." Here he referred to the "armed struggle" that brought about the rule of the Taliban in Afghanistan. (4)

This was their position in 1992. In the intervening years they have evolved a more moderate position, one that condemns terrorism along with U.S military actions that create collateral damage. (The realm of philosophy–*moral relativism*: here they equate a purposeful act of murder with a horrific accident. One incident is by intent and one a very regrettable accident. Shakir is guilty of the moral equivalence that is all too common in today's world.) Be that as it may his message is one of tolerance and peace and that is certainly not heard often in the realm of Islam. However once again, as always, with Islam there is a big but. He also states:

> "'Every Muslim who is honest would say, I would like to see America become a Muslim country ruled by Islamic law.'" He also states that he wishes to achieve this 'not by violent means, but by persuasion.'" (5)

Certainly the declaration of non-violence is a very good thing, however "the but" lies in the Muslims' overriding desire to convert the world, and in this case America to *Shari'a* law. Putting aside for a moment the draconian nature of *Shari'a* let's examine his, and many other Muslims' reasoning. They say that America is a corrupt and bankrupt culture and that we are an immoral people. I will deal with this issue at some length in the Chapter 43 *Culture*, however for now let me merely state that: "beauty is in the eye of the beholder."

What they think is immoral is not necessarily so. To a large extent what Islam sees as immoral is the freedom of movement, expression and action that we in the West hold extremely important to our happiness and well being. That is the essence of our culture. Freedom!

Shakir and Yusuf say that the *Qur'an* holds the essence of morality for all mankind and since *Shari'a* flows from the *Qur'an* it would establish a moral base for behavior. Well if one studies the *Qur'an* it is clear that the areas that deal with moral behavior in a very broad sense are not so different than the Judeo-Christian teachings. (Close enough for our purposes here.) The point is if America is corrupt and the Judeo-Christian ethics have been the foundation of our entire history for many centuries, what is it in Islam that would be so much better. Careful examination of their, and Islam's position in general, yields that it is the use of the stick that will bring about the desired behavior (remember Khomeini's quote). Well what stops the other religions in America from dealing with "immorality" with a stick as well and thereby achieving the same result Islam claims it will achieve? The answer is our individual FREEDOM and our society's separation of church and state.

Another very revealing point of Shakir's and Yusuf's goal of an Islam ruled America is their desire to achieve this "not by violent means, but by persuasion." Indeed! How many people do you know that have all the personal freedoms that Americans enjoy would, if given a choice, choose the repressive form of government that is a product of *Shari'a* in every Muslim country? I imagine that when the choice is against *Shari'a*, the stick that Messrs. Shakir and Yusuf have behind their back becomes quite evident and if resistance persists there is always *dhimmitude* for the *infidels.*

Westerns are not coerced into behavior that they do not wish to follow (within the bounds of an impartial rational secular body of law). *Shari'a* in America could only be achieved by the ***death of our Constitution and The Declaration of Independence.*** Similarly the institutions that still protect what is left of European freedoms would also be destroyed. Messrs. Shakir and Yusuf are like all the statists and dictators that came before them; they believe that morality can be achieved at the "end of a gun!" *Shari'a* in America would destroy America in every sense that Americans have come to understand, live by and all too often take for granted. The fact that Islam thinks the culture is corrupt does not mean that it is or that we think it is. If they are so interested in morality they should preach the elimination of the slavery that is common in many Islamic countries. Eliminate repression of, and violence against women, eliminate all of the terrorists murders of the innocent.

One example of the moral superiority they speak of: the school in Beslan, Chechnya in 2004, where Islamic terrorists killed one hundred fifty children. And before the killings there were three days of torment and torture of the children, withholding water to all of them and then raping and killing the young girls. What degree of twisted religious logic could possibly allow these terrorists to think they were doing Allah's bidding?

When the Shakirs and Yusufs of the world are joined by an out pouring of Islamic protest over barbaric acts like those in Chechnya and 9/11 then let them come and preach to us about moral superiority otherwise they are nothing more than smooth and fast talking con men playing at being shocked by short skirts!

If the West is looking for a weapon against radical Islam it is the continuous articulation of the superiority of Western culture and its underlying philosophy and the loud proclamation of the practical accomplishments that were and are achieved under that philosophy. Further, compare the human condition of living within the West against the human condition of living under *Shari'a* and the type of societies that exist within *dar al-Islam*. We will examine the specifics of the "weapon of philosophy" in the Chapter 43 "Culture."

One Islamic woman summarized the philosophical war between the West and Islam quite succinctly:

> "It's a clash between a mentality that belongs to the Middle Ages and another mentality that belongs to the 21st century. It is a clash between those who treat women like beasts, and those who treat them like human beings." (6)

The un-alterability of our foundational culture, its philosophy, its freedoms, and its institutions and beliefs must be made an irrevocable absolute. It cannot be suspended for any group at anytime for any reason in any context. That is the line in the sand that we must draw. That is the first weapon we have to fight with. That is the philosophy we will not vary from for any reason. That is the greatest weapon we have–the moral certitude of a superior philosophy and the culture it gave birth to and the will to fight for it with every means at our disposal.

40 Political

COMPLACENCY

In the face of an advancing hostile culture the West continues to be complacent, especially in America. Complacent in the sense that we think that this issue of terrorism and Islam will recede into the dark corner from which it came, just give it time. In a very real way we feel that we are invincible. Whether this comes from arrogance or the fact that we are the only super-power is immaterial. It is wrong thinking and it is foolish. We can fall just as Rome fell and the many other civilizations before and after Rome that were, in their day, the dominant civilization. There is no permanence in life, everything always changes. The question is: is this our turn to collapse or do we have a future?

Indeed our complacency is further enhanced by the confusing information we use to form opinions regarding Islam. The President talks about the "religion of peace" and has known terrorist sympathizers working in the White House and the administration and there exists too cozy a relationship with the Saudis. While at the same time he appears to be a staunch fighter of terrorism and in fact he is in many ways. Unfortunately he fights as though terrorism had nothing to do with Islam. The overwhelming voice of the media talks about "fundamentalists" as though they are the exception to a large moderate population of Muslims that are crying out against terrorism. Also the mainstream media spends a disproportionate amount of time bashing America and making it almost seem that the enemy is really not "terrorists" but "insurgents" or "freedom fighters," and that the addressing of grievances will cure the situation. And of course we must always negotiate, even though nothing has ever come form negotiating with Islam. And nowhere does the mainstream media or the intellectuals ever state that we are in a real global war for survival. In fact one must question whether they understand the issue or not.

Further masking the increasing dangers is the fact that we are a nation, and perhaps a World, of sound bites. The depth at which we study or try to understand an issue is too shallow to yield effective and true knowledge. The average person will rightly claim the lack of time as a reason and that he relies on the professionals, i.e., politicians and the "intelligentsia." But both classes have come up far too short to fill the vacuum. The intellectuals have abdicated their responsibility of critical thought and evaluation of issues in broad historical contexts and instead have opted for almost universal agreement within a narrow context of *multiculturalism* and *political correctness*. It seems that it is always “wrong” to speak out against Islam. The universities should be bastions of diverse dialog and differing opinions that bubble over into the national consciousness (as they appropriately were for the Civil Rights era) and thereby help form the national dialog. Instead they have become stale *politically correct* factories of sameness.

The big problem with politicians is that most are not anymore knowledgeable than their constituents when it comes to these complex issues (for some of the same reasons). Alternatively many understand but have hidden agendas. The degree of intensity and volume of dollars spent on lobbying in Washington effectively limits the amount of truth a politician really wants to understand. If he knew the whole story he might not be able to accept the contributions with any degree of maintaining his conscious. I’m sure that this sounds cynical and perhaps it is to some degree but given the diversity and quantity of ill formed, sound bite driven opinions on just the War on Terrorism and Iraq, etc., I am at a loss to believe anything else. And then there is the situation where a good percentage of Congress (this time its the loyal opposition) argues against every piece of legislation that can help our war against terrorism and encroaching Islam without offering concrete alternatives that go beyond political rhetoric. Given this almost lackadaisical approach to Islam how really dangerous can Islam itself be? It would be unusual for the population not to be complacent given an environment of this nature. (Obviously complacency here does not include fear that another terrorist attack will hit America. However that is viewed as a horrific but narrow and transactional event not a threat to our very existence.)

For many of the politicians, intelligentsia and media mainstream it is not that the issue is too complex, it is that it is too clear. The clarity creates a real danger of having to act decisively and strongly and against the grain of mass opinion (opinion they have spent years molding), so better to cloud the real issue with “sidebars of fluff”, the existence of weapons of mass destruction, Abu Ghraib, collateral damage, right wing conspiracies, left wing appeasement, a war that can’t be won, etc. If we are to believe these voices none of which express the degree of alarm that they should be expressing; then why worry about a few fanatics. They can cause damage but little else. We will watch this phenomenon pass as so many others have. That is not the answer History supplies concerning past civilizations that were also trapped in their own myopia and complacency as they collapsed.

With this as the intellectual climate it is near impossible to create a consistent foreign policy. There are just too many divergent positions and agendas. It is the people that have always been the driving force and once again they must rise to this challenge for it is only they that can create the imperative for the needed political agenda, one that is based on the self-interests of the U.S. in full recognition of the life and death struggle that we are involved in.

CONSISTENT U.S. DOMESTIC AND FOREIGN POLICY

The U.S. appears to be fully engaged in fighting terrorism (and most of Europe as well) but at the same time they shy away from fighting the cause and the "generator" of terrorism. As discussed before it is the religion of Islam. Despite the protestations of the Islamic leaders and lobby groups such as CAIR, AMA and the EAD, it is first, last and always the religion itself that from time to time throughout its 1400 year history triggers a new *jihad* for world conquest. It is a religion that, by Islamic scholars own words, must be followed literally because the *Qur'an* is the word of Allah. And the words in the *Qur'an* are quite direct and explicit in their exhortations to world conquest. How many people outside of Islam and particularly in Washington have read any part of the *Qur'an* so that they could better understand where the people that are terrorists and their supporters are coming from? Since many of the dictates within the *Qur'an* express the ideas that the West is fighting, it should be "required" reading for every politician and military officer. This might help form a consistent foreign policy, not necessarily in every detail but at least in terms of direction and recognition of the nature of the enemy.

The first step to achieving consistency in domestic and foreign policy toward Islam should be the elimination of all policies that are inconsistent, perhaps obvious but not easy. In parallel the government must develop a set of long-term bi-partisan strategic objectives and a specific actionable plan that will curtail Islam's expansion. The tragic truth today is that we don't even have a consensus within the Congress of who is the enemy. Everyone has an idea that "terrorism" is an enemy but few even realize that terrorism is a tool not an enemy. It is the highest level of leaders of Islam that manage, fund and leverage the tool that are the real enemies. If you eliminate the "head", the terrorist will dissipate like so much polluted smoke. If we don't eliminate the head we will be fighting terrorism for generations or until they wear us down while their brethren continue to infiltrate and slowly change Western culture. In the end we will lose.

The domestic policy changes must include federally mandated reversal of all publicly funded special accommodations to Islam that in any way impinge on the separation of church and state. Any special requirements the religion of Islam requires must be developed and funded privately as they currently are for Jewish and Christian sects. There can be no difference among religions from the governments' (federal, state and local) perspective. Along with this all religion based and oriented lobbying groups and contributions to politicians must be outlawed. Religion (all religion) has no place in the secular world of government. In the long run special accommodations can only breed contempt, anger and resentment within the population. These are not emotions conducive to the evolution of a harmonious society. Until the War on Terrorism and the expansion of Islam is stopped there should be no Islamic migrations to this country. We have got to understand that being at war with a religion is in many ways no different than being at war with a country. In the ways that it is different we must deal with the exigencies required of us. The most important of these is the safeguarding of tolerance toward Muslim citizens and the protection of their inalienable rights. If America is to hold its head high in this "war" then it must not repeat the mistakes we made with respect to the Japanese citizens in the U.S. during WW II. As I said in my preface to this book the overwhelming majority of Muslims are not the enemy and if Malek Chebel's ideas (27 Things to Change in Islam) begin to take hold they are part of the solution.

Implicit in every aspect of our foreign policy must be the means to achieve our ends; diplomatic, economic, military and we must become as determined and ruthless (not to be confused with belligerent) in the pursuit of our goals as the enemy is with respect to the pursuit of their goals. A policy of this type must span political parties and terms in office. This is not an issue of partisan politics it is a long-term life and death struggle. We must not be afraid to use our strength nor should anything be ventured that does not benefit the U.S. or significantly hurt the enemy. We are too prone to expending resources for too little gain.

The war in Iraq is a perfect example. It is an ill-conceived venture but not for the reasons that are consistently put forth.

Iraq was clearly a state that sponsored terrorism. It was also clearly anti-

American and would do anything to hurt America. It was also feared that Iraq had weapons of mass destruction, and whether you accept that or not it was used as one of the tactical reasons to go to war. The stated "strategic idea" behind the war was to topple the dictator Saddam and replace the regime with a democratic state. A democratic state in the midst of a sea of totalitarian fundamentalism was supposed to ferment unrest in the other states and hopefully expand the influence for democracy throughout the area. The entire plan was one of those ideas that look good on paper but something is lost in translation. The problem was two fold: first it is near impossible and unrealistic to take a people that have lived under a total dictatorship all their lives, and in fact for endless generations and in a part of the world that knows nothing else, and expect them to evolve and prosper in a democratic society overnight. The second reason is Syria and Iran.

Iraq is predominately Sunni and Iran is Shiite. Sunnis and Shiites have been in conflicts for centuries. Because of this Iraq was in effect an excellent counterbalance to Iran's expansionist desires and influence in the Middle East. To topple Iraq without addressing the need to eliminate Iran was simply crazy. One might say that this is hindsight. Not true, there were many people that said exactly this during the buildup to the Iraq war. It was not that the people that said it were any smarter than the administration it was that the administration had to deal with partisan politics. It was a real stretch that we went to war in Iraq at all but to take on Iran as well would have been politically impossible. Ergo we should NOT have gone to war with only Iraq. If we do not have the correct plan and backing for the real and strategic war we are wasting life, resources and time and positioning the country as "trigger happy," and all for little gain.

The issue was and still is that The Congress doesn't get it. They do not yet understand that we are already at war with Iran and have been since 1979. Iran is the central clearinghouse for all terrorism. Hamas, Hezbollah, et al; and now there is evidence that Iran is attempting to take over control of al-Qaeda. Without Iran many of the worst terrorist groups dissolve (unless another state steps up to fill the vacuum and if it does we should destroy that state too).

The entire insurgency in Iraq is funded and supplied by Iran and uses Iran as a safe haven. In the north the insurgents used Syria as a safe-haven and we did nothing about it because of Washington politics. The military watches in frustration and our men are killed or wounded.

So what have we achieved in Iraq. We have in a very real sense gained little (unless we use Iraq's location as Iran's neighbor as a base for operations in the future). We have lost a couple of thousand American soldiers and billions of dollars while Iran now reigns supreme in the Middle East; the Iraqi counterbalance is gone. When the insurgents take over the section of Iraq that borders on Iran, Iran will have also gained much of the Iraqi oil fields. Hezbollah has been dispatched to start a war with Israel (*and the French think that Iran is a stabilizing influence in the region.* It is clear why Islam does not worry about Europe.) And Iran continues its nuclear program essentially unencumbered by the West.

And perhaps worst of all it would appear that because of Iraq, America has lost its taste for war just when that seems to be the only thing that can turn the tide–an all out total destruction of Iran's capability to go nuclear or to ferment terrorism. In short the toppling of the regime just as was done with the Taliban. Many will think that statement absurd, war mongering, lunacy, etc. however that is because we continue to refuse to accept Iran's continued provocations across forty years as acts of war. I guess we are waiting for Iran to get the "bomb."

How much different the outcome would have been had we not gone to war without a total commitment? The issues should have been fought in the realm of politics, if lost in that realm no war would have been better than a half-hearted non-strategic attempt at–(what?) eliminating a dictator. That's not good enough after all we consistently support so many other dictators.

The Taliban is only marginally worse than the dictators we have supported throughout the Middle East and the Islamic world in the past. We like to think of these dictators as better but in truth they are no better and often worse. The repression of their people, and through their policies the assurance that the population will remain largely ignorant, creates a fertile ground for the imams and mullahs to plant the seeds of Wahhbism. This does not say that by freeing them of a dictator and raising their standard of living we could eliminate radicalism. The nature of Islam is what in the end breeds the radicalism; however, experience and history have shown that supporting the dictator has never been to our long-term benefit. While there is a very real danger that through our actions in support of a dictator we are perceived as being hypocritical in that we position ourselves as proponents of democracy. What a self-defeating policy.

Some examples: Egypt, the Shah on Iran, Arafat, even Saddam by Europe. It is also the support we give to these dictators that generates distrust of the U.S. in the minds of the populace being subjugated to the horrors and lack of freedom inherent in such dictatorships. We are supposed to be the example of a free society, how can we hold our heads high and believe this while we support any dictatorship that avows that they will help in the suppression of terrorists. They are terrorists themselves, of the worst kind; they lie about what they are. And where is the citizenry of the West that allow this hypocrisy to pass as policy?

So a good first step (after the destruction of the Iranian regime and its nuclear capability) might be to begin to "do battle" with Saudi Arabia. The official line from Washington is that the Saudis are giving us a great deal of help rooting out terrorists and further helping in fighting the war, etc. All true but are they really helping the U.S. or are they using us to help them to prevent their overthrow from within? This kingdom is rotten through and through. The family of Saud sold their soul to Wahhbiism generations ago in order to stay in power and today they do everything to foster radicalism throughout the entire world. This is not an ally.

In the Chapter 28 *A Matter of Policy* we saw how the al-Azhar University of Cairo and the Wahhabi Imam Muhammad bin Saud Islamic University in Saudi Arabia spread their message of hate across the Islamic world from the Middle east to Europe, America and Asia. Where is a Western University teaching the lessons of the Age of Enlightenment, the nature of democracy, of the American Constitution both in Cairo and Riyadh? We allow the Islamic world to join our universities, we allow them to teach Islam and create private schools, why is it not reciprocal? Why isn't it a quid pro quo? The politicians would say that it is because we have freedom of religion and speech, etc. True enough but this merely indicates that as Americans ***we still can't get our minds around the fact that we are at war with a religion not a specific nation***. Would we allow Nazis to set up special schools here in the U.S. to teach courses on the "joys of Nazism" in the 1930s and even 40s? Why not? The answer is clear to all, but when it comes to a religion we haven't yet understood the nature of the enemy we are at war with. If we did, many issues of foreign policy would become considerably simpler, at least in formulation. Nothing in this war is easy or what it seems. (Being at war with a religion absolutely does NOT mean becoming to Muslims what the Nazis were to the Jews.)

Our artists, writers and satirists criticize Islam and its ways and they receive death threats, *fatwa*s, from imams, mullahs, clerics (the "holy men" of Islam). Why don't we put an exceptionally attractive bounty on each "holy man" who issues a death threat against a person in the West? The PC crowd will dismiss this as "lunacy from the right" but why should we allow the enemy to set the rules. If someone threatened you with death would you allow his wishes to proceed unchallenged? There was a time when being an American or British, etc. citizen carried an implied protection that was recognized everywhere. Now it signifies "target." What has changed? Why shouldn't systematic "applied self defense" be utilized?

In an age before *multiculturalism* Britain dealt with cultural problems in a very effective way. There existed during the British Raj in India the practice of "suttee." This was the horrific tradition of burning widows alive on the funeral pyres of their dead husbands. General Sir Charles Napier said to the perpetrators of this barbaric custom:

> "You say that it is your custom to burn widows. Very well. We also have a custom: When men burn a woman alive, we tie a rope around their necks and we hang them. Build your funeral pyre; beside it, my carpenters will build a gallows. You may follow your custom. And then we will follow ours."

Could anything be simpler and in a very eloquent way more just?

CONSISTENT FOREIGN POLICY IN OTHER WESTERN DEMOCRACIES

The comments regarding consistency that apply to the U.S. also apply to the rest of the Western world. Of course it is far more difficult for the U.S. to exert pressure on its allies, exhorting them to be consistent in their approach to Islamic relations, when the U.S. is an equal offender. Here are some examples of the disaster the lack of anything resembling consistency can cause. Although it is Israel who is the inconsistent country in this case it is partially the fault of the Clinton and Bush administrations for continually pushing Israel to negotiate with the Palestinian terrorists as well as any other M.E. country that is on the offensive against Israel.

After two decades of attempted and failed negotiations between Israel and the PLO, Israel unilaterally decided to abandon Gaza leaving it to the Palestinians. The policy is called "disengagement" and its purpose is to unilaterally achieve security for Israel without the endless unsuccessful process of negotiation with the Palestinians. The policy has evolved in parallel with the building of a security wall surrounding a large portion of Israel. Although the wall has certainly dramatically lowered terrorist attacks within Israel the "disengagement" policy is a failure.

Upon Israel's withdrawal, Gaza was immediately taken over by terrorists (Hamas and Islamic Jihad) with broad popular support. The newly "freed Gaza" proceeded to once again use rocket attacks against Israel. This was their highest priority, more war instead of using Gaza as a base to begin country building and forming ties to civilization, both Islamic and Western. The next step was an incursion into Israeli territory. During that action an Israeli soldier (Cpl. Gilad Shalit) was kidnapped and a number of his comrades killed. Israel should not be surprised at the Hamas action. Given a free rein in Gaza, Hamas began to dig a network of tunnels from Gaza into Israel for the purpose of continuing the war. It is critical to understand the objectives and motives of one's enemies (an understanding America desperately needs). The PLO is not interested in a country it is interested in destroying Israel. The policy of disengagement did not give Israel more security it gave it less.

So Israel is confronted with two choices; letting the incursion go unpunished and forget the kidnapped soldier (very unlikely) or attack Gaza and attempt to free the soldier (most likely). There is a third choice that I didn't list and that is to attempt more negotiations but after years of fruitless talk this option should be out of the question, or is it. Israel has once again begun "negotiations" with Hamas while saying they won't negotiate with Hamas! Literally! The following is the framework of the situation.

> First, Olmert states that Palestinian Authority Chairman and the head of Fatah, Mahmoud Abbas are responsible for bringing about Cpl. Gilad Shalit's release.
>
> Second, they say Hamas better watch out because they're going to get it.
>
> Third, they say that Hamas won't get it until later.
>
> Finally, while stipulating that they will not negotiate with Hamas, Olmert and his associates are negotiating with Hamas.

An interesting editorial comment on the insanity:

> "As for the details of the latest Israeli-Palestinian conflict—this Theater of the Absurd has long since become tedious. Here are all of the recognizable elements, repeated again. The minions of Hamas, the party that now controls the Palestinian quasi-government, attacks an Israeli military post—and Israel seeks to "cooperate" with the Palestinian Authority's leaders, as if they were not at war.
>
> "Then disappointingly Condoleezza Rice calls for calm on both sides and tells Israel 'to give diplomacy a chance to work' (it hasn't in 40 years so why now?). Meanwhile, the Palestinians tout a new agreement that 'implicitly recognizes Israel's right to exist'—except that it was drafted by imprisoned Palestinian terrorists and explicitly authorizes terrorist attacks on all of Israel.
>
> "This is all normal in the one arena of global politics that has been most thoroughly surrendered to the rule of brazen irrationality." (1)

At this point Israel was about to withdraw 80,000 settlers from the West Bank as part of the "disengagement "policy. The Gaza experience has proven to be a complete failure so how can Israel possibly go forward with the West Bank plan? Somehow I believe they will. Such is the nature of exhaustion.

And speaking of exhaustion it appears that the one thing the French are never exhausted of is doing things that undermine Israel and the West for diplomatic and economic gain. The French worked hard at getting the U.N., U.S., Israel and Hezbollah (Lebanon) to agree to a ceasefire in the Hezbollah–Israeli War. The basis would be that the U.N. would supply a multi national force comprised of French (2000 or more troops) Turks, Malaysians to police the border between Lebanon and Israel to prevent Hezbollah attacks against Israel. Hezbollah would disarm and Syria would stop channeling supplies to Hezbollah (from Iran). Hezbollah and Israel would withdraw from the Lebanon/Israeli border. On the second day of the agreement France said that it could not supply more than 200 troops because the plan that ***they*** brokered was not specific enough. Hezbollah continued to be rearmed by Syria so Israel launches an incursion 60 miles into Lebanon against Hezbollah. Kofi Annan castigates Israel for the infraction of the ceasefire agreement but of course doesn't mention Hezbollah's infraction. The French with their 200-man army in place begin to lobby for contracts to rebuild Lebanon. And we like fools continue to trust the French, who have undermined us in every way possible for a decade or more and who are in Islam's back pocket (thanks to the EAD) and the UN that is first, last and always completely anti American.

At this writing the ceasefire is holding but it is only a question of time until Hezbollah feels strong enough to take another run at Israel and/or take over Lebanon. Such has been the experience for decades.

The frustration of constant failure and over forty years of failed peace talks have not been enough for Israel and the West to learn that they are dealing with an enemy that is completely unyielding. Even when we think that we have finally achieved success it always turns to smoke in our hands. We continue to talk because we do not want to face the truth of the situation. So we try alternate means of achieving a rapprochement with the various Middle East factions; we yield endless variations of concessions and accommodations only to be frustrated once again. The only real solution is the sad truth as stated by Benjamin Netanyahu's dictum that "the way to fight terrorism is to fight terrorism—to fight its perpetrators as consistently and as persistently as possible, robbing them of any realistic hope of achieving their aims by force." How much better off the West, including Israel, would be if we had a stated public policy of "if you hit us we hit you twice, if you want to negotiate come to the table with items you will concede or don't call us." That is consistency.

Truth is often ugly.

TERRORISM

The elimination of terrorism is critical for the obvious reason of eliminating the fear generated by the continual threat to life, life style and property. Most significant however is that the West not allows terrorism to "exhaust" us. It is this process of wearing down the potential victims of terrorism that is the real goal of terrorism. The exhaustion in turn leads the West to adopt policies of capitulation and appeasement toward Islam whether as an explicit reaction, as in the case of Spain, or as the result of subtle and incremental changes in our psychology. However the complete understanding of this strategy needs to be factored into all of the West's dealings with Islam.

Rhetoric aside, today we deal with Islamic states almost as though they were completely independent of terrorism, as though the entity of terrorism was distinct from the states that sponsor terrorism, the states that fund terrorism and the state that is the generator of the foundational fanatic ideas that instigate terrorism. All that seems to be necessary for the West to not include an Islamic state in the category of sympathetic to or supportive of terrorism is for the state in question to verbally denounce terrorism, even in the mildest way possible. The truth is the Islamic countries, particularly in the Middle East and including Pakistan and Afghanistan, are all terrorist states to varying degrees. And the West must make them understand that we know it and as long as this is the case we will do everything possible to undermine those Islamic states.

Simply put the only way to eliminate all terrorism is to destroy the supporters of terrorism. We can go on forever spoiling airplane attack plots, etc. but there will always be one that we miss. It doesn't take much to unsettle the equilibrium of the Western way of life and its economies. It is five years after 9/11 and the Islamists are still planning air attacks. Does anyone think they will stop? Does anyone really think that negotiating will put an end to terrorism? Only if we destroy the terrorist's source of funds, training and logistic and intellectual support do we have a chance of eliminating mass terrorism.

The issue is not how to achieve this end; the issue is do we have the will and can we put together the political consensus, particularly in the U.S., needed to launch the solution.

IMMIGRATION

Europe became *Eurabia* due to a massive influx of Muslim immigrants with a high birth rate whose passage to Europe was aggressively funded by Arab oil money. However the total lack of Muslim integration into European society itself was made possible by the Europeans' implementation of the doctrine of *multicultural tolerance*. The problem America faces is both similar and different depending on the context. We do not have an acute assimilation problem with Muslims in America, at least not yet. But it is growing and it can reach a critical mass if left unchecked. However we do have a rather significant problem with *multiculturalism*.

Immigration should be about an individual's right to "life, liberty and the pursuit of happiness." The people who emigrate to the U.S. overwhelmingly come to this country seeking these "inalienable rights." The greatness of America is a direct consequence of these principles and the people that came here to achieve them in their own lives. We have a very long history of welcoming and ***assimilating*** immigrants. This includes granting political asylum to those fleeing from political persecution. However the critical element of our history of immigration has been assimilation. The people that came here wanted to become Americans with all that this implies. With every distinct ethnic wave of immigration, by the second generation or third at most, the children were Americans in all ways. The process of assimilation took place through education, the schools, through learning to speak English, through neighborhood and normal peer pressures at every level of society and through the work place. The immigrant wanted to "fit in." They experienced the implicit "rightness" of the American experience and culture and the freedoms it supported, encouraged and guaranteed. They kept the best of their culture of origin alive in their hearts and in all of the simple ways that gave poignancy to their lives in America while adding to the "folk culture" of America. They all made the America they chose to live in the better for it. But the key point is that they assimilated and the citizens of America would expect nothing else.

This was an age where Americans thought that ours was a great culture, a superior culture. This was an age before *multiculturalism*. We will not return to this "age of assimilation" if we do not scrap the concept of *multiculturalism*. We must ensure that what has gone wrong in Europe, or perhaps more accurately "*Eurabia*," does not happen here. Replace *multiculturalism* with what? That is the question. The answer: re-embrace the founding fathers' concepts that served us so well throughout our history. The culture and system that made America great must be taught in the context of it being a superior culture. A basic tenet of that culture is the belief in the equality of individuals and peoples. Captured in that thought is all the evidence a rational person needs to understand the "superiority" of a culture that keeps that thought and its practice as a cornerstone of its society and laws.

America should not attempt to absorb a migratory wave of people who have nothing in common with us and who have completely different values, while having no desire to be assimilated into our culture and many of whom work diligently and fanatically to destroy the West. This principle makes at least a significant part of the Islamic immigration fundamentally different from any migrating people in history or others currently migrating to this country from all over the world.

America does not want to emulate the growing cultural problem that is appearing all over Europe.

> In "1999, when I lived briefly in a predominantly Muslim neighborhood, I took in the fact that the city was divided into two radically different and almost entirely separate communities. One of them, composed mostly of ethnic Dutchmen, was secular, liberal, and (owing to a very low birthrate) dwindling steadily; the other, composed of immigrant Muslims, lived in tradition-bound, self-segregating enclaves whose autocratic leaders despised democracy and whose population (thanks to high birth and immigration rates) was climbing rapidly. This division, I soon realized, was replicated across Western Europe. Clearly, major social friction-and more-lay down the line." (2)

The picture painted by Mr. Bawer, who is quoted above, is not pretty and bodes poorly for future cultural developments in Europe. I don't know if Europe can reverse this malaise but it is not too late to prevent it from occurring in America. Even as these words are being written the latest migration statistics on Muslims shows a dramatic increase in numbers since 9/11. "In 2005 more people from Muslim countries became legal permanent United States residents–nearly 96,000 - than any year in the past two decades." According to the N.Y. Times (September 10, 2006). And the trend is growing. In the same article Ahmed Youssef one of the émigrés is quoted as saying that he is opposed to the war in Iraq. Well of course he is (so are many Americans) but the point is that it is a good bet that all 96,000 émigrés are against the war in Iraq and most likely against many other of the items in the war on terrorism. However they personally are not the enemy but we are at war with their culture and their religion how else can they feel. One really can't blame them; it is normal for them to be "sympathetic" to Islamic causes and points of view. But that is exactly the point. The charge of bigotry aside unfortunately the point being made is the truth regardless of appearances or even motivation.

No Islamic immigration should be allowed in the U.S. until the course of Islam is changed and the war with Islam is over.

MULTICULTURALISM

Enough has been said about *multiculturalism* except perhaps one thing–the teaching hopefully will be ended except in courses on contemporary mysticism. It is a flawed and damaging premise and one that is logically incorrect, i.e., that all cultures are equal or of equal value. They are practically, logically and metaphysically not equal.

WOMEN

Central to the goal of stopping the advancement of Islamic fundamentalism is the secularization of Islam. And central to that goal is the furthering of human rights; and there is no better place to start then by freeing Islamic women from a repressive existence. These are goals that can only be achieved by a dedicated effort carried out over generations. It is not a "one administration" task or even a single generation's.

Western women have been a force for fundamental change within our societies for centuries. Especially in the past century the women's rights leaders, organizations and movement have been a catalyst for some of the most dramatic changes western culture has undergone since the industrial revolution. All of these changes have not only furthered women's rights and equality but also in a broader sense, contributed to the liberalization and advancement of Western society. As such women have attained a level of power, influence and equality never seen in History and thereby represent an unparalleled force for change in the world. That power and influence must be enlisted in a movement to bring the same level of freedom to Islamic women. It is up to Western women to actualize the potential for change that women in general represent and to instigate its initiation in other societies. By exploiting political pressures, education and communication the West can begin the process that will help to free 500 million women from a repressive existence and change a central practice of Islam. This will represent a meaningful crack in the wall of the "Islamic State."

The reason to emphasize the role of women in winning the battle against fundamentalist Islam lies in the fact that the emancipation of even a small percentage of the 500 million Muslim women will create over time an inexorable pressure in Islamic society to move toward humanist teachings and secularization.

Not only are the women a driving force for this evolution but also the children born to them will be educated and exposed to many ideas of which freedom will be a dominant concept and experience in their family lives. As this spreads outward from the home there will be no going back to the feudal system of today's Islam. In two to three generations the numbers will dramatically grow and in so doing will change the face of Islam and the world. By the third generation the process will be past the point of critical mass if it is not derailed by force. (And attempts at force will be inevitable.) And the West should use all of its political and economic resources to prevent the movement from being stopped by force. Societies evolving ideas and practices of equality and freedom do not breed suicide bombers or terrorists while being far more attuned to assimilation. This in turn lessens the influences of fundamentalist Islam.

The process as presented is aimed at all of Islamic society however for practical reasons the first wave of pressure and protest must be aimed at Islamic practices within Western countries and secondarily within Islamic countries. The methodology of achieving the goal within Western countries is merely ***to enforce existing laws not now being enforced within Muslim communities***. (Primarily European but increasingly in American communities as well.) The same pressures applied to Islamic countries will meet with a resistance far more difficult to overcome. The point is not to allow the counter-resistance to slacken the effort. The more Islam is kept off balance and defensive in the realm of morality the better it is for the West to counter their expansionist drive.

An optimum starting point in this effort would be the American Feminist movement. Through their ability to rally women to a cause both domestically and internationally they could begin to put the kind of pressure on the United Nations, Human Rights Watch, heads of state, Congress and foreign governments to bring this issue to the forefront of public attention. This would not only create awareness and act as a pressure against Islam but it would also allow the public to become more aware of the Islamic issue in general. The spotlight of truth has an excellent chance of reversing many of the kinds of abuses that are so much a part of Islamic advancement. It would be like that period in our history when women led the battle that helped change their position in the U.S. and helped further the entire civil rights movement. And as History has shown it caused the adoption of these rights on a global scale throughout the West.

Earlier we saw the quote by an Islamic leader who said: "we will conquer you through the womb of our women." This concept needs to be reversed. *We must conquer them through the wombs of their women.*

The long-term objective must be the complete liberation of Muslim women to the extent they wish to change their existence. The process will be slow but it will progress if the early programs maintain the consistency and focus the early women's right movement did. Many women absolutely rebel against their position in the Islamic world. They wish to become emancipated and free to live a life they choose. The major freedoms these women seek are: education, freedom to choose a mate for love not as a parental obligation or to choose a career, to be free of polygamous relationships, from male abuse, rape, from beatings, genital mutilation, freedom from being a victim of an honor killing, etc. In short to be treated the way any human being deserves to be treated, as an individual with the same inalienable rights.

The resulting impact on Islam will be to move it to a point of a moderate religion where its precepts are left to the realm of the spiritual and *Shari'a* gives way to the secular laws of advanced democracies. In this way Islam will join Christianity and Judaism.

The resistance from the Islamic leaders and many Islamic men will be relentless and loud. The issue will be trivialized and the claims of abuse positioned as gross exaggerations and the results of *Islamophobia*. They do not want to overturn the status quo. They have lived like this for fourteen hundred years, who are we to try to change their religion. Then I would say don't live in the West. It is our culture if you don't like it or can't follow our laws and norms you are free to leave. No matter the counter pressure and public relations campaign against the movement the program cannot waiver.

There are "radical women", true heroines, already blazing the trail and fighting the battle against this "gender apartheid" and violent and oppressive behavior against women in the Muslim world. These are just a very few stories that provide a view into the nature of the evil that must be fought and at least one of the weapons in that battle.

Unni Wikan was born in Syria to a middle-class family and raised a Muslim. She began to reexamine her religious beliefs after a traumatic incident. She witnessed the murder of one of her professors, a respected medical schoolteacher. The murderers were two Muslim Brotherhood terrorists shouting

"Allahu akbar!" (God is great!). (The professor was too liberal for their taste.) Over time she became a secularist and started writing for the Arab American Web site Anneqed.com. She also became a strong critic of the intolerance and violence that was increasingly associated with Islam. In what must be the most courageous of acts for a female Muslim, she rejected the hatred of Jews and the institutionalization of anti-Semitism that is universal in the Islamic world. She had been indoctrinated with this propaganda since she was a child, but she had the clarity of thought and reason and strength of conscious to reject it. In her books she tells several stories to illustrate the denial of individual rights.

Norwegian-born girl Aisha was about to be transported by her parents to Morocco to be married to a stranger. Knowing this Aisha went to the Norwegian child protection authorities and begged for help. The Norwegian authorities refused to get involved for fear of appearing *culturally insensitive.* (3)

> Another "protected" tradition is "honor killing." The family honor is restored through the murder of a female relative who is seen as having sullied it-by, for example, being raped. There are many true stories of this practice where girls are brutally murdered by their families. This happens throughout Europe. (4)

The victim is secondary in almost all these cases, subordinated to a misguided "respect" for immigrant-group traditions. (A condition unseen before in Western history.) The degree of moral equivocation that must take place for such a conclusion to exist at all in Western law enforcement is shameful.

Arab-American psychologist Dr. Wafa Sultan shocked the Muslim world when she took part in a debate on Al-Jazeera in February 2006. Her opponent was the Algerian Islamist cleric, Ahmad bin Muhammad. The two debated Islamic teachings and terrorism. She attacked the Muslim world for being mired in a "medieval" mentality and she dubbed the war on terror not simply a clash of civilizations but

> "a clash between civilization and backwardness, between barbarity and rationality, between human rights on the one hand and the violation of these rights on the other, between those who treat women like beasts and those who treat them like human beings."

She is now in fear for her life and is under constant guard.

(Note: Ms Sultan's whereabouts were a secret for fear of her life

> unfortunately, the New York Times article revealed the Los Angeles suburb in which she and her husband reside, as well as other personal information. The NYT must have thought it was a need to know for the public. Since then a blog called Neocon Express has started a campaign to get a number of private security firms to donate equipment and services for Sultan's protection.)

It is so rare in this world of twisted logic to see such moral clarity. Compare Dr. Sultan's forceful pronouncement of the issues the world faces with the "sinister reasoning" by European authorities that allow them to turn a blind eye to murder, kidnapping and rape in the name of religious freedom and the desire to be "sensitive."

Brigitte Gabriel is a Lebanese Christian journalist who, with her family found refuge from persecution in Israel. There she began to see the evil inherent in the anti-Semitism she grew up with and has rejected. She now travels all over the world lecturing and writing about the persecution she suffered at the hands of the Islamists. She is also a staunch defender of Israel on American college campuses. In addition she has become a powerful voice for restoring Arab-Jewish relations. Gabriel now lives in the United States where she founded the American Congress for Truth, an organization devoted to providing information about the Middle East conflict and the dangers of Islamic totalitarianism.

Nonie Darwish is an Arab woman has worked diligently to bridge the gap between the Arabs and Israel. She is also a defender of America's battle against Islamic terrorism. A former Muslim who was born and raised in Cairo and the Gaza Strip (in later life converted to Christianity) now lives in the U.S. where she writes and speaks about the problems associated with the Muslim world. She recently stated: "Hundreds of millions of other Muslims also have been raised with the same hatred of the West and Israel as a way to distract from the failings of their leaders." (5) She has started a web site ArabsforIsrael.com.

A woman who diverged from the norm of "acceptance" to take on Muslim culture is professor, author and activist Phyllis Chesler.

Phyliss Chesler was a prominent figure in the American feminist movement but has left because she rejected the anti-Americanism and anti-Israeli sentiment that seemed to consume the movement. She is now a strong critic of American feminism. In her book *The Death of Feminism: What's Next in the Struggle for Women's Freedom*," she has criticized modern feminism and its current direction. Chesler also provides a powerful voice in the battle against Islamic sexism. As described in an article titled: *How Afghan Captivity Shaped My Feminism* (an article from: Middle East Quarterly) Ms Chesler describes her experience as a Muslim wife to an Afghani man who she thought was a moderate. Upon a visit to his family in Afghanistan she was immediately shrouded in a veil, her passport was confiscated and she became a virtual prisoner. She was able to escape back to the U.S. only when some friends helped her. Since her return she has become outspoken about the Islamic abuses of women.

> (These stories are a brief synopsis by Suzanne Fields who originally published them, and many others of courageous women in the *Washington Times*.)

The stories and the issues they raise are succinctly encapsulated by a statement made by Oriana Fallaci, in her book *The Rage and the Pride* when she asked why so many women in Islam "cannot go to school, cannot go to the doctor, have no rights whatsoever, who count less than a camel."

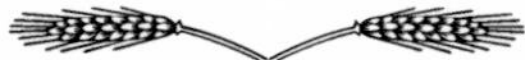

The reader may think that the "weapon of women" is an impractical solution to terrorism. Perhaps if viewing only the short term this is true. However women changed the face of America over a long term and as we have seen there are many women within Islam working to change Islam the same way. Claiming how "this" can't work prevents the first steps from being taken. It will take generations no doubt and will not succeed by itself but it is a very powerful element for change and we need to "jump start it."

"THE LOYAL OPPOSITION"

The success of a free country depends as much on a "loyal opposition" as it does on good programs. It is through an intelligent dialog between differing groups concerning the setting of goals and the various methods of achieving goals that a consensus can develop. The problem in today's "dialog" is that no one listens, especially politicians. (As the saying goes: God gave man two ears and one mouth and they should be used proportionately.) The primary preoccupation among politicians seems to be with re-election and making points against the opposition. Whereas this may be minimally acceptable in issues not dealing with survival it is completely irresponsible when we are faced with an enemy as determined as Islam and when a unified strategic plan and set of tactical counter measures are essential to our survival as a culture.

Perhaps if an environment such as this existed prior to the Iraq war then the correct war might have been fought–against Iran, Syria and Iraq as the whole they really are in the context of terrorism. Or if not feasible then an agreement on biding our time and working the issue using other means, at least until the time for a war was right. The war, in a political sense, was largely approved by the opposition because of the fear of being labeled as "against the war on terrorism." The war was focused on Iraq because of fear of not being able to politically justify and execute a strategic thrust that would be essential to real success. Of course the WMD issue played a supportive role for the "Iraq alone strategy" but that proved incorrect and if it turned out to be completely true as stated, the remaining issues that we fight today would still be with us, i.e., the real danger in the form of a very belligerent near nuclear Iran and an always terror supporting Syria and Iran. And still Iraq struggles against the "insurgents" sponsored, funded and even supplied by Iran. What a mess! Is there a plan for a real solution to the problem? Hardly what we have is a - "put points on the score board" -opportunity for the opposition and cries for "surrender". Good news for Islam bad news for the country.

One could argue that a pull out form Iraq would cut our losses, etc. But that again is the short-term political opportunity speaking. The Iraq problem is a small piece of a much bigger issue and until we as a nation face that issue the problem will just get worse as the "loyal oppositions" just in-fight the country to its demise.

41 Economic

The fuel that drives all of the world's terrorist organizations is oil, more specifically the income that the oil generates for the "Islamic Enterprise." The West's insatiable demand for oil creates a level of wealth of such enormous proportions that Islam is able to fund not only all of their basic needs but also all of the terrorist activities for past decades and for decades in the future.

Two points that this statement implies about the Islamic "civilization" when compared to the West. The West ***creates wealth***. The oil they buy is used to fuel the engines of commerce that in turn create the greatest standard of living for the greatest number of people ever in the history of the world. The money the Islamic countries receive for their oil is turned into palaces, and to fund armies that are used to help repress their populations and to build terrorists training camps, i.e., factories of death.

Putting this thought another way in 2005, as in 2004, the ***world economy*** grew by about 5 percent, according to the International Monetary Fund (IMF). Furthermore the IMF projects similar growth for several years to come. This is faster growth than in all but a few peak years in the 1980s and 1990s, and it's in vivid contrast to the long periods of stagnation or contraction in history. The greatest engine of this growth is the United States, which ***produces more than one fifth of world economic product and whose gross domestic product has been growing at around 4 percent.*** The other engines of growth are China and India, each with about a sixth of the world's people, and with economic growth of 10 and 8 percent, respectively. However their growth is very much coupled to the purchase power of the U.S. economy.

The demand for energy in the United States is ever growing. In fact, we consume 22.8 percent of the world's energy supply but also generate about 22 percent of the world's GDP. From the world's perspective that is a good deal because that "fuel" (the production) in turn fuels the world's economies. Of course we are always accused of being energy gluttons and greedy, etc. Even our left leaning politicians join the world chorus but little is ever said of the benefits and enormous productivity we bring to the world (represented by that 22% of global GDP) in exchange for that energy we use.

During the same period of Western driven economic growth and prosperity there were 14,000 deaths from Islamic fundamentalists related incidents and the remainder of Islam produced nothing except for the oil that would not be produced if Westerners weren't the ones engineering, operating the wells and refining the oil. But the United States is the Great Satin. By what moral compass do these accusers of the U.S. navigate to this conclusion?

It is time for the "devil to get his due." The U.S. must remove the money that it provides the Islamic Engine, by eliminating in the shortest period possible all dependence on Middle East oil. Before launching into the "how," it is clear that even if the U.S. succeeds in becoming energy independent the remainder of the world will for a long time be buyers of Middle East oil. The elimination of the U.S dollars from the income flow will be felt however, and going forward at least some of the programs that help the U.S. severe its dependence on M.E. oil can help do the same for other importers of oil.

There are three ways to neutralize foreign oil as a "weapon" used against us–increase domestic and non M.E. based oil production, the widespread use of nuclear energy and the nationwide adoption of alternative fuels, specifically ethanol and coal. All three of these energy sources must be pursued in parallel; first because ultimately they will all be needed at least through a transition period that will take ten or more years and secondly because of the different time periods needed to mature each of the alternative options.

OIL EXPLORATION

A statistic that every American should keep in mind is that 72% of all oil used in the U.S. is used for transportation: cars, light trucks, trains, etc. If we are to seriously impact our dependence on foreign oil than the 72% must be dramatically impacted or alternatively the oil used to maintain the current usage percentage must come from within the U.S. The best course would of course be to achieve both a reduction in oil needs and an increase in U.S. based oil supply.

American oil consumption is rising, from more than 15 million barrels a day in the early 1980s to more than 20 million today. It is likely to continue to increase–another 33% over the next 25 years, according to the U.S. Department of Energy—the reason is quite simple, crude oil is an incredibly useful substance. Some 40% of our oil consumption is for cars and light trucks; 32% for buses, railroads, ships, heavy trucks and agricultural machinery. An additional 17% goes into petrochemicals to produce products from plastic to paint. In the face of the substance's vital importance and the projected increase in the growth of usage and the instability of supply sources, one would think that the U.S. is doing everything possible to increase our domestic sourced crude oil. Well not exactly.

America's domestic petroleum production has significantly declined, from 10 million barrels a day in 1970 to about 5 million barrels today. Our brilliant strategic solution has been to increase importation of oil to more than 12 million barrels a day. This represents about 65 percent of the nation's total oil supply. In addition we import about 20 percent of our natural gas. Looking at this situation critically it is easy to conclude that we have ceded control of one of our most critical resources to foreign unstable even hostile governments. How have we managed to leave ourselves so vulnerable? The summary form of the answer is simple. Although the problem was first recognized as being acute in 1973 when the first oil crisis occurred the country did nothing positive to address the growing problem during the ensuing thirty-three years, and in fact has labored diligently to make the problem worse. The reasons for this incredibly dangerous lack of attention and action to a problem that has proven to be catastrophic in its unintended consequences, i.e., funding terrorism, and lethal in its longer term consequences, i.e., complete disruption of our economic life, are found in the complex workings of fragmented, narrowly focused politics.

For many years our political "leaders" of both parties have striven mightily to render themselves completely ineffectual in addressing the issue while simply decrying the situation as our dependency and vulnerability continue to grow. And even still American energy companies are restricted, by the federal government, from exploring for oil in the areas where the greatest untapped oil reserves are found–the deep sea, government land and Alaska's North Slope. The Heritage Foundation declares that the U.S. "is the only nation in the world that has placed a significant amount of its potential domestic energy supplies off-limits."

Our country's political establishment, from Congress to the Presidency, has ***worked for a third of a century to prevent increases in our energy supply***. They have been editorially supported by most of the press and all of the environmentalists. This may be good short-term politics but it is a disaster long term. It reminds me of the man that is falling off the roof of a skyscraper and half way down says that everything seems to be all right.

In 1980 President Carter imposed a "windfall profits" tax on oil companies, which raised $40 billion rather than the $227 billion he had promised. But instead of easing the energy shortages as he stated it would, the tax reduced domestic oil production by between 3% and 6% and gave imported oil a competitive advantage. Of course this advantage translated into increased imports of foreign oil by about 10%.

In 1990 the first President Bush issued a presidential directive forbidding access to about 85% of Outer Continental Shelf oil and natural gas reserves. In 1998 President Clinton extended the moratorium through 2012.

In 1995 President Clinton vetoed a budget bill that would have allowed oil exploration and drilling in part of the Alaska Arctic National Wildlife Reserve (ANWR). At the same time to the west of ANWR the Prudhoe Bay fields were delivering oil through the Alaska pipeline to the U.S. market without damage to Alaskan land, the greatly loved caribou or other wildlife. ANWR contains up to 16 billion barrels of oil, so Clinton's veto today is costing America about a million barrels of oil each day. Yet Congress has repeatedly defeated efforts to open ANWR to exploration. (The environmental lobby is very powerful.)

Exploration is not the only aspect of our energy policy that Congress has labored diligently to cripple there is also the lack of oil refining capacity. We have not built a new refinery since 1976. After Hurricane Katrina, a bill to streamline the "refinery permitting process" and encouraging the building of refineries on closed military bases was blocked in the Senate Environment and Public Works Committee when every Democratic senator, along with Jim Jeffords (I., Vt.) and Lincoln Chaffee (R., R.I.) voted "no."

In addition to the Congressional war on oil refinery the states of the union have created a patch quilt of refining restrictions and regulations that prevent an optimum flow of gasoline across the country. As an example, gas refined in say Texas can't be sold in California and so on. Not only has this created a nightmare of logistics for the oil companies (and by so doing added to the price of a gallon of gas), it has created spot scarcities. Natural gas fares no better.

Adding to the illogic of the situation there is enormous concentrations of clean natural gas in the Intermountain West but these reserves are currently off-limits. This is even stranger when one realizes that the land is neither wilderness nor park but merely government land. The gas would be able to supply all energy needs to 50 million U.S. homes for the next 60 years while producing income for the federal coffers. Furthermore ninety percent of the deep sea is off-limits to drilling, including 420 trillion cubic feet of natural gas (we currently consume about 23 trillion cubic feet per year, so that amounts to a 19-year supply) and 50 billion barrels of crude oil. This alone could replace current levels of oil imports from the Persian Gulf for many decades to come. Yet the House of Representatives in May 2006 voted 217-203 to block the opening of some of the Outer Continental Shelf areas to natural gas exploration and drilling.

Those opposed to tapping America's resources argue that deep-sea energy exploration poses a significant environmental risk. The environmentalists cite an incident of a major spill that occurred almost 40 years ago. As serious as a major spill can be, the fact is that the technology involved in deep-sea exploration and drilling has gotten to the point that the risks are dramatically reduced through technologies such as enhanced safety, blowout prevention systems and shut-in valves. Regulations have also improved and the strict adherence to these preventive measures is common practice in the industry. The combined impact of these advances proved their efficacy during the devastating hurricanes (Katrina and Rita) in 2005 when virtually no oil or natural gas was spilled even from rigs in the vicinity of these significant storms.

Moving onto the land, the North Slope (ANWR) is the never-ending saga that Hollywood could make an epic film about. The U.S. Department of Energy has estimated that ANWR could hold as much as 16 billion barrels of oil. That is an amount equal to 30 years of imports from Saudi Arabia. (The little kingdom that spends a good percent of the money it receives from our oil purchases on proselytizing extreme Islamic fundamentalism.) ANWR at peak production is estimated to yield approximately 1.5 million barrels per day, or about 7.5 percent of this country's daily usage. The amount of oil is so great that it is enough, according to experts, to impact world prices. However this source of "black gold" is unfortunately also off limits due to the powerful environmental lobby. The lobby has defeated every attempt to open ANWR. Their claim is that production would harm the environment. Yet President Clinton's Department of Energy published an extensive report in 1999 entitled "Environmental Benefits of Advanced Oil and Gas Exploration and Production Technology" that found, "from the tundra of Alaska to the wetlands of Louisiana, a host of advanced technologies enable the oil and gas industry to produce resources far beneath sensitive environments."

The report goes on to describe techniques such as building ice roads for moving equipment that simply disappear without a trace when summer comes to the Arctic and directional drilling that allows many wells to be put down from a single location. These and other techniques would enable the production of oil and gas using just 2,000 of ANWR's 19,500,000 acres. Can we not afford to impact just 0.000103% of the North Slope to help national security and enable a step toward energy independence? A new national poll released by PACWEST Communications of Portland, Oregon shows Americans overwhelmingly (over 60%) favor gaining access to American oil and gas from ANWR. However Congress seems to know better or to know better lobbyists. How easily politicians forget whom they work for.

What is equally interesting and potentially positive for the economy is the diversity of the companies that are involved in oil and natural gas development. Smaller, independent oil and natural gas companies already develop 90 percent of our nation's wells and produce 82 percent of American natural gas and 68 percent of the crude oil. (1)

Were the deep sea, government land and ANWR to be opened for development the economic boom would be considerable as well as almost immediately reducing the price of oil. Many experts say that a significant component of the current high price of oil is the continuing uncertainty of oil supplies. The ability of the U.S to produce a great deal of oil in the next decade would immediately relieve price pressures due to this uncertainty.

The existing political context with respect to energy policy can be summarized as follows:

> A demonstrated inability to develop a comprehensive long range energy policies and programs,
>
> A long history of political divisiveness,
>
> Disastrous interference in any proposed independent domestic energy policy that had any chance of addressing the needs of

> the country in the long term,
>
> The acute urgency of the problem given increasing dependency on hostile energy sources and
>
> The use of the out-flowing energy dollars to support terrorist activities.

Juxtaposed these against:

> The overwhelming new evidence of the soundness and safety of developing these resources that have been off limits for an unreasonable time,
>
> The potential economic gain from their development,
>
> The choking off of a large amount of terrorist funding.

One would think that at this point, given the critical issues at stake, there might be some support for aggressive forward movement to develop the strategic energy program that the country has lacked for more than thirty years. In stead we are offered more of the same stale bromide driven drivel.

Sen. Hillary Clinton's energy speech to the National Press Club in May 2006 is all too typical of what is behind the energy problem. I do not mean to pick on Senator Clinton (she expresses a position that is typical of all too many in Congress) but in that she may be running for president her views are quite important. Her speech was a model of *political correctness* but of no real substance. She clearly stated that she is for wind power, solar power and increasing the amount of oil stored in the Strategic Petroleum Reserve. Although certainly good things they can be easily shown to be a woefully inadequate for addressing our needs. Unfortunately she did not stop there, she further stated that she was:

> For a windfall profits tax on oil (though she doesn't call it that), which would, as in 1980, reduce domestic oil production,
>
> For higher taxes on oil companies so government, rather than the market economy, can regulate energy production,
>
> Against the construction of additional nuclear power plants–America's cleanest source of energy–because of her "real concerns" about the "quality of the oversight provided by the Nuclear

Regulatory Commission." (That translates into not enough governmental control over an industry that is too hot to touch politically),

Against ANWR drilling (she has voted against it half a dozen times), and against additional offshore drilling,

For greatly expanded ethanol production–good news but greatly subsidized–bad news. (More on this later.)

What is always tragic to watch in Washington is the way the goals stated are so good but are impossible to achieve with the programs that are put in place to achieve them. Senator Clinton's overall goal is "reducing our dependence on foreign oil by at least 50% by 2025." But the programs she proposes are completely incapable of achieving anything like the energy generation level she claims as her goal. As always with politicians the year for the realization of the goal is always well beyond their terms. She and her ilk are against absolutely every program that has the capability of working. In fact none of the programs alone, proposed herein, can achieve the goal of energy independence, it will require a number of them together and perhaps all.

Senator Clinton avoids any program that might have any degree of controversy, e.g. expanding nuclear power, drilling for the proven reserves of oil and gas off our coasts, and the gradual eliminating of the ethanol import tariffs to allow a great inflow of these alternative fuels. All of these are *politically incorrect* energy policies that the Washington establishment will not permit. Why? That is the appropriate question. The really sad thing of course is that the avoided and defamed policies are the exact correct policies that would have an excellent chance of bringing the U.S. to a point of real energy independence and in turn deal a real blow, in a peaceful and passive way, to terrorists states.

NUCLEAR

Impacting the 72% figure (percentage of oil used for transportation) is the highest priority goal but the remaining 28% must also be reduced, at least in part. Of the remaining 28% of oil usage 3% is expended on electric generation. Nuclear power can go a long way in helping to achieve reduction by replacing oil as a fuel in the generation of electricity. The immediate reaction might be that only 3% does not seem to be enough to warrant the "risks" of a conversion to nuclear power. Two things undercut that opinion. The first is that the 3% itself represents an enormous amount of oil. The second is that many automobile companies are building hybrid cars and looking at a transition to full electric vehicles. (Toyota is committed to the development a plug in car. This is in addition to its hybrids.) The combination of these technologies will lift the 3% to a much higher figure, as more and more vehicles over time will require some degree of generated electricity to run. This program therefore would fall under the category of "getting in front of the problem."

At the current time there are 104 commercial nuclear generating units operating in the U.S. under license by the U.S. Nuclear Regulatory Commission (NRC), and although they generate 20% of the total electricity the absolute number is very small in a country the size of the U.S. and with an electricity appetite as gargantuan as ours. As a side-benefit these plants provide clean energy while avoiding the 700 million tons the CO2 that would otherwise be released into our atmosphere each year. The positive environmental impact on carbon emissions of an expanded nuclear generating capability would be enormous.

The problem is however that up to 2005 we have stopped building nuclear power plants. No new U.S. reactors have been licensed since 1978—the year before the accident at Three Mile Island. The major reasons have been safety fears, government regulation and ironically aggressive environmentalism.

Mitigating this situation to some extent, in 2005 President Bush proposed the *Nuclear Power 2010 Initiative* to facilitate plant construction. The combination of this initiative and the escalating price of oil has caused sixteen companies to express interest in building plants and another twenty five new nuclear plants are under consideration. A byproduct: the construction of the two new units is expected to create more than $9.2 billion in economic activity and 5,600 new jobs.

An interesting point on the potency of nuclear generation of power is that the core pellets of fuel required to generate electricity needs for a family of four for one year fits into the cubic volume of a child's crayon.

CONTAINMENT

Three Mile Island was in at least one sense NOT a disaster. Although the plant did experience a partial melt down of its core reactor and did release some radioactive gases, it did so as the result of three levels of system failure compounded by human error and still, with a screw-up of that colossal nature, no significant radiation harm was done to the surrounding area nor to any of the surrounding population. The levels of redundancy built into the containment and safety systems performed to the point that they prevented Three Mile Island from becoming a disaster like the one at Chernobyl (a considerably inferior technology). This is not a reason to celebrate of course, but it does demonstrate a certain degree of sophistication and reliability of design. Perhaps many will not be persuaded by this argument but in fact today's nuclear power plant design and particularly their containment and safety systems have evolved to an extremely high level of reliability, to the point of being truly safe. The 104 existing plants in the U.S. have demonstrated an excellent record of safety as have the significantly larger number throughout the Western World.

SECURITY

Since 9/11 the security at nuclear generation plants has undergone enormous upgrades. Permission to enter a plant can take weeks to acquire and that is only after an extensive background check. The points of entrance and egress are kept to a minimum and are manned by armed guards with automatic weapons. The buildings have many internal levels of barriers consisting of razor wire and concrete blocks. Internally armed guards patrol the buildings. In addition electronic alarms and surveillance is everywhere. The actual cooling towers contain no radioactive material. The buildings containing the reactors are the strongest structures built. The entire complex of buildings is built to sustain the worst possible tornadoes, hurricanes, earthquakes, fire, floods, internal explosions, etc.

SAFETY

Ever mindful of the enormous requirement for safety the industry over the past ten years has dramatically improved the safety in existing plants and the design of new plants. In fact the safety factor is between 10 and 100 times safer than existing models. This figure is hypothetical (provided by the industry depending on existing plant comparison). The NRC has stated that until the new designs are applied to new plants those figures are impossible to assure. However the point is that the industry has done a great deal to improve the safety factors of plants. Furthermore the industry, on an international level, shares all new designs and improvements.

STORAGE

The other major safety concern is the storage of spent nuclear fuel cells. The spent nuclear cells, although beyond their useful life, are extremely dangerous and highly radioactive for thousands of years. Because of this they must be stored in a facility that is impervious to time and environment and at the same time extremely secure.

The federal government had planned to act as a central depository for spent cells at a new facility at Yucca Mountain in Nevada. The depository would service the entire industry, however lawsuits have delayed the implementation of the depository. The lack of this facility has forced nuclear power plants to alleviate the problem on their own through the deployment of "on-site dry storage facilities."

Spent fuel rod assemblies are initially placed in wet storage for cooling over a planned period of five years. The wet storage capacity exists on the plant site but is viewed as an intermediate process. At some point the spent cells must be moved from the cooling phase to a permanent facility. Because of the delay in the opening of Yucca Mountain the spent fuel pools are filling to capacity. Yucca, even when or if it does eventually open, won't be ready to receive spent fuel until 2015. Therefore a solution needed to be found that would alleviate this growing problem.

Dry storage facilities utilize a prefabricated concrete unit on a concrete pad. When the fuel assemblies are ready for dry storage, the transfer is accomplished underwater placing the spent cells into steel reinforced canisters. The canisters are then removed and filled with an inert gas (helium) and then moved to the dry storage facility. The facility itself is an enormous structure that is designed to withstand natural disasters like hurricanes and tornadoes while sustaining no damage or allowing an impact to the environment or people. Furthermore dry storage is not a new or unproven technology and is in use currently by half of U.S. nuclear power plants. Most of the remaining reactors in the country are currently applying to implement dry storage facilities.

ENVIRONMENTAL

The environmentalists are split over the issue of nuclear plants. There is a major faction that is against any new deployment of nuclear energy. (One could also state without any exaggeration that they are also against every solution that has any chance of working.) There is also a group of environmentalists that are very positive on nuclear generation most notably: Patrick Moore, the founder of Greenpeace, Stewart Brand the founder of the Whole Earth Catalog and the noted British conservationist James Lovelock. They argue that the elimination of an enormous amount of greenhouse gases would be an overwhelming benefit. Whereas the opposition states that the nuclear industry is capitalizing on fears associated with greenhouse gases. They are both correct but so what. The move to nuclear generation would dramatically reduce greenhouse gases and the industry is probably using the issue as an advertising point. That fact does not change the need. The environmentalists are the greatest group for fear-mongers in Washington so why do they get upset so easily when the tactic is used against them?

NON U.S. NUCLEAR

Thanks to the rising oil prices and ironically the environmentalists there is a growing demand for nuclear energy generation elsewhere in the world. The global warming problem and the implementation of the Kyoto treaty, have made nuclear power an extremely attractive energy option to both the public and to politicians, since nuclear has no CO2 emissions.

South Korea, Taiwan and Japan import nearly all their energy, while China imports almost half the oil it uses and India is nearing the 70% level. It is not surprising that these, the largest Asian economies, are searching for different ways to increase domestic production of energy.

Nuclear power generation is undergoing a dramatic resurgence in these Asian countries. China and India between them have 10 new nuclear reactors under construction and nine at the planning stage. Another 43 have been proposed.

It should be noted that these countries are also increasing their use of ethanol (production is forecast to grow by 300% over the next five years) and of wind power (which is still only a tiny portion of needs). However there is no doubt that nuclear is their major response to the dual pressures of oil prices and environmentalism.

COAL

Although a high percentage of new power plants should be nuclear there will always be reasons where this may not be the best solution to specific generation problems. In addition existing oil burning electrical generation plants cannot be converted to nuclear but they can be converted to coal.

U.S. produces one billion tons of coal per year. This represents 35% of world's total production. U.S. coal deposits contain more energy than all of the world's oil. The U.S has a 250-year supply of coal at the current rate of consumption. In the past the major problem with coal has been its emissions. However with the advent of new "scrubbers," the technology that processes the after-burn emissions, coal has been able to conform to the Clean Air Act. To improve emissions further the industry is working on improved scrubbers and processes that will reduce emissions to near zero

What makes coal especially attractive is the speed with which it can be implemented. Whereas nuclear plants can take ten years to come on line and even new oil exploration can take years to develop and reach the marketplace coal is the fastest method of off loading oil usage. Even though it only impacts the 28% oil usage figure (or the 3% electric generation figure) it is a big step in the right direction. Currently 50% of our electrical generation requirements come from coal plants.

ETHANOL

The oil glutton of our society is transportation. Reducing the 72% of oil consumption used in automobiles, etc. is the real goal we must reach in our quest for energy independence. The two-fold thrust of greatly expanded oil exploration and development coupled with alternative fuels is the only solution that has the impact potential required to eliminate imported oil. Unfortunately ethanol is not without its problems.

To begin with ethanol is a renewable, clean burning fuel produced from corn, soybeans, sugar cane and sunflowers crops and based on proven technology that has existed for decades. In fact the first Ford Model T was designed to run on pure ethanol. The Energy Bill of August 8, 2005 was the first official commitment to expand the use of ethanol in the U.S. It is projected that by 2012 ethanol usage will reach 8 billion gallons, up from 3.4 billion gallons in 2004. The increase in production will require an increase in deployed acreage from 10 million to 18 million acres. However this is still a tiny percentage of what must be produced to offset the use of gasoline to an extent that is meaningful.

In addition ethanol is a heavily subsidized energy source. Ethanol producers receive a 51-cent-a-gallon federal subsidy, which costs the government $1.4 billion last year at current production levels. The domestic producers are also protected from international ethanol imports by a 2.5% tariff and an import duty of 54 cents a gallon. The problem with these subsidies and tariffs is that they distort the real market opportunities of what should be a new industry. If in fact the market were open to full competition the price of ethanol would drop thereby encouraging its usage as an alternative fuel. By distorting the price through the duties and subsidies the government is assuring ethanol's parity with oil but in actuality it is undercutting the potential of off setting the use of oil with ethanol on a greater scale. The government's objective is to protect the farmer whereas its objective should be to do everything possible to encourage the use of ethanol.

The government is the last entity one would choose as a model of efficaciousness, however given the strange world of energy regulation and its Byzantine legal regulatory environment only the government can help the current situation in that it must change laws and tax codes to enable ethanol to be successful. Some examples: dramatic tax breaks to automobile manufacturers for every ethanol car produced, sizeable tax credits for individuals who convert their cars to ethanol, equally aggressive tax treatment for pumping and distribution organizations that convert to ethanol, etc. The point is the government needs to be in a "world war" mind set in its approach to energy independence and it must do everything possible to help the war effort and ethanol is part of the frontline.

The government should eliminate the foreign tariff on ethanol. Without a tariff the foreign production of ethanol would increase to take advantage of the opportunity presented by an emerging industry. In that most of these countries are in geographic areas where a sugar cane crop could be used to produce ethanol it would become more economical in a shorter period. Sugar cane yields far more ethanol per acre cultivated than does corn or soy but sugar cane is an impossible crop to grow in large quantity in the U.S.

However a new crop is emerging that has the potential yield of sugar cane and it can grow well in the U.S., more of this shortly.

There is however one context within which a subsidy would be necessary and one where it would be beneficial for a very short timeframe. OPEC has proven to be quite astute at manipulating the price of oil to assure that it remains the major energy source that it currently is. If OPEC sees a real threat to their exports they will respond by lowering the price of oil to the point that it undercuts the competitiveness of ethanol. Normally this type of competition is exactly the way the consumer would benefit but in the case of a real war the last thing we want is for the enemy to destroy a strategic development. To prevent this the government should introduce a variable external tariff on foreign oil to directly correspond to the amount of an OPEC cut. In this way OPEC could not use its considerable pricing muscle to cause a move away form ethanol, at least in the U.S.

The ethanol production/cost is also an issue. Producing ethanol requires diesel fuel for tractors to plant and harvest the corn and fertilizers, and pesticides, many derived from oil, to allow it to grow. It is estimated that it takes about seven barrels of oil to produce eight barrels of ***corn-based*** ethanol. This may be true in the initial stages of production but the issue as stated does not examine the longer-term production dynamics that the expanded use of ethanol will create. The fuel needed for tractors and transportation, etc. will at an early phase of the evolution of the process be converted to ethanol and replace diesel or gas. In addition better crop yields and future pipelines will help to reduce the per barrel cost of production; which in turn will increased demand due to lower price per gallon at the pump, thereby assuring ethanol's growth.

Also on the horizon are better ethanol source crops and technologies for producing ethanol. One such crop is a bamboo-like plant that sprouts 11 feet in just one year. If South Dakota were planted with this crop it is estimated that it could produce enough ethanol to dramatically reduce dependence on Saudi oil.

One man that is betting on the future of ethanol is a multi-millionaire technology entrepreneur who has invested tens of millions of dollars in an ethanol project utilizing the bamboo like plant. "Mr. Khosla's current bet is on next-generation ethanol. He believes, with all the passion of a techno-evangelist, that we can get most of our vehicle fuel from the American Midwest rather than the Middle East, and we can do so simply by growing it." (2)

The tariff in the short run could remain to help farmers through a transition period but it should be just that, a transition period to adjust to the production dynamics of the ethanol production cycle. Within a couple of years the subsidy should be reduced to zero and the price of ethanol should normalize across domestic and international growers.

Through ethanol production and usage Brazil has achieved the complete elimination of gasoline as a fuel for automobiles. 100% of the automobiles in Brazil use ethanol as their fuel. In Brazil's favor is the use of sugar cane as the crop that is used to create ethanol. Perhaps the sugarcane crop can become a viable export staple of the countries in South America that are capable of growing it. It is vastly preferable to support the economies of South America then the Middle East.

The methods used to convert automobiles to burn ethanol, to convert the retail stations to store and pump ethanol and the fuel's transportation from point of crop production through refinery, distribution and storage facilities then to retail stations are all known and proven technologies. That does not mean it is a trivial conversion but it is the kind of thing America does so well if the government does its part in the initial phase and then gets out of the way.

OTHER SOURCES OF ENERGY

The bad news for Senator Clinton's energy plan and the die hard environmentalists is that wind and solar power make up less than one-half of one percent of the electricity we use on a typical day and those figures are unlikely to change anytime soon. The technologies are just not practical because of yield, cost to produce and climate. Solar cells are much too costly to build for large-scale generation purposes and wind turbines would require enormous "farms" to be even practical at this time. (Although the technology is improving and is estimated to be commercially viable on a large scale in the near future, so wind is a possibility.) Furthermore the wind and sun in most parts of the country are inadequate to allow for the generation of commercially viable electric generation. Where it can work it is too little to be meaningful on a national needs level and even in these places the environmentalist object to the damage done to the landscape or in several cases the ocean where wind farms were planned.

To complete the energy picture 18 percent of electricity is from burning natural gas and 6.5 percent by harnessing the energy of water moving through dams.

The real volume impact solution for our energy needs in the next ten years comes down to two things that are practical and can be achieved while bringing us to the brink of energy independence. They are ethanol for transportation and new oil sources to be found on the North Slope and deep-sea.

We don't have a real shortage of energy we have an over abundance of politicians, special interest groups and lobbyists. The three in tandem may not want to, but they are undercutting the best interests of the country and all are doing it in the name of the country. "The road to hell is paved with good intentions."

42 Military

> "People are calling for a cease-fire in the interests of peace. But there have been more cease-fires in the Middle East than anywhere else. If cease-fires actually promoted peace, the Middle East would be the most peaceful region on the face of the earth instead of the most violent.
>
> Was World War II ended by cease-fires or by annihilating much of Germany and Japan? Make no mistake about it, innocent civilians died in the process. Indeed, American prisoners of war died when we bombed Germany." (1)

In our national conscious, ***war should be classified as a last resort action*** or in self-defense. Americans do not normally think in terms of first strike wars. However it is also true that self-defense does not just mean after we are attacked. If we know that we are in danger of an attack in any form whatsoever how can we not respond before hand to prevent it? And this certainly includes terrorists. One might argue that negotiations might change the course of events and that is certainly worth an honest attempt but when all else fails and there is a "clear and present" danger then action is required. Certainly the number of peace talks and talks-to-talk-about-what-we-will-talk-about-when-we-finally-talk-about-peace, have been so numerous as to become blatantly ridiculous. Yet we seem to have this Pollyanna way of believing that talks will solve any situation.

However even with the elimination of this mind-set of the desirability of more talks we still seem to have a significant problem when confronted with a critical situation such as Islam and the war on terror and that is our seeming inability to fight a war to win.

> "The West has so lost confidence in itself and in its spiritual, cultural, and political values that it is defenseless before violence–in which case absolutism will triumph and Muslim fantasy of superiority will come true." (2)

These words are a harsh indictment.

Assume that there is broad based agreement and military action is planned. Then it must be to win. To most that may sound obvious but in fact it is not. Since WW II we have not fought a war that we fought to win. Many will take issue with that statement but the record is what it is. There are always impediments to full wining strategies. We mange to rationalize each situation with terms such as proportionate response, containment, limited action, fear of proliferation, avoidance of collateral damage and almost all of them turn out to be political expedients placating some domestic or international extreme position that our young fighting men pay the price for. I ask the question: How can we commit troops to an engagement in which we are not using all of our resources to win? If we commit to war then nothing, no issue whatsoever, should stop us from the pursuit of absolute, total and overwhelming victory.

We have this irrational fear of collateral damage and negative international opinion. As for negative opinion we have that in abundance with the policies we currently utilize, does anyone think that "foreign public opinion" can be worse and who really gives a damn when our citizens' lives and the welfare of our country are at stake? We go through such insane lengths to avoid collateral damage that we endanger our own troops in the process. This makes us weak not morally better than our enemies. What is moral about risking our men and women in the armed forces to avoid killing even small numbers of the enemy's populations? It is altruism; it is not rational morality nor is it good military strategy. There is a big moral difference between targeting the innocent (as the terrorists do) and having them accidentally harmed in a conflict. I am not saying we can be cavalier about collateral damage but it is impossible to prevent it entirely. If we cannot accept this fact of war then don't fight, give up and be a country of pacifists. It will be glorious for about a year or so.

And if we are going to fight we must use the weapons and all the force and destructive capability that are required to win.

The modern term that is the leper's bell of warfare is "proportionate response." Never in the history of the world has such a ridiculous euphemism for suicide existed. If you are attacked you destroy or surrender since "proportionate response" is nothing more than slow surrender with maximum casualties. When Pearl Harbor was attacked the response was not to find some Japanese base and bomb it. The response was an all out war against an aggressor. The U.S. has every legal and moral right to fight to destroy the aggressor until he is totally defeated and is no longer a danger to us. The outcry against this position will be "how uncivilized!" It is not "civilized" to yield to slow suicide, or surrender to aggressors.

The current Iraq war is a perfect example. Iraq per se was a mistake as explained earlier but now that we are there why do we spend endless tormented and twisted months attempting to fight "insurgents" instead of where they come from and who gives them arms and refuge. Everywhere you look in the Middle East (and even outside the Middle East), if you ask who is the biggest threat to American security and interests in general and the War on Terrorism specifically and the answer is now, and always has been, Iran. Iran supports Hamas in the Palestinian territories, Iran supports Hezbollah in Lebanon, Iran supports the Assad dictatorship in Syria, Iran supports and gives refuge, funds and training bases to al-Qaeda and to the Shiite militias in Iraq. Iran is supporting them all. There is even evidence that it was Iran that instigated Hezbollah's attack on Israel and thereby began yet one more war in the area.

Iran is the real war, and it's time we started fighting it. Are we waiting for Iran to get the nuclear weapon that they would not hesitate to use on us through terrorist attacks and on Israel directly as they have said. So why are we trying to talk to Iran? Why are we trying to build a consensus that we know will not work even if it can be built?

Immediately after 9/11 a Congressional "declaration of war" should have launched a real war, a war to win; and the targets should have been ALL of the state sponsors of terror–Iran, Iraq, Syria and Afghanistan and very stern warnings to Pakistan and Saudi Arabia to stop their support of the Islamic terrorists or we will.

It should have been a full mobilization backed by and fought through the use of every weapon in our arsenal short of nuclear (only because of its far reaching impact cross border not that it might kill large numbers of the enemy). It should have been focused and utterly destructive. It should have borne the same degree of commitment, urgency and lethality we brought to WW II. That is a war that is being fought to win. That is the use of power. If you don't use it then you really don't have it. Nothing less is worth the effort to fight because we always loose in negotiations and we always will. One can only negotiate with an enemy of such fanatical beliefs as Islam from a position of absolute overwhelming power and strength. The enemy knows this and they know that we are afraid of our power and so they "bully" us. It is therefore they that have the power not us. They will do anything to win and we always do "not enough."

I am trying to be provocative because these questions need to be answered at some point sooner then we may care to think. ***The World Trade Center sneak attack murdered almost 3000 innocent lives*** (600 more than Pearl Harbor) and the world of Islam celebrated this "declaration of war" against America and they danced in the streets. There was no mystery as to who the state sponsors of terrorism were or are. Certainly there was no lack of knowledge as to what countries were and would continue to be the cancer in the Middle East. We took the politically expedient "solution," the more politically correct solution, we took the solution that would unsettle public opinion the least and we have wasted four years, billions of dollars, almost 3000 more American lives and accomplished little; and in the end we will still have to fight Iran or take the long appeasing road.

As an aside: in the aftermath of 9/11 non Islamic world opinion was pro American at first, but dissipated in a matter of weeks as it always does. How quickly they forget. And so one must wonder "what does it really matter." It is an unfortunate truth of world politics: only real power is respected.

The following passage was used in the Preface of the book but it is an appropriate reminder at the end just what we are dealing with. From the Ayatollah Khomeini, quoted in an 11th-grade Iranian schoolbook:

> "I am decisively announcing to the whole world that if the world-devourers [i.e., the infidel powers] wish to stand against our religion, we will stand against their whole world and will not cease until the annihilation of all them. Either we all become free, or we will go to the greater freedom which is martyrdom. Either we shake one another's hands in joy at the victory of Islam in the world, or all of us will turn to eternal life and martyrdom. In both cases, victory and success are ours." (3)

Iran WILL drop a nuclear bomb on Israel when they can (unless Israel goes first). A terrorist organization WILL try again to bring mass death and destruction to the shores of America the first chance they have to slip through our defenses. The terrorist states would and perhaps WILL try to detonate a nuclear device in America. There is no amount of destruction and death, innocent or not, that will stop the Islamic fundamentalists from continuing their *jihad* against America first and the rest of the West in time. Do you really think otherwise? Is there any words or events from Islam in the past decades that can cause one to believe these statements exaggerations?

What if in fact the U.S prosecuted a war of the magnitude suggested herein would we win the war with Islam? Certainly in the military sense we would and that would stop large-scale terrorism but winning is a broader context then just a given military framework. The issue would still exist–how do we change the mind-set of Islam?

One might argue that after a devastating war such as was discussed previously the receptivity for Western ideas, etc., in a conquered land would hardly be ideal. To an extent that is true, but as a model I would offer Japan after WW II. There was no changing the Japanese militaristic mind set prior to WW II, however afterward with excellent programs and wise policies, diplomacy, aid and help in economic development (and dealing from a position of absolute strength) Japan rose from ashes and in fact Japan became a Westernized country and an economic powerhouse and ally. It is not impossible. ***It would of course be far better to succeed in the realm of ideas before a war is necessary***. But we may not have that luxury.

43 Culture

THE WAR OF IDEAS

Although I have been arguing for a vigorous approach to a shooting war it is not a long term winning strategy when confronting Islam as a whole and with respect to Islam's aggressiveness in an historical perspective. A shooting war would deal to a large extent with the issue of terrorism and its supporters and it might even deal a deathblow to the weapon of terrorism at least for the current time. However in the long run Islam cannot be defined by a single country or alliance of countries, it transcends that designation. (This is why the example of Japan from the previous chapter may not be completely realistic.) It is a global religion that contains a mind-set that is, at all times, antagonistic to the West and its culture. In actuality it is not just the West; it is any non-Islamic culture. Even if a war is to come and it is completely successful we will still be left with the issue of Islamic expansion of the non–violent type. That which Islam does not win by the sword they can win by infiltration enabled by Western accommodation and/or ignorance of the expansionist process. It is therefore necessary to win the war of ideas. It is necessary to work with the Islamic humanists to bring about the separation of the secular and spiritual within Islam. Only then will the world be on an "even playing field" with Islam.

To begin within the modern intellectual community of Islam and Islamic thought have been greatly influenced by the Egyptian activist Sayyid Qutb. In the late 1940s Qutb spent two years in America exposed to a lifestyle based largely on "a good time and fun." "He was disgusted by everything from church dances to the Kinsey Report," Bernard Lewis states. The Great Satan is "neither an imperialist nor an exploiter but a seducer". It is the seductive appeal of American culture that appalls the Muslim intellectuals.

A member of the terrorist group the Muslim Brotherhood, lamented that the influence of American culture, by way of movies and television, was "a real invasion" of the Islamic world by the West. So even an uncoordinated non-intellectual "presentation" of Western culture is perceived by much of the Islamic world as an invasion. Imagine what the potential of the impact might be if the real and foundational values of the West were projected instead of so much base pop culture.

A well-articulated "picture" representing the best of Western Culture and humanistic ideas might put the Islamic world in an intellectually defensive position for a change. Overtime it might even help initiate a "grass roots" movement for reforms.

The Saudis are already greatly influenced by satellite TV and smuggled DVDs. There is currently a campaign to allow movie theaters, which are outlawed in the kingdom. And recently a Saudi actress starred in a Saudi-made film about a young woman's struggle against the limitations imposed by Wahhabi fundamentalism. The purpose of the restrictions on movies, television, art and literature is to prevent individuals from thinking about the dogmas foisted on them by an oppressive culture and fundamentalist imams. But Western influence keeps breaking through and knocking down the barriers to thought. And we are doing so with the most trivial of views of our culture.

In February 2006 the Al-Jazeera hosted a debate between Dr. Wafa Sultan (an Arab-American psychologist and Dr. Ahmad Bin Muhammad, an Algerian professor of Religious Politics. The debate was posted on the web site of the Middle East Media Research Institute (MEMRI.org). The debate received over 3 million hits. During the debate Ms Sultan exhorted fellow Muslims to reject the fundamentalist mind-set and join modernity. She also urged Muslims to free themselves from the shackles of anti-Semitism. Most stunningly, she compared the behavior of Jews and Muslims in the face of oppression. She said, "The Jews have come from tragedy and forced the world to respect them with their knowledge, not with their terror." Subsequently Ms Sultan did an interview with Rabbi Tovia Singer on Israel National Radio in which she was quite outspoken about the problems within Islam. Her expressed thoughts have had a considerable impact on audiences.

Predictably Ms Sultan was denounced as a "heretic" by the cleric with whom she debated on Al-Jazeera, and he later dubbed her "more dangerous to Islam than the Danish cartoons," thereby unwittingly providing a glimpse into the very mind-set Sultan criticized. But almost as a knee jerk reaction to criticism the death threats immediately began.

Malek Chebel believes that while Islamism is very popular in the Arab world today, there is also a growing reform movement against it: "Today, a certain Islamic trend is progressing in the right direction, even if we do not see it or do not want to see it." He further states that in the long run Islam will be forced to accept change in order not to be left behind by other civilizations. He says that this will happen through "addressing a number of issues Muslims do not want to address right now: the aspirations of young Muslims, equality between men and women, and, most importantly, the preeminence of the individual over the community." (1) One might add that Mr. Chebel could be proven wrong if Islam dominates. It would then be free to deploy *Shari'a*. On the other hand Mr. Chebel's position is correct if Islam can be contained.

It is becoming quite evident that in many ways the "War of Ideas" began years ago but has been and still is non-focused and exists as a random set of events. Yet some of these random events have created interesting results. Imagine the impact that could be realized with a concerted effort at the communication of real ideas.

The "War of Ideas" must be fought with books, movies, television shows, and most especially the Internet. The goal should be to promote what is often derided as "*cultural imperialism*," the spread of the ideas and values of the Enlightenment to the countries of the Middle East. But to be most effective it must be done with the same degree of organization, planning and direction that a shooting war is done with.

When thinking in terms of a "War of Ideas" it is critical to understand what ideas it is that we wish to project. Unfortunately the Islamic World's exposure to the West is currently predominantly through TV shows and films that are essentially entertainment aimed at the lowest common denominator. The best proposal that I have ever heard for projecting the real ideas and ideals of the West to the Islamic World was presented by Juan Cole, a notoriously anti-Israel, leftist professor of Middle Eastern studies at the University of Michigan. The proposal is really simple and that is exactly why it is so brilliant.

Professor Cole's proposal is to hire skilled linguists to translate into Arabic the classic works of American political thought, especially those works that deal with freedom of religion, division of powers, sovereignty of the people, and equal rights, most notably the essays and speeches of Thomas Jefferson, James Madison, Tom Paine, Benjamin Franklin, Martin Luther King Jr., and Susan B. Anthony. In addition a short, solid but representational history of American Jews and other minority groups in America. Professor Cole also wants to subsidize Middle Eastern publishers to print these books in large numbers and at low prices. He suggests that we pay the fees to book dealers throughout the region to display the books prominently. (2)

In the same way that the proposition that women will be the most important weapon against radical Islam and terrorism going forward Mr. Cole's idea has great power but is obviously a long term proposition. Since the struggle with Islam is 1400 years old it should not be a issue to initiate a set of solutions that will take a couple or more generations to bear fruit. And also like the "women solution" this one is aimed at the intellectuals and students. The effect of both will be to instill in a core of intellectuals and the young of the universities the set of values that came from The Age of Enlightenment. The power of the ideas and concepts are such that once understood, they cannot be ignored. Inexorably they will permeate the culture over time and dramatically contribute to the process of secularizing Islamic society.

The West has never approached Islam with intellect, only with weapons, war, money and often arrogance. Our culture appears to be shallow, militaristic and mercenary and above all devoid of real values. It is no wonder that the fundamentalists can create in the mind of the average Muslim a view of the West that is horrendous, immoral and oppressive. The irony is that the West has the very best communication skills and technology in the world. Yet we don't communicate anything of substance. Our message needs to change, to encompass all that is essential and wonderful in the West and when it does the skills we possess must make that message omnipresent in the World of Islam. It is in this way that we can begin to engage the "enemy" in the realm of ideas.

The underlying premise that must be present in all of the ideas the West uses to influence Islam is its unapologetic support for the individual and for individual rights.

WESTERN CULTURE

In reviewing the evolution of a complex society any number of measurements can be utilized in gauging the success of the society and its culture. High on any list of measurement would be "life sustaining." If a society is not life sustaining then it would have to be a culture that is oppressive in the extreme.

> *Life sustaining* must mean more that subsistence. In a societal context the concept of life sustaining must be both life

expectancy and *quality of life*.

> The essence of the *quality of life* within a society is its ability to support the *actualization* of human potential, unencumbered by government, religion or other citizens. A human includes all people regardless of race, religion or gender.
>
> *Actualization* means the *freedom* and ability to grow and achieve goals that are not harmful to the others in the society.
>
> *Freedom* means the right to choose all aspects of your personal life without the intervention or permission of others.

It is only with these concepts that one can create an appropriate framework for evaluating the degree of success of a society. Change one element and it is always at the expense of some group or individual in the society and the result therefore is a diminution of "life sustaining."

The West in general and America specifically, since the Age of Enlightenment, has evolved a society that is unparalleled in human history in terms of creating an environment that has provided a cornucopia of advancements in the arts, sciences, technology, engineering, in biology and agriculture, wealth distribution on a scale never imagined, a life expectancy that increases every year. An American born in 1920 had a life expectancy of 54 years and in 1985 had a life expectancy of 75 years. The worldwide average is about 60 as of 1992. The American female has a seven-year premium over males. And the numbers are improving for all. (3) In addition there exists in America a standard of living higher than that of even royalty in any other period of history. However this could not have been achieved were it not for the highest level of personal freedom that has ever existed. In fact one can trace the progress in knowledge with the growth of freedom in a society. In every period of history where human freedom was curtailed one can clearly see the slowing of growth in the sciences and arts.

As we have seen, it is particularly interesting to trace the history of Islam's long decline from its medieval achievements in architecture and mathematics, etc. to its current abysmal state, with virtually no intervening achievements. The comparison dramatically demonstrates how the repression of the individual so common in societies driven by religious doctrine also represses all progress.

Even in the arts the decline is startling. Some of the most beautiful art of the medieval period as well as the adornment of architecture was achieved in the Islamic world during its "free thinking" renaissance. Compare that with, not only the decline over the past ten centuries but also, the current attitude expressed by Islam toward art in general. The example of the monuments of ancient Egypt is a point in question. The scientific, humanist mindset of the West views them as archaeological treasures to be studied. The blindly fanatical mindset of the Muslim world views them as worthless remnants left by pre-Muslim *infidels*. This clearly was also the mindset of the Taliban when they purposely blew up the ancient, gigantic and magnificent Buddhas in Bamiyan, Afghanistan in complete disregard for their intrinsic beauty, historical importance and the outcries of much of the civilized world.

Art is the concretization of man's metaphysical values. The Taliban certainly expressed, through their barbarism, their real philosophical foundation, the worshiping of death and destruction. With a world-view of this extreme evil how can they value the individual human being?

The West is certainly not without its problems and faults but it is also the culture that has contributed more knowledge and scientific achievement to the world than any other in recorded history. In every field of endeavor the quantum leap in understanding and advancement is truly without precedent. Whether in medicine or electronics or cybernetics, in automation and food production and safety along with abundance, in short in every life enhancing way possible the West has advanced mankind. Contrast this context of achievement with the major achievement of Islamic society in the past millennium–the suicide bomber.

> "It may be that Western culture will indeed go: The lack of conviction of many of those who should be its defenders and the passionate intensity of its accusers may well join to complete its destruction. But if it does go, the men and women of all the continents will thereby be impoverished and endangered." (4)

A Closing Thought: Islam as it is currently structured and practiced cannot exist with the culture of the West. We are in a war for survival and only one culture will be dominant in the world of the 21st century.

> "The gods by whom this kingdom stood are gone.
> Gone from the shrines and altars.
> You defend a city lost in flames.
> Come, let us die...the conquered have one safety: hope for none."
>
> *The Illiad*, by Virgil about the fall of Troy. (5)

But the question that only history will answer is whose is the kingdom that will fall. In the long run history has shown that it is wise to be on the side of freedom but of course we live in the short run.

Appendix A

From Chapter 11 Islam and Women FGM Quotes

"How can we leave our daughters uncircumcised? The government can do what it wants and we, too, will do what we want. We will all circumcise our daughters, no matter what the punishments. [Khaled al-Sharif, Abnob tribe member, quoted in news report, "Egyptian Fundamentalists Ignoring Female Circumcision Ban," 6

"Until recently, it never occurred to me that there was anything strange about women's circumcision." [Ahmed, 32-year-old Sudanese veterinarian, interview, p.124, Prisoners of Ritual: Odyssey into Female Genital Circumcision in Africa, Hanny Lightfoot-Klein, 1989]

"We are brought up to believe that all sorts of evil things will happen to us if we are not circumcised. [Eclas, 43-year-old Sudanese biology professor, interview, p. 116, Prisoners of Ritual: Odyssey into Female Genital Circumcision in Africa, Hanny Lightfoot-Klein, 1989]

Question: "Do you ever feel angry when you…realize how you have been deprived?" Answer: "No, because that is the culture here. They do it to everybody." Question: "Do you know other women who feel the way you do?" Answer: "No…they feel they have to follow custom. Even educated people still do it as before." [Fahtma, U.S.-educated Sudanese mother of four children, interview, p. 134, Prisoners of Ritual: Odyssey into Female Genital Circumcision in Africa, Hanny Lightfoot-Klein, 1989]

"She plans to take only half the clitoris (from her daughter). She must have some sort of circumcision, she says, or people will look down on her. [32-year-old Sudanese practical nurse with 9 years of education in the capital. From "Interviews with Women" History #6, p. 254, Prisoners of Ritual: Odyssey into Female Genital Circumcision in Africa, Hanny Lightfoot-Klein, 1989]

Often in the Muslim world female circumcision is stated to be the same as male circumcision. However this is blatantly false. Although one might say that there are certain advantages in the context of cleanliness this issue can be addressed without so drastic a step with respect to women. Most often a woman will lose the ability to enjoy sex as the result of this procedure. If this was the case for men there would be such an outcry as to be heard around the world.

Islamic female circumcision is not limited to the African continent, it is also practiced in Europe as well, although not as widely. Often the European authorities turn a blind eye to these events. However, there are cases where the local Muslim politicians have tried, fortunately unsuccessfully, to make this practice legal in some countries in Europe.

Appendix B

Taken from www.thereligionofpeace.com

"There have been over 6,000 terrorist attacks committed by Muslims since 9/11/01 (a rate of about three or four a day). This number is incomplete because only a small percentage of attacks were picked up by international news sources, even those involving multiple loss of life. We included an attack if it was committed by Muslims in the name of Islam, and usually only if loss of life occurred (with a handful of exceptions where there were a very large number of injuries). In several cases, the victims are undercounted because deaths from trauma caused by the Islamists may occur in later days, despite the best efforts of medical personnel to keep the victims alive.

We usually don't include incidents related to combat, such as in Iraq and Afghanistan, unless it involves particularly heinous terrorist tactics. Unprovoked sniper, drive-by or roadside bombing attacks on military personnel serving normal police duties are sometimes included depending on the circumstances."

The web site contains a list that goes on for endless pages detailing every single terrorist attack in the world over the past several years. The list is inclusive of almost every country in the West, The Middle East and Asia as well as many locations in Africa. A perusal of the site is recommended to grasp the scope of world terrorism today.

Appendix C

From Chapter "The Direct Results of Political Correctness

Twenty Areas known as Terrorist Hot Spots

Dallas and ARLINGTON, TEXAS
DENVER
Tucson, Arizona
San Diego
Los Angeles
San Francisco and Santa Clara
Seattle
Detroit
Chicago metro area
Plainfield, Indiana
Kansas City, Missouri
Oklahoma City, Oklahoma
Boston
New York metro area
Philadelphia
Washington DC and Maryland and Virginia suburbs
Raleigh, North Carolina
Orlando, Florida
Tampa, Florida
Boca Raton and Fort Lauderdale, Florida

The Seven Areas of Highest Muslim Density

Falls Church Virginia: The Washington suburb, where one in every ten residents is Arab, provided refuge to the hijackers, who attacked the Pentagon.

El Cajon, California" Two of the 9/11 hijackers received aid and comfort the San Diego suburb, which has a 3% Arab population.

Bridgeview, Illinois: Known as the "American West Bank," the Chicago suburb is home to a huge population of Palestinian refugees, as well as several Hamas terrorist fronts under investigation.

Lackawana, Ne York: The al-Queda cell known as the "Lackawana Six" was based out of this Buffalo suburb which has a 6 percent Arab population.

Jersey City, New Jersey: Nearly 35 of the population is Arab in this city next door to New York, where Blind Sheikh Omar Abul Rhaman led a mosque and plotted to blow up New York buildings and landmarks.

Dearborn, Michigan: This Detroit suburb where Arabs account for one of every three residents, has become a prime target of FBI counterterrorism investigations.

Hollywood, Florida: This suburb of Fort Lauderdale–where Padilla and l-Shukrijumah lived, along with one of al-Quida hijackers–also has a high concentration of Arab and Muslims, according to the Census Bureau table.

The information in this appendix is taken from the book *Infiltration* by Paul Sperry pp 64,65. The sources of Mr. Sperry's data is Homeland Security documents and documents from The Census Bureau both from December 2003

Acknowledgements

A book of this scope cannot be written without referring to a broad range of sources and relying on the thinking and investigative work of many fine minds and researchers. Especially important to this work are:

The works of Bernard Lewis, Phylis Chesler, Bat Ye'or, Andrew Bostom, Ibn Warraq and Paul Sperry. In addition to the CAIR and Anti-CAIR Web sites Mr. Sperry's book *Infiltration* was particularly helpful in understanding the workings of the CAIR organization.

I would also like to thank Mr. Louis J. Freeh, The Wall St Journal, Fairleigh Dickenson University Press, and Prometheus Books for their permission to include many of the more extensive quotes found in this work.

Special thanks to my wife for support and advice and to Neil Zuckerman and Richard Lopez who took the time to read the manuscript and provide good and helpful advice. Any shortcomings are certainly all mine.

Bibliography

The *Qur'anic* quotes used throughout this book are taken form "The Koran" by N.J. Dawood, Penquin books.

Chapter 2 Tolerant

1 From the BBC report of March 2006
2 Fom the text of *Muhaqqiq al-Hilli*, a 13th century scholar.
3 The Arab Mind by Raphael Patai
4 The Aeropagitaca John Milton's
5 "23 Years: A Study of The Prophetic Career of Mohammad", by Ali Dashti.
6 From the AP BAGHDAD- April 2006.)

Chapter 3 Dhimminitude

1 Statistics and quote from Abolish–American Anti-Slavery Group and The British Anti-Slavery Society
2 From The *Dhimmi*: Jews and Christians under Islam by Bat Ye'Or.
3 Ibid

Chapter 5 Benevolent

1 John Wesley on Islam from *The Doctrine of Original Sin*, 1841–ix 205.
2 The *Legacy of Jihad* by Andrew G. Bostom M.D.)
3 Dates and locations of pogroms taken from*: "Anti-Semitism: The Longest Hatred"* New York: Schocken Books. 1991 and Dershowitz *"Case for Israel"*.)
4 Geography and statistics from "The Decline of Medieval Hellenism in Asia Minor and the Process of Islamization from the Eleventh Century through Fifteenth Century"–Berkley and Los Angeles: University of California press, 1971, pp 166-167)
5 Geography and statistics from "The Decline of Medieval Hellenism in Asia Minor and the Process of Islamization from the Eleventh Century through Fifteenth Century"–Berkley and Los Angeles: University of California press, 1971, pp 166-167)
6 The population numbers are from the year 2002 and are taken from the

Internet web site of *Worldwide Population Statistics.*
7 An Introduction to Islamic Law by Joseph Schacht. Oxford 1982.–
8 *The End of Faith* by Sam Harris.
9 The Law of War and Peace in Islam: A Study in International Law–London–Luzac 1940 p.62)

Chapter 6 The Roots of Hatred

1 From George Vajda's 1937 research essay available from *Josiah* the Brown University Library.
2 *Apocalyptic Muslim Jew-hatred*–by Andrew G. Bostom from The American Thinker web-site.
3 Ibid and Article 7 of the Hamas Charter
4 Ibid
5 www.palastinefacts.org
6 Ibid
7 Ibid
8 From papers of the Judeoscope web site.

Chapter 7 The Nature of Islam

1 Quotes from The Global God: Multicultural Views of God by Alain Besancon.
2 Ibid
3 *Summa Theologica* by St. Thomas Acquinas.
4 *Atlas Shrugged* by Ayn Rand
5 *The River War* by Winston Churchill
6 *The Crusades: The World's Debate* by Hillaire Belloc
7 The American Annual Registry 1827-29 & found on two Web sites ***www.bigpicweblog.com*** and www.danielpipes.org
8 *Writings on Empire and Slavery* by Alexis de Tocqueville
9 Manifesto for an Enlightened Islam, Malek Chebel.
10 Why I Am Not a Muslim By Ibn Warraq
11 Ibid

Chapter 8 The Collective and Group Think

1 Letter published on www. judeoscope.com.)
2 Ibid

Chapter 10 The Hypocrisy of the Leaders of Islam

1 Canadian Lebanese Human Rights Federation letter

Chapter 11 Islam and Women

1 *Voices Behind the Vail* by Ergun Mehmet Caner)
2 Position Paper on Honor Killings by The Muslim Women's League April 1999
3 The Institute for the Secularization of Islam by Azam Kamguian
4 Statistics from UNICEF.
5 *The Arab Mind* by Raphael Patai

Chapter 12 Human Rights

1 The Spirit of Allah: Khomeini and the Islamic Revolution by Amir Taheri

Chapter 13 The Nature of the Battle

1 *The Islamic Question* by Roberto A.M. Bertacchini and Piersandro Vanzani S.I.

Chapter 16 A Different War–Terrorism

1 *Unholy Alliance* by David Horowitz
2 The details of this story were taken from various news reports including the Wall Street Journal, Associated Press, Front Page Magazine and the Internet. All dated between June 3 and June 6, 2006
3 Incidents, activities and quotes regarding mosques from *Infiltration*, chapter 11–by Paul Sperry

Chapter 17 A Different War - Subversion

1 From Daniel Pipes at www.danielpipes.org)
2 Ibid

Chapter 18 CAIR

1 FrontpageMagazine.com–several issues
2 *Infiltration* by Paul Sperry.
3 Ibid

Chapter 19 The Euro-Arab Dialog

1 *Euro-Arab Dialogue* by Saleha al-Mani
2 Ibid
3 Ibid
4 The Third Reich and the World" by Charles Block
5 *Eurabia* by Bat Ye'or
6 *Report on Islamic summit 1974*, Pakistan, Lahore 22-24 February 1974 (Karachi) pp 222-23

Chapter 20 Infiltration

1 Almoudi: What His case Means to Muslims by Falasten M. Abdeljabbar in The American Muslim February 2004 p20
2 WorldNetDaily.com posted July 28, 2006

Chapter 21 Population Growth

1 *An interview of Paul Bowles* by Brendan Bernhard and re-quoted in his review of the book *The Force of Reason* by Oriana Fallaci. Bowles was the author of *The Sheltering Sky* and many other works
2 Garrett and Hardin in *The Tragedy of the Commons* - article Science #162, 1968 pp 1243-1248
3 The Tragedy of the Commons Revisited by Beryl Crowe
4 *Eurabia*, Bat Ye'or
5 *The Islamist Challenge to the Constitution* by David Houck Middle East Quarterly Spring 2006
6 *Muslim Community Development Initiatives*, by Marya Morris, American Planning Association, April 25, 2004

Chapter 22 Jihad

1 The *Noble Qur'an* Muslim Students Association, University of California
2 Mecca Islamic Summit Conference of 1981
3 *Islamic Imperialism* by Efraim Karsh, p23
4 *The Arabs: A Short History* by Phillip K. Hitti p. 36,37
5 *Islamic Imperialism* by Efraim Karsh, p23
6 Hatred's Kingdom by Dore Gold
7 *The Legacy of Jihad* by Andrew G. Bostrom, MD
8 Source Washington Post April 29, 2006

Chapter 23 Shari'a

1 Wikipedia
2 *The Shari'a* by H.A.R. Gibb
3 Manifesto for an Enlightened Islam, Malek Chebel
4 *The Muslim World* Volume 28, by Charles Watson
5 Why I Am Not A Muslim by Ibn Warraq
6 Ibid
7 Ibid

Chapter 24 Islam and Treaties

1 *The Cease-Fire* by Tashbih Sayyed, Ph. D from *Muslim World Today* website, August 11, 2006

Chapter 25 Palestine

1 The Arab League Secretary Chedli Klibi in an interview.
2 www.***medea.be/index.html?page=&lang=&doc=1144***
3 The Force of Reason by Oriana Falacci
4 Who Is to Blame for Grief on the Beach? By Charles Krauthammer, Washington Post, June 16, 2006

Chapter 26 Lebanon

1 "A House of Many Mansions - The History of Lebanon Reconsidered" by Kamal S. Salibi

Chapter 27 *Multiculturalism* and Political Correctness

1 Wikipedia
2 Ibid
3 Story from Wall Street Journal, March 23, 2006
4 Euro-Arab Dialog: The Relations Between the Two Cultures, by Derek Hopwood
5 *Eurabia*, Bat Ye'or
6 *The Coming Armageddon* by Barry Shaw http://www.mideasttruth.com/forum/

Chapter 28 The Direct and Lethal Results of Political Correctness

1 *Pacifists Versus Peace* by Thomas Sowell–townhall.com July 21, 2006
2 *Infiltration*, by Paul Sperry
3 Summarized from a speech given by Dame Eliza Manningham-Buller (Head of MI5) at Queen Mary College on November 10, 2006

Chapter 29 Support From the Left

1 *Radical Son* by David Horowitz
2 Unholy Alliance: Radical Islam and the American Left, by David Horowitz
3 Ibid
4 Ibid
5 *Feminism's Blind Spot* by Sarah Baxter in the New York Times August 13, 2006
6 The Chronicle of Higher Education, by Phyllis Chesler

Chapter 30 The Double Standard

1 *Illiberal Europe by* Gerard Alexander, Daily Standard, April 3, 2006.
2 Ibid
3 Quotes from CNN web site posting.

Chapter 31 The Media

1 Wall Street Journal, June 26, 2006
2 Cynthia Ozick New York Observer May 10. 2004 part of an anthology following *Those Who Forgot the Past: The Question of Anti-Semitism* by Ron Rosenbaum.
3 Summarized by the author from articles In *The International Herald Tribune* by Elaine Sciolino - 3/31/2003, 12/4/2003, 1/4/2004.
4 Manifesto for an Enlightened Islam, Malek Chebel
5 Newsweek, June 19, 2006
6 *Jewish World Review*–article written by Jack Kelly, a former Marine and Green Beret, was a deputy assistant secretary of the Air Force in the Reagan administration
7 *Los Angeles Times*, June 26 by Faye Fiore

Chapter 33 Cowardice, Hopefulness or Stupidity

1 *The Force of Reason* by Oriana Fallaci
2 National Catholic Reporter, October 22, 1999
3 *The Jewish World Review* by Jonathan Tobin September 20, 2006.
4 *Word War IV* by Norman Podhoertz
5 *Infiltration* by Paul Sperry
6 Ibid
7 Ibid
8 *Democrat, Hampered FBI Probe In Detroit*, by Paul Sperry from WorldNetDaily website March 13, 2003
9 *Infiltration* by Paul Sperry
10 *View From The Left*, Jerusalem Post, December 26, 2003

Chapter 34 A Matter of Policy

1 Bourrinet, *Le Dialogue Euro-Arabe*. These machinations are discussed in detailed by Al-Mani in *Euro-Arab Dialogue*
2 Euro-Arab Dialogue by Saleh Al-Mani
3 Ibid
4 Islam and Dhiminnitude by Bat Ye'or
5 From ***www.medea.be/index.html?page=&lang=&doc=1144*** Note: The proceedings were recorded in French. All of the information was derived from the translation into English using the Google Language Translation Services.
6 *Euro-Arab Parliamentary Dialog*, Damascus, 1998, EAD, PAEAC, MEDEA
7 An editorial from the WSJ Sunday, June 25, 2006, by Louis J. Freeh who was the FBI director from 1993 through 2001
8 The French Betrayal of America by Kenneth R. Timmerman
9 Ibid
10 *Frances Next President* by David Twersky article in the NY Sun August 8, 2006. The quote was widely covered by many newspapers domestically and in Europe in main news and editorials..
11 *Free World* by Timothy Garton Ash

Chapter 35 The Lack of Consistency in Foreign Policy

1 Quote from article in the *Washington Times*, by Rowan Scarborough, June 23, 2006
2 Gen. Casey quoted in article in the *Washington Times*, by Rowan

Scarborough, June 23, 2006
3 *Israel's New War* by Caroline Glick, Jerusalem Post April 28, 2006
4 Quote of Richard Miniter from *Israel's New War* by Caroline Glick, Jerusalem Post April 28, 2006
5 *Meet the Press*, Rep Murtha (D), June 18, 2006
6 The Wall Street Journal "Best of the Web", James Tarantino June 22, 2006
Chapter 36 The Humanist Muslims

1 *In the Beginning There Was Man, Not Religion* by Omran Salman Bahraini Reformist–The Middle East Media Research Institute, April 13, 2006.
2 Why I Am Not a Muslim, by Ibn Warraq
3 Middle East Media Research Institute, April 12, 2006
4 *The Future of Islam* by Judea Pearl in FrontPage Magazine June 30,2006
5 Reason and Revelation by A.J. Arberry
6 The London's Daily Telegraph April 10, 2006

Chapter 37 The 27 Proposals for Reforming Islam

1 The Manifesto for an Enlightened Islam by Malek Chebel was originally written in French and seems not to be available in English at least through the sources I tried. Therefore the information presented herein was summarized from the MEMRI web site and was authored by Nathalie Szerman, Director of MEMRI's Research for the North African Reformist Thinkers Project.

Chapter 38 The Elusive Solution

1 *A Sermon for the West* a speech given by Oriana Fallaci at The American Enterprise Institute on January 10, 2003

Chapter 39 Philosophical

1 *Islam Unveiled* by Robert Spencer
2 *The Arabs: A Short History* by Philip K. Hitti and *Islam Unveiled* by Robert Spencer.
3 *Islam Unveiled* by Robert Spencer
4 The New York Times *Two American Muslim Clerics* by Laurie Goldstein, June 18, 2006
5 Ibid
6 Quote from Wafa Sultan in a debate on al Jazeera TV, transcript available at ***www.memri.org***. Ms. Sultan is a secular Arab-American psychologist living

in Los Angeles

Chapter 40 Political

1 Jerusalem Post, June 27, 2006 by Caroline Glick
2 *Crisis In Europe* by Bruce Bawer The Hudson Review - April 18, 2006
3 *Generous Betrayal*, by Unni Wikan
4 *For Honor's Sake* by Unni Wikan
5 ArabsforIsrael.com

Chapter 41 Economic

1 Mella McEwen, Oil Editor *Midland Reporter-Telegram* 7/4/2006
2 *Washington Post*, by Sebastian Mallaby July 25, 2006

Chapter 42 Military

1 Pacifists Versus Peace by Thomas Sowell on Townhall.com
2 David Pryce-Jones; evaluation of points made in *Islam Unveiled* by Robert Spenser. Mr. Pryce-Jones is a noted writer on Islamic subjects and wrote the forward for Islam Unveiled.
3 An 11th-grade Iranian schoolbook quoting Ayatollah Khomeini

Chapter 43 Culture

1 Manifesto for an Enlightened Islam, Malek Chebel
2 *Barnes & Noble Goes to Baghdad*, by Fred Kaplan, Slate.com, April 28 and The Intellectual Activist - TIA on-line
3 *Technological Risk* by H.W. Lewis
4 Cultures in Conflict: Christians, Muslims, and Jews in the Age of Discovery, by Bernard Lewis
5 As found in *Europe Conquered* by Irina Oberman The Stanford review.

Further Readings

Many books influenced the writing of this book among them the following ones are of special note.

Mr. Bernard Lewis, professor emeritus at Princeton, author of:

- What Went Wrong?: The Clash Between Islam and Modernity in the Middle East
- The Crisis of Islam.
- Middle East: A Brief history of the Last 2,000 Years.

Other Authors:

The Legacy of Jihad by Andrew G. Bostom, M.D. and *Islamic Imperialism A History* by Efram Karsh together these encyclopedic works are a must read for anyone wanting to see the Ten Step process enfold in great detail.

Manifesto for an Enlightened Islam, Malek Chebel. Provides an in depth discussion of the reforms that need to be implemented within Islam. Malek Chebel is a renowned anthropologist and a specialist on the Arab world. In 2004, he established the Foundation for an Enlightened Islam. The organization is based in France.

The Clash of Civilizations and the Remaking of the World Order by Samuel P. Huntington

An Introduction to Islamic Law by Joseph Schacht. Oxfoed 1982

Infiltration by Paul Sperry. Mr. Sperry provides an extensive set of documentation on the methods and events of Islamic infiltration into the American culture and government.

The Koran Interpreted by Arthur John Arberry

Islam Unveiled: Disturbing Questions about the World's Fastest-Growing Faith by Robert Spencer

Indoctrination U, by David Horowitz - A survey and study of university's curriculum and teaching practices. Avaialable on FrontPagemag.com.

The Shia Revival by Vali Nasr is vital reading for an understanding of the Iraqi insurgency (Sunni vs Shiities). Chapter 4–Khomeini's Moment–is particularly informative in understanding a great deal of the reigning politics of the Iran/Iraqi relationship.

The Islamic Question by Roberto A.M. Bertacchini and Piersandro Vanzan S.I.

On Liberty by John Stuart Mill's published in 1859–"The most fundamental principle of a freely operating liberal society is the right to the "freedom of opinion".

"The Death of Feminism: What's Next in the Struggle for Women's Freedom," by Phyllis Chesler

Web Sites of particular interest:

www.anti-cair-net.org

www.danielpipes.org and www.danielpipes.org/article/1705

http://www.sezame.info/index.php?action=article&id_ article=75430&print=1&P, July 2004. Interview by Hakim Al-Ghissassi. *Sezame* is a French-language monthly dealing with French North African news. See other reports in the North African Reformist Thinkers Series: "French Moroccan Progressive Author on 'The New Islamic Thinkers,'"

http://memri.org/bin/articles.cgi?Page=archives&Area=ia&ID=IA26406 ; "Tunisian Reformist Researcher on Discrimination Against Christians in Egypt,"

http://memri.org/bin/articles.cgi?Page=archives&Area=sd&ID=SP1103 06 ; "'Manifesto of Liberties' - A Muslim Association for Freedom in the Arab World"

http://memri.org/bin/articles.cgi?Page=archives&Area=ia&ID=IA27306

INDEX

9/11

A

B

C

D

E

F

G

H

I

J

K

L

M

N

O

P

Q

R

S

T

U

V

W

Y

Printed in the United States
86857LV00003B/13/A

9 781425 130817